The
Naked
Trader

The Naked Trader

How anyone can make money trading shares

3rd edition

by Robbie Burns

HARRIMAN HOUSE LTD

3A Penns Road
Petersfield
Hampshire
GU32 2EW
GREAT BRITAIN

Tel: +44 (0)1730 233870
Fax: +44 (0)1730 233880
Email: enquiries@harriman-house.com
Website: www.harriman-house.com

First edition published in Great Britain in 2005 by Harriman House.
Second edition published in 2007 and reprinted 2008, 2009 and 2010.
This edition published in 2011.

Copyright © Harriman House 2011

The right of Robbie Burns to be identified as the Author has been asserted in
accordance with the Copyright, Design and Patents Act 1988.

ISBN: 978–0–857191–70–0

British Library Cataloguing in Publication Data
A CIP catalogue record for this book can be obtained from the British
Library.

Certain images copyright © iStockphoto.com
Figure data and information copyright © respective owners and sources
Cartoons copyright © Pete Dredge 2011 and Roy Mitchell 2005
Author photo by Jim Marks

Set in Plantin, Clarendon and Eurostile.

Printed and bound in the UK by CPI Group (UK), Croydon, CR0 4YY

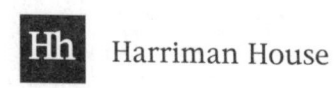 Harriman House

Contents

About the Author

Robbie Burns has been a journalist and writer since he graduated in journalism from Harlow College in 1981. After starting life as a reporter and editor for various local newspapers, from 1988–1992 he was editor of ITV and Channel 4's teletext services. He also wrote ITV's daily teletext soap opera, 'Park Avenue', for five years.

He then went on to freelance for various newspapers, including the *Independent* and the *Sun*, and also helped set up a financial news service for CNN. In 1997, he became editor for BSkyB's teletext services and set up their shares and finance service. While there he also set up various entertainment phone lines in conjunction with BSkyB, including a *Buffy the Vampire Slayer* phone line that made him nearly £250,000.

He left full-time work in 2001 to trade and run his own businesses, which included a café in London that he later sold, doubling his money on the initial purchase. While at BSkyB, Robbie broadcast a diary of his share trades, which became hugely popular. He transferred the diary to his website, **www.nakedtrader.co.uk**, which became one of the most-read financial websites in the UK. Between 2002 and 2005 he wrote a column for the *Sunday Times*, 'My DIY Pension', featuring share buys and sells made for his pension fund which he runs himself in a SIPP. He managed to double the money in his pension fund from £40,000 to £80,000 in under three years, as chronicled in these articles. By mid-2011 he had turned it into £250,000. Robbie now writes a weekly column for ADVFN.com.

Robbie has made a tax-free gain of well over £1,000,000 from trading shares since 1999, making a profit every year, even during market downturns. His public trades alone – detailed on his website – have made more than £900,000.

He lives in a riverside apartment on the Thames with his wife, Elizabeth, and young son Christopher. His hobbies include chess, running, swimming, horse racing, and trading shares from his bedroom, erm … naked. After all, he wouldn't be seen dead in a thong … (you might catch him in Speedos).

Acknowledgements

Thanks to my wife Elizabeth for her support and putting up with me moaning constantly while I was writing (and rewriting) the book. Also, thanks to all the contributors to the real-life stories section.

Finally, thank you to my editor for his always valuable contributions (especially the boring chart stuff I'm too lazy to do myself) – and for making sure everything is as accurate as it can be. If there are any spelling misstakes they are his fault and not mine, okay?

Preface

Welcome to the Crazy World of Shares

Ever wondered whether you could make money by buying and selling shares? And maybe eventually quitting that damn job to do it? Being able to tell the boss to stuff it?

I think you can – whatever your age, job, status or character defects!

I did it. And honestly, I am not a planet brain, I'm not great at maths and I'm pretty lazy. So if I did it, you can too!

This third edition of *The Naked Trader* will be your best friend if you want to learn how to make money from shares. I'll reveal to you common-sense stock market knowledge that's taken me more than 14 years to learn. You can learn from the things I've got right – and learn even more from the things I've got wrong. Not to mention things that other people have got right and wrong, too.

Oh, and don't worry – I speak plain English, not the financial gobbledegook others hide behind. I hope you'll gain from my experiences without having to trawl through a lot of boring old financial twaddle found in so many other books about the market.

Is this book for you?

Who is this book aimed at? Well, anyone interested in making money from trading shares. For starters, it's perfect for total beginners to the stock market – the first bits of the book, for instance, are all about exactly what your first steps should be, and all the core information you absolutely must know (but for once written in a way that won't give you concussion).

But it's also very much for those of you who are already trading, and who want to improve. It's packed to bursting with strategies and helpful hints that have all worked for me. I think that should also make it equally interesting to the more experienced investor, who perhaps wants to try out some new ideas.

And no matter your experience, if you have ever bought books about making money in the markets before, but found yourself collapsing off your chair in boredom after five minutes, this book is for you too. Trading isn't dull, so there's no reason for a trading guide to be a papery equivalent of Ovaltine. That's why this one isn't.

The only trading topic this book doesn't cover in any great depth is technical analysis. So if double bottoms are your thing, I'm afraid you'll need to look elsewhere. [Oo-er, missus, etc. – Ed.] I'll touch on them briefly. [I bet you will. – Ed.] But that's all. [I'm out of innuendoes now. – Ed.]

Put simply, this book will teach you everything you need to know about how to make money from shares – and without giving you a headache. I've got a low concentration threshold myself. If I can write it, you can read it!

Robbie
London, 2011

Introduction
Trading Shares, Eating Toast, Making Money

When I wrote the original *Naked Trader* back in 2005 I thought it would be a one-off. I never expected it to sell many copies. I had felt there was a gap in the market for a simple-to-read book on how to make money from shares, written by someone who has really done it full-time, but I was stunned when it turned out that gap was pretty big and the book went on to be a bestseller. Three years later I wrote the second edition, which sold even more than the first one.

I'm so pleased that my writing seems to help people. The emails from those who tell me they've never even bothered reading a whole book before, but have managed to finish *The Naked Trader*, are very satisfying indeed.

This completely updated third edition is designed to be read from scratch, so there is no need to buy the previous two editions. In fact, if you bought one of those, I hope you will find this new edition worth getting too. It's a top-to-bottom revision, adding another four years of market experience to the core material of the earlier books, with tons of refinements and new stuff throughout.

Why a third edition?

Markets change and move fast. Since I wrote the last edition (2007) many things have happened in the world of shares, and I've learned a lot too. I only want to bring out new editions when I think I've got something genuinely new and valuable to add, and the time definitely feels right now.

This book contains lots of new strategies and ideas that have arisen out of the past four years of trading. In that time, my trades have actually become more profitable, and I've been able to refine a number of new techniques that are definitely worth passing on. In fact, since the last edition I've become a millionaire. [It's true. He dresses like Mr Monopoly now. – Ed.]

So if you bought either of the previous editions and enjoyed them, I hope you will like this one just as much. Of course, there is some ground that has to be covered for new readers, and old hands may find some of this familiar.

But much else is new, and everything else has been updated, refreshed and spring-cleaned. This is still the one book you need to get started in trading, as well as a source of seriously decent strategies for making that trading worthwhile.

Jargon-free, common-sense advice

If you've never traded a share before it doesn't matter, as I'll guide you every step of the way. And if you have traded for a while and have made losses, I am confident I can put you on the road to long-term stock market success by getting rid of your bad habits.

If you have traded shares for a while, but you're struggling to make money, I hope you'll find some of my strategies useful.

You won't find any inexplicable stock market jargon in this book – I write in plain English. You won't have to start scratching your head and think,

'Has he lapsed into Esperanto?' I'm going to explain how to buy and sell shares the easy way, and guide you to the winners. I'll be taking you through every step and explaining all the silly jargon.

The fact is: stock market investment is easier than you think.

Brokers and tipsters love to spout jargon because it makes them look clever, and helps persuade you to part with your hard-earned money as a result of their 'advice'. But I'll guide you through all that nonsense so that *you* can make your own decisions and do your own research.

This is not a get-rich-quick book (sorry!)

One thing I certainly can't do is promise that £10,000 you have spare is going to become £100,000 overnight as a result of reading this book.

Though I have become a millionaire, it has taken me many years. Building a fortune from trading takes time, and you will make more money by growing your money slowly than by trying to make a million in a year (you won't succeed, and the flame-out could be pretty disastrous).

You know those ads:

> *"Make £400 a day from the markets ... "*

> *"Become a stock market millionaire with our software ... "*

Come on, you've always known in your heart of hearts that when something sounds too good to be true – it is!

This book is about building your wealth slowly and surely – with realistic targets and time frames. Using discipline, good stock-picking techniques and avoiding the mistakes new investors nearly always make, I believe I can make you richer. But you just aren't going to become a millionaire overnight.

I became a millionaire, but believe me, it took loads and loads of nights!

Trading shares is an exciting roller-coaster ride with plenty of thrills and spills. I really hope that excitement comes over in *Naked Trader*.

If you have never bought or sold a share before, I hope I'll arm you with the information you'll need to start trading. This includes everything from how to buy a share to getting real-time prices.

Then I'll tell you everything I've learned over 14 active years of trading. You'll learn what makes shares move and what to watch for before pressing that buy button. I can also reveal how to make money by backing shares to go *down*. And I hope to provide you with tons of useful info you just won't find anywhere else.

Whether you have a small amount to trade, or you've inherited £100,000, I hope after reading this book that you will be well-armed to enter the fray.

So, get a cup of tea, put your feet up and welcome to the crazy world of shares. Oh, and never forget the toast.

Part I
Rat Race, Exeunt

"Money can't buy friends,
but you can get a better
class of enemy."

– Spike Milligan

Escaping the Rat Race

My story

In about 1998 I remember sitting in a grim office overlooking a dismal carpet warehouse on the A4 and thinking: "Is this how I want to spend my life?"

I was earning quite a bit, but I wasn't happy. I didn't want to be in a horrible office working for a big company anymore. I knew what I wanted: freedom!

I quit the rat race in 2001 and have never looked back. I love my lifestyle. No moody bosses or targets. Just me! Of course there are no office politics – but I can live without them!

I now sit at home in my office overlooking the Thames, with my feet up, putting on a trade here and there and relaxing. My wealth continues to build in the markets over time.

Luckily for me, I realised working for someone else – unless you absolutely *love* what you do – is a mug's game. You're just there to pay the mortgage every month.

So while I worked for BSkyB, I also worked for myself. I had a shiny Reuters machine on my desk (after the cleaner had been), and I learned everything about the markets through practice.

I quickly realised I could make a lot more money trading than in my full-time job, and in 2001 I quit to trade more or less full time. Before this, though, I had to get some extra money to trade with.

The delectable Buffy

So while still employed I started to develop other income streams – one of which, incredibly, included a *Buffy the Vampire Slayer* information line. This made me £250,000 over four years! It simply involved me reading out the latest Buffy news on my phone at home – eager viewers would call a line to hear the recording, and I made money out of each call. Sadly the series ended in 2000, and so with it the line.

I started it for a bit of a laugh … but on its first day the guy who owned the phone company called me and said: "Bugger me, it's just taken £400!"

Happiness is … residual income

And I sold mobile phones and cut-price phone calls and energy for a company called Telecom Plus. And still do now, actually, from time to time via my website. I got – and still get – a cut of every phone call made or energy used by customers that have signed up through me. It's called residual income and it pays all my bills even now. I still earn from customers I sold to in 1999!

Armed, therefore, with a huge pile of cash, I quit my job and decided to trade full-time.

Waiter, there's a fish in my fish pie

However, I did want a bit of a fallback in case I wasn't such a great trader, so I bought a café near a tube station in Fulham. That proved a lot of fun and I made quite a bit of money. My wife and I improved it till it made £1,000 a day instead of £300 – it was very successful.

So successful, in fact, that it actually became a pain in the neck. More customers, which led to more staff, which led to more problems. Classic growing pains.

Sometimes staff didn't turn up and I found myself making coffees at 7am! It involved all kinds of problems: firing staff; talking to customers complaining there was fish in their fish pie; and dealing with all the mess a café brings.

The worst incident I can remember was when all the staff were sick, and I was on my own behind the counter trying to deal with a large queue of people.

So I shouted out to the café: "I need help! Anyone want a short-term job? £10 an hour." And one of the customers came to my rescue and started serving. There was a lovely community spirit and I met a lot of great people.

But with my son arriving on the scene it became too much effort to run it, and enough was enough.

I had originally intended it to be the start of a chain, and I nearly bought a second café, but decided in the end I didn't want to be a retail mogul. Too much effort – I'd rather have less money and enjoy relaxing.

So I sold the café for roughly double what I paid for it. Interestingly, running the café helped my trading because a café business is quite complex, and learning the accounts helped me evaluate stock market businesses.

A lazy life

So now I just trade and run my website **www.nakedtrader.co.uk**.

I also hold five to six seminars a year, where I show readers my techniques using live markets on a large screen. I really enjoy them and it gets me out of the house too.

And it's amazing how many share picks come out of these seminars which go on to make me plenty of dough.

It's also good fun to meet readers and have a drink with them. If you want to come to one, see the info on the seminars at the end of the book. Maybe we'll have a drink together sometime!

The markets have certainly made me very happy. There are plenty of other people like me around who have managed to quit their office jobs and trade. And they, like me, are nothing special. All it takes is some discipline, determination, and – I'm afraid – some trading capital. I can help you sort out the discipline and determination, but you have to come up with some capital.

I hope *The Naked Trader* will put you on the first rung of the escape ladder. Trading stock markets really is much simpler than you might imagine once you see past the jargon. And I promise you won't find any of that here.

What sort of trader am I?

I suppose I am more of a medium-term investor/fairly frequent trader than a day trader. Maybe I should be called the Naked Investor. I expect you imagine a *trader* to be someone sitting at a desk all day feverishly buying and selling shares.

Well, that's not me at all. I don't want to be like that. I want to be, oohhh … drinking tea and eating toast. Having a snooze. Going to the gym. Watching the racing. Sitting in the garden with a good book (or a bad one – I always fall asleep, whatever the book is like. Especially if it is a finance one). And I enjoy playing with my son. And, okay, basically I'm a bit lazy (is it time for a nap yet?).

What I hope you'll learn is that **you don't need to spend 40 hours a week in front of a screen watching every move the market makes.** And it is even possible to trade or invest if you have a full-time job, as long as you can get some peace and quiet on the internet at work at some point during the day.

In fact, that may be the best way to start trading. Begin by making some extra money while you're working, and learn the tricks of the trade.

Instead of spending all day emailing your friends, getting addicted to Facebook or Twitter, fiddling with your iThing or BlueBerry, spend a bit of time at work learning how to invest.

Keep this book handy

I suggest you keep me handy, even when you think you've sussed out how to make money. Because, even if you've read the book once or twice, you may need me again if you fall into bad ways – and believe me, you will be tempted. And I will always be here for you to skim through …

Anyway, I really hope you enjoy the book. You don't need to read it all in one sitting. Read it in bits and let it sink in. Take it on holiday and read it on the beach. Keep it handy when you're going through a bad trading patch. Don't take it on a date, though. There just isn't room for the three of us in the relationship.

A Day in the Life of a Naked Trader

Dear diary ...

6AM

I'm in bed of course! What on earth is 6am? I know people in the *Sunday Times*' 'A Life in the Day' column always wake up at 6am, go running for five miles, have power breakfasts, make executive decisions and are dressed and at their desks by 7am. But this day-in-the-life is an honest one. I will be asleep. And if you try and wake me up I will hospitalise you. It really is quite simple.

7.15AM

My young son Christopher awakes on the dot of 7.15am and so promptly brings us all hurtling out of the Land of Nod.

I grab some tea and toast and head for my trading desk (well, it's just a desk with a computer on it). I lift the blinds up on my office windows and I always smile: I think I have the most spectacular view in the whole of

London. I live right by the Thames, just off the towpath. And because I'm opposite a wetlands centre, I see the river, trees and the sky! No buildings are allowed to be built on the opposite bank. The view (which the government will no doubt tax shortly) is so great it always reminds me how lucky I've been and how glad I am that I got into buying shares so I could afford to buy the apartment without a mortgage.

Actually this hour is one of the most important parts of the day, because at 7am every morning companies report their results and release announcements. First thing to do is to check whether there are any announcements on shares I own.

If there are, I try and quickly judge whether I need to take any action. Is a report looking a bit dicey … any question marks come up? How are profits looking? Should I sell and take my gains, or perhaps buy some more?

Next I check the spread betting firms to see how the FTSE 100 is set to open. They tell me – and pretty accurately – whether it looks likely to be a good or bad opening, which often sets the tone for the first couple of hours.

However, I tend to mainly hold smaller companies, so if the FTSE 100 is scheduled to open lower it doesn't necessarily mean I've got to worry: they aren't listed on it.

Then I click on a few reports to see if anything catches my eye. Sometimes a company report looks good, so I make a quick note to check on it later. Or a company might, say, announce it is hoping to move to the main market from the junior market. I would make a note of that, as it would mean that in the future I could buy it tax-free in my ISA.

7.56AM

Four minutes to make a fresh brew and some more toast before the market opens at 8am!

8AM

The stock market opens at 8am and my monitors of various shares suddenly spring into life. Always interesting to see how your shares are starting the day.

The first half an hour of the market is important, and I whizz through all my positions to check nothing is tanking for any reason. However, one thing I think I have really learned since I wrote the last edition is: it usually isn't worth trading during the first hour of the day, regardless of whether or not a share of mine is racing up or down. That's because there is always an initial overreaction by the market to news, and this can be magnified early in the day when there are fewer people buying and selling.

It's easy to get caught out. So I always wait for the markets to settle and simply watch with interest.

On the smaller shares, market makers will often mark a share up or down because the share has been tipped in the press. By the opening, a share will often already start higher or lower – you can never deal at last night's closing price!

8.30AM

Everything begins to calm down and the gaps between the buy and sell prices – the spreads – start to narrow. But it's rare at this time that I would either buy or sell. This is the time my son, Christopher, needs to be taken to school, and either myself or Mrs NT do it. I hate driving, so if it's a reasonable day I will cycle to school with him. If it's ridiculously rainy or a cold day, Mrs NT will drive him in.

I love cycling with him, especially on a lovely sunny day. The fact I'm not a day trader, having to be hunched over a screen from market open to close, suits me. After all, the whole point of quitting full-time office work was to relax and enjoy having time to do other things.

9AM

Time for a look at the email inbox. I get quite a few emails, sometimes more than 100 a day, and I answer them all, unless they are abusive or the person is obviously mad. [Finally, an explanation. Wait – what? – Ed.]

Sometimes people become aggressive if I try and tell them it's their fault they've been losing money, not the market's fault – a lot of people tend to blame everyone but themselves. But blaming the market is meaningless, and it's dangerous for a person's trading. I'd rather warn them, on the off chance that the red mist won't descend, than send them a bland email agreeing with them just for a quiet life.

The hardest emails to answer are those with the subject line: 'Just a quick question'. Of course, that means it's an extremely long and complicated one! So if the email is very long or complex it goes into a folder marked 'pending' and I answer it at the weekend. Otherwise I try to reply as fast as I can and keep the inbox clear. The ones I hate ask me whether they should buy or sell a specific share. I have to reply that I can't give an answer to that, as you have to be a regulated advisor. I wouldn't want to in any case. If I tell someone to buy something and it goes down it will be my fault, and ditto if I tell them to sell and it goes up!

9.45AM

Mrs NT usually heads off to play tennis. I have a look at the markets and see what's happening. This is about the time of day when I might consider a trade. Or not. Sometimes there isn't anything I need to do, sometimes there is. I never rush anything. I usually call a friend – the only other person I know well who also trades shares – to have a chat about today's market, and discuss if there is anything one of us has spotted. It's good to have someone like this to talk to, as he can often bring up negatives about shares I am interested in and vice versa.

10AM

Time for another round of tea or coffee and toast. And a read of the paper. If it's a sunny day I might do that outside in the little garden I have by the river. I'll then come in and have a good look through the current portfolio. It is divided up into spread bets and shares held in an ISA – both of which enable me to avoid paying any tax on profits.

Is there anything bothering me, anything about to produce results? Anything I should take a profit on? If there is something that is on my mind to buy or sell I'll look at Level 2, which gives me a snapshot of how many buyers and sellers there are around. It gives me a good idea of whether my trade is sensible, and a final push to either make the trade or leave it till later.

These days I only push a buy or sell button if I really feel the time is right. The absolute worst thing to do is to make a boredom trade.

Things are generally busier for me if the markets are going down, as I might then have a shorter-term spread bet open, betting on the market to carry on falling, and that takes a bit more looking after.

If I feel like it, at this time of the day I'll also either do some research on anything that came up when I was looking at news stories earlier, or do a bit of web surfing. I don't tweet and I'm not on Facebook, as both look too addictive.

11AM

Markets tend to go quiet around 11ish, so time for a bit of exercise. One might be able to trade naked, but now it's definitely time to don my shorts as I'm off for a slow run. I go around the Thames, up over Hammersmith Bridge, down past the wetlands centre and back over Putney Bridge. It's lovely, like running in the country but living in London – best of both worlds! I take an iPod or a radio and listen to my usual rubbish dance music.

11.45AM

Quick shower and back to the markets. At about this time I look through my shortlist of potential buys and see if any are rising. Is it a good time to buy? I try and suss out the mood of the market and will trawl through Level 2 again to see if anything looks likely to rise. This is probably the best time of the day to buy.

12PM

Wednesdays I'll write up my website update, which I quite enjoy – though it takes some time to write. I blog about my life, a bit about things in the news that annoy me and then any trades I made in the last week. Often I've forgotten what I traded, so I have to go through my accounts.

On other days I'll reply to more emails. Again, it could be anything! Could be someone interested in a seminar, wanting some info about some aspect of the market, perhaps wanting me to make a speech (I never accept), or do an interview (I rarely do). Often someone asks to advertise on my site. I refuse as I want the site to remain independent, and I wouldn't want to advertise tipsters or systems and suchlike, as I don't believe in them. I turn down some big sums, but would rather that than get emails along the lines of, "I bought this via your website and now I live in cardboard".

12.30PM

Time for lunch. That might be a sandwich or something, or me and Mrs NT might meet up for lunch somewhere. Or I might meet a friend. I may go and practise some golf, as I am just starting out! The only exception is Wednesdays, when I am probably still writing stuff for my website update … the sacrifices I am willing to make for my loyal readers!

1.30PM

The market sometimes changes at 1.30 pm. This is because in the US it's 8.30am in New York, when they often release important economic data. The FTSE 100 as a whole, and individual shares, can suddenly move quickly in one direction or another, depending on what is announced. It doesn't affect me that much usually, but if it's a down market and I am betting on the FTSE 100 to fall, I might quickly close that bet and take my profits if news from the US is good and likely to make the FTSE 100 pick up a bit.

1.45PM

If it's a nice sunny day I'll go for a sleep and a laze in the garden. Otherwise, a cup of tea and a KitKat, Twix or Yorkie bar! Told you I was honest – this is definitely not a diary c/o the *Sunday Times*!

2.15PM

This is when I'll have a look at my higher-risk shortlist of shares. I buy some high-risk shares for my pension, which I run myself in a SIPP (self-invested personal pension). I'm sensible in my ISA and spread bet accounts, and so view my pension fund – or at least around half of it – as a place to open the throttle up a bit and try a few dangerous picks. I will often buy high-risk oil or mining shares in it. This satisfies the gambler I know is in me, and it doesn't matter much if one dives. I've actually done rather well with it, though this kind of thing can easily leave you looking like a prat (and is definitely not to be recommended for money you can't afford to lose).

2.30PM

The Dow Jones opens across the pond, where it's now 9.30am in Manhattan – and where it goes, UK shares tend to follow. I check through the main portfolio again. The worst time is when a share goes down quite a bit and I have to decide whether to get rid of it or not. If the market is going well, it's unlikely I'll place any more trades for the day. If it is going very badly, I might consider buying a good share that seems to have dropped purely because of the market-wide panic selling.

3PM

I'll usually have a chat with my share-buying mate to see if he has discovered anything. On Wednesdays I'll check through my website update and see if it all makes sense and then publish it. If I make a terrible error, someone usually puts me right straightaway.

A new update generally means a whole lot of new emails to reply to after people read through what I've written and comment on it. Sometimes I get a rude email if I mention I've sold a share that someone really likes. If it's close to a seminar I might read through some questionnaire answers from those coming, to start to judge what to cover on the day.

3.30PM

It's school run time. Either me or Mrs NT does the honours. If it's a nice day and the market is quiet, I'll do it. I am usually the only dad doing pick up. If the market is very quiet I might even call it a day at this point and go straight to the park with Christopher for a sit down and an ice cream.

4PM

Time for a last look at the portfolio as the market shuts in half an hour. How have I done today? What did I miss? How much money did I make or lose? When you have a lot of money in the market (I have more than a million usually), it can be up or down £10,000–£20,000. It took some getting used to this. Over a month I could end up down or up by £50,000 plus!

4.30PM

That's it! The market's shut: hurrah! I have a final look through and close ADVFN down for now and turn off the computer. This is time for playing with my son. We might go for a swim, or a game of football, or do his reading – anything that we feel like.

5.30PM

Time for tea. Mrs NT tends to do it, though I do my best Heston Blumenthal impression about twice a week. We try to eat healthily, but pizzas, chips and sausages do sneak in sometimes. We try and make sure Christopher has something decent, but he is always on the hunt for sugary things.

7.30PM

Time for Christopher's bath and bedtime. It is so rewarding being with him all the time. Being a stay-at-home trader gives me precious time with my son which could never be achieved as a full-time worker. Some of the dads round here leave home at 5am and don't return till 9pm, never seeing their children. Not something I could do.

I enjoy doing the bedtime story. Once a week, though, we get a babysitter in and Mrs NT and I go out for dinner with friends or to the cinema. We think it's important to get out for some 'us time' once a week at the very least.

8.30PM

Nothing on TV, so time for a cuddle with the Mrs! The next 5 ... I mean 30 minutes are censored ... I watch *The Apprentice* if it's on, or *Dragons' Den*. I also like *Curb Your Enthusiasm* and *Have I Got News For You*. Sky Atlantic, which shows all the new HBO programmes, is good too. But there's so much old crap on these days that I find I'm watching less and less. And I really hate most UK sitcoms and soaps.

9PM

I check to see where the Dow Jones closed. This always has a big effect on how my shares might start the day tomorrow. I also spend a little time doing research on companies flagged up from this morning's news stories, and check to see what's being launched on the market in the next few days. And I might look through some share lists and see if anything new comes up. More emails usually ping in and I get through some of those.

9.30PM

If there is a seminar coming up in a week or so, I do some preparation work. I never intended running seminars and have only been doing them relatively recently. I don't do that many, maybe five a year, but people seem to really enjoy them and they are very rewarding personally. The feedback is always good and I'm glad to be able to help.

So many nice people come and we have great fun chatting over lunch and in the bar afterwards. I read through replies to questionnaires I have sent delegates in advance and they really help me plan the day – I try and give people what they want. There is a lot of interest in Level 2 at the moment, which the professionals use to judge good entry and exit points. I explain Level 2 in depth and try and make what is complex simple. A lot of the day also depends on what's happening in the markets.

We've even started friendships with people who've attended the seminars. A very nice couple who actually live near us have become great friends. I also made friends with someone who became my dentist, and a lovely couple who live in Switzerland.

The seminars came about by accident as a suggestion from a reader. I was really nervous doing the first one, but now I love the days and stay at the hotel the night before and after. I need recovery time afterwards – you just try and talk non-stop for ten hours and you'll see what I mean!

If there's no work to do, I might curl up around about now with a book – on the terrace if it's warm.

10PM

I have a check of the news and hope Robert Peston isn't on it – his presence usually indicates economic trouble! Sometimes we watch something we Sky-plussed. Or even half a movie, which we'll finish off the next day. By now the computer is most definitely off till the morning!

10.30PM

If we went out, we usually get back around now. The babysitter also does the ironing which is rather handy, so now we just have a chat, a decaf something and then …

11PM

… off to bed and I'm asleep the moment my head hits the pillo—zzzzzZZZ …

Part II
Getting Started

"The safest way to double your money is to fold it over once and put it in your pocket."

– Kin Hubbard

Is Trading Right for You?

Who are you?

First, the warning

Okay, I feel like a right boring old fart starting with a warning. After all, you bought this book because you wanted to make some money. And you *can* make money on the markets.

It's just that, over the years, I've met or read of people who have totally screwed up and instead of making money they lost it. In fact, later in the book you will read some terrible stories from traders who had disasters.

Some lost nearly everything. One or two lost a fortune but then managed to get back on track. But some reckless traders have lost houses and even their marriages.

NAKED TRADER
Old Fart Warning

There have been various times in the markets when shares have slumped, taking people's money with them in spectacular fashion. Like 2000–2002.

May/June 2006 was also pretty bad, as was August 2007. And let's not get into the Lehman implosion. The point is, shares don't just go up – they can go down a lot, too.

Don't think you'll get rich quick. It won't happen. But if you take things easy, are careful with the amount of money you put in, and learn from your mistakes, then I am happy to encourage you – because your chances are good.

(Of course, if you do get rich quick, go ahead and email me with the subject line 'Na-na-na-na-naaaah!' – and feel free to send me some cash as proof. Preferably used 20s.)

Can you afford to trade shares?

Before you buy a single share, I do urge you to look at your finances carefully and honestly. Ask yourself:

1. Where is the money coming from that I am going to use to trade?

2. Can I honestly and realistically afford to lose a lot of it?

3. Where the hell is the remote control?*

It's unlikely you will lose all the money you put into investing – if you are careful and follow the rules laid out in this book – but it's not impossible. It is quite possible that you could lose 20–30% if the market runs against you for a while.

Maybe you have £10,000 spare sitting in a building society account not earning much interest. Will you feel okay about it if you end up with £6,000 after six months of trading?

-   If the answer is 'yes' to the above question, then go for it!

-   If the loss of the money would devastate you, keep it in the nice safe account and just wait till you can realistically afford to trade.

Perhaps you've suddenly come into money unexpectedly – say, £50,000! Great – as you weren't expecting it and, presuming your financial status is okay, then no reason why you shouldn't invest around £15,000 of it.

---

*Under the second-to-left cushion on the sofa.

Are you a compulsive gambler?

Let's presume you have the money to play with. One final thing to check: are you a compulsive gambler?

- Do you bet on the horses, buy scratch cards, go to the casino, play online betting games on a regular basis? And does that give you a feeling of excitement?

- Do you feel unable to stop doing these things because they are really enjoyable, even if you are losing?

- Do you hide your bets from your partner? (Under the sofa's a good place, but not the second-to-left cushion.)

If the answers to any of the above are yes, then give this book to someone else (or chuck it, so they have to buy a new one). Going into the markets will just be enabling your current addiction – and losses on the markets can be difficult to control.

Your temperament is also wrong for trading. To trade, you need to be cold and unemotional like Mr Spock, but you will feel the same rush when buying a share as you do when backing a horse. So as an *EastEnders'* scriptwriter might say, "Leave it aaht!"

In summary, then, don't trade if:

- you can't afford to lose some of the money

- you are likely to get emotionally involved

- you have, or could have, a gambling problem.

However, if you feel you are sensible, level-headed, have a few quid spare and want to give it a try, then go for it!

Okay, warnings over – let's get on with it!

What Do You Want From Your Trading?

Develop a money strategy/income streams

Before you launch yourself into the wild world of shares, you need to ask yourself why you're doing it.

- What sort of return are you after?

- Are you a high-risk, high-return hotshot or do you just want a few extra quid?

- Are you looking to build wealth over a long period?

- Just want a bit of fun?

- Make a bit extra to buy a new car?

- Hoping it will help pay school fees for your kids?

- Provide a better retirement?

- Or do you want to become a full-time trader?

Think about what you want from the market, because what you want (and how much you want it) will really affect how you trade.

Make more money by not relying on the markets

I believe it is easier to make money on the markets if it is *not* your main source (or would-be main source) of income.

If you're currently in a full-time job, you should do what I did and think about new income streams that will let you quit and trade but still have a fallback. I did a Buffy phone line and became a distributor for Telecom Plus, selling telephony and energy in my spare time. Think about things you could do, or find to do, to make extra cash alongside your trading.

Is there anything extra you could do at work to build up money for yourself? Or any contacts who might give you freelance work? See if you can find yourself some new income. It's one of the ways to eventually quit work.

The reason I suggest more than one source of income is that you will be more relaxed when trading. If you are trying to make trading your only source of income you will be much more stressed – and therefore more likely to snatch at profits, not cut losers, and not make enough money.

How much money do I need to start trading?

The question of how much money you need to start trading comes up a lot. If you only have £500, there really isn't that much point because of dealing commissions. You also won't really be able to get yourself a balanced portfolio (AKA a broad range of shares). And you will want some balance in there.

With around £500, I reckon you're better off waiting till you've built a bigger pot. In the meantime, it's definitely worth 'paper trading'. In other words, give yourself (say) 50 grand in pretend money, and play the markets on paper – keeping a record of buy prices for shares you go in for, and then how they perform, and what you sell for.

A lot of successful traders start this way, though it will never be a perfect replica of the real thing. (Extraordinarily, one can be a little calmer when only risking a fictional fortune.) Also, if paper trading, no return trips please to the Bank of Me, Myself and I, and its magic money-making biro when paper trades go the wrong way. Haven't you heard that credit is impossible to get these days?

So what's a reasonable figure? I would say that once you have around three grand or more, you have enough to start putting real money into the markets.

How much money do I need to become a full-time trader?

The amount of money you need to become a full-time trader depends on how much you think you need to live on, and how much you think you can make from investing. I reckon realistically full-time investors can and need to aim each year to be making 20–25% on the money they have invested. This is with dividends (the profits paid out by a company to its shareholders) paying for their trading costs.

This means that, if someone has trading money of £100,000, a full-time trader is someone who can get £25,000 out of it with the right discipline, and is happy living on that amount of money. If you need more to live off, you'll need to invest more.

It is possible to make more than 20–25%, of course, but you'd have to be really good or have a couple of lucky breaks. The point is, you have to be realistic about it. I have people who email me to say they have started being full-time traders with just £10k. I think they are bonkers. It won't happen. Some people think they can do it by using leverage – in other words, debt on-demand that supersizes the amount they can buy and sell – in spread betting. However, what often happens is that instead of making more money they go bust. Spectacularly! Losing not just their own money, but money that isn't theirs … My view is: don't use the credit you can get. Use genuine money.

Reader spot – no margin for errors

"I tried a £50k day trade using leverage, without having the money to settle. My position lost 10% and I had to sell other shares to cover the shortfall on a bad day for the FTSE 100. What did I learn? Don't day trade with someone else's money – they'll definitely want it back!"

And above all, please … as said, only use money you can afford to lose a lot of – even 50% of it. Heck, all of it. You have to be prepared for such an outcome, or you just won't be able to trade in peace. And bad things do sometimes happen … So if you have £10,000, ask yourself – will I be okay if a lot of that, God forbid, goes down the drain? And only put in as much as you *are* okay with. Then you're safe.

 # Types of Trader and Investor

I've met loads of traders/investors over the years. Everyone is different and everyone has their own idea on how they will make money.

Mr Small Cap Oil/Miner

Yeah! He thinks he's going to make millions from finding the next big oil company and puts his money only into small oil and mining shares in the hope of finding a 'multi bagger' (a share that will multiply numerous times over in value). Problem is, though he might find the odd good winner or two, he will often also end up with busts or overnight 50% fallers. While there is nothing wrong with backing oil and mining shares, they should be part of an overall balanced portfolio. Having just oil and mining stocks isn't the best of ideas. They're risky things!

Chances of success: 1/10

Mr Day Trader

Thinks he's going to make a mint from being a *day trader*. Anyway it sounds cool doesn't it? Imagine at parties! "What do you do?" "I'm a day trader!" "Wicked!"

Day traders were common in the markets in 1998–9 and many gave up their jobs to day trade. And then went back to their jobs again.

Same thing in 2006–7 before the credit crunch and recession struck.

Day trading means buying shares and holding them for not very long – just taking lots of small profits. Trouble is, most people lose at day trading and that's a fact. Indeed, about 95% lose. It takes an awful lot of effort and it's very stressful too. With commissions and spreads, it's very hard to make enough each day to live off. Mr DT may easily get into denial and think he's making money when he's not. There is the very exceptional day trader who can do it, but you need to do it full-time and concentrate on it. Very hard.

Chances of success: 0.5/10

> **Q.** How come the conga line kept on breaking up at the day trader's party?
>
> **A.** Not many of them were willing to go long.

Mr Chart Guy

Has decided his charts are the True Answer and will only trade shares from looking at a chart.

He examines things like Fibonacci ratios and Bollinger Bands (personally I like Bollinger but can leave the bands). He also looks at things like moving averages and MACD divergence and likes to draw pretty lines all over the charts to prove something is a buy or a sell.

Now don't get me wrong – there *is* the odd person out there who does manage to make money from charts alone, but I think they are few and far between. My view is those going for just charts are missing out on the whole picture. Charts should be used, but in conjunction with other methods outlined in the book.

Chances of success: 3/10

Mr System Addict

Now here's the chap that just loves to buy trading systems. He'll be clicking on all the ads that offer to turn £2,000 into £75,000. He can't think of anything better than plugging in the latest amazing system that tells him when to buy or sell a share.

He just can't believe it when his system signalled a buy and yet the share went down! What is wrong with the share?! The system says it was going up! Especially as it was all meant to be so easy. The people that sold him the system said so. And they know what they are talking about, don't they? I'm afraid the truth is that you have to do a bit of work to make money in the markets.

Chances of success: 2/10

Mr Safe and Steady

A bore but – crucially – one without imagination. He'll only buy something he considers safe. So companies like utilities ('people always need power') or Tesco ('people always need to eat'). Nothing wrong with that necessarily, but he only likes them because he *thinks* they're boring, which isn't a great reason.

He probably does okay in the long run, and he may end up making more money than he would just leaving it in the building society. The thing is, while he won't lose very much, you do need to take *some* risk to make money.

Chances of success: 6/10

Mrs Long-Term Investor

Notice the Mrs here – most women who trade are longer-term investors because they don't take as many gambles as the men.

Mrs LTI doesn't buy that often and is quite cautious. But she will do her research and will probably hold for long enough to make good profits.

And you know what? Mrs LTI should do well. Her problem may be eventually holding on for too long and she needs to learn to take profits some time.

Chances of success: 8/10

Mr Medium-Term Investor

Buys and holds shares for anything between three months and two years. Does some careful research. Sticks to stop losses. Takes profits when it's sensible to do so. Keeps an eye on his shares but doesn't necessarily wet-nurse them all day. Prefers smaller companies (with growth prospects) to the FTSE 100 ones. Sounds a bit like me! I reckon the best chance of being a winner.

Chances of success: 8.5/10

Mr Analyser

Take the first four letters of his name and you know what I mean. This trader tries way too hard and analyses everything way too much. So much so that he'll end up not buying shares that could go up quite a lot, just because he has over-analysed and got too worried.

Chances of success: 2.5/10

Mr Accountant

Loves poring over every detail of a company's accounts and takes great joy in PEG ratios and acid tests and all that. Thing is, he misses the point of the market, which largely ignores all that. If you look at all the ratios and the small things, you'll never buy a single share and miss loads of good opportunities. I've often talked to accountants. They tell me they often get too scared to trade, and that is no good at all.

Chances of success: 4/10

Mr Short

Mr Short thinks the market is always too high and everything is too expensive, so he would rather bet on shares to go down. He shorts all the time rather than buying, and enjoys being a bit of a maverick. One thing he's forgotten: over time shares go up more than they go down. So he's asking for trouble. Bull markets last way longer than bear ones and he is likely to make big losses during a long-term bull market. Shorting is fine in the right circumstances but not all the time.

Chances of success: 1/10

Mr Quick In and Out

As well as fairly obviously being useless in bed, Mr Quick in and Out may have trouble making much money in the markets. This character looks for something that's going up, and hopes to hop on board and get out quick if it starts to go down. But the problem is that he is typically trying to find shares that have plunged and yet he thinks will rebound quickly – and he could end up holding some real shockers that don't rise again for long. For every one or two small successes, he is going to have the odd awful stinker that will bring his whole portfolio down.

Chances of success: 1/10

Mr Bottom Picker

Yes, I know what you're thinking, that title sounds a bit gruesome. But if you're into such things, then good for you, not really my cup of tea to be honest but I have an open mind.

Mr BP just *loves* shares that have suddenly plummeted, preferably on a profits warning. He'll get up in the morning and the first thing he'll do (well maybe after a wee) is scan the list of the worst performing shares and get stuck in. The reasoning is: "It's oversold."

He'll buy in and then start to worry a bit when it doesn't immediately start going up. It dips a little more the next day, but, "Hey, it was nearly double the price the day before yesterday so it'll go back up and I'll make loadsamoney." Except it often doesn't, and what was meant as a short-term trade becomes a "long-term investment".

Of course, every dog has its day, and it has to be said that Mr BP would have been right on the money in early 2009, when the banking crisis subsided and lots of shares that had plummeted suddenly began to seriously pick up again. (But of course not all shares did …)

Chances of success: 3/10

Mr Scaredy Cat

This type of trader sells the moment the market starts to go down a bit. They are scared of the slightest drop in the market. They then buy it all back again when it goes back up.

Trouble is, once all the costs of commission and spreads are taken into account, their profits are never going to be huge, even if losses won't be that big either.

Chances of success: 3/10

Mr Bulletin Board

Mr BB spends his life on the bulletin boards – you wonder how he gets the time to do anything else. He reckons himself as a bit of a guru. He's everywhere, telling people what he's bought. The buy is usually backed up with a pretty chart. He boasts about how well he's doing.

The funny thing is, if one of his buys tanks stupendously it's forgotten about, while if he buys something that goes up, he will continue to remind the other people on the bulletin boards. The winners remembered, the losers forgotten. Whatever you do, don't follow Mr BB's tips. Do your own research!

Chances of success: no idea!

Mr Penny Share

Loves his low-priced shares and won't buy anything else! Prefers to buy shares under 20p because they could double, treble or become ten baggers (a ten-times increase in value). More likely, they will go bust rather than double or anything else. I'm afraid 'look after the pennies and the pounds will take care of themselves' doesn't apply here.

Chances of success: 0.5/10

Mr Footsie Player

Doesn't bother much with shares and prefers to play the indices, i.e. putting money on the whole FTSE

100 (or other index) to go up or down. Usually believes he has found some kind of super system which tells him when to buy and sell. Will be on the bulletin boards making predictions, most of which are wrong but somehow he persuades himself he is always right. Most people lose playing indices. If Mr Footsie Player tells you he's winning, take the boasts with a cupboard-full of salt. Especially as more than 95% of index traders lose!

Chances of success: 1/10

Why did I write about these characters? Well, though they're mostly caricatures, their flaws are very real and very common. (Their virtues are less common, but just as achievable.) I think it's worth thinking about them so that you can decide the type of investor you are or want to be.

And now you know the types, you'll hopefully be able to recognise when you're falling into trading styles that are less than ideal. It's easy to do – that's why lots of people have done it!

The Trader's Toolkit

Introduction

Good news!

I give you full permission to skip the next few pages if you have already traded lots of shares via the internet and know how to do it, or if you read the last edition of this book and have already traded. However, if you take the plunge with the beginners and read it anyway, it won't do you any harm – not least because all the how-to-get-started stuff has been updated for this edition!

So, for those who know how to look up a real-time share price, have bought shares, have an online broker account and know a little bit about the markets, this is your last chance to get yourself some tea and toast and move directly to page 57.

If you have never, or hardly ever, bought shares over the internet, then there is *no* escape. You need to read this chapter.

No skipping, right?

I promise you, it's not that boring. In fact, it's way easier than you might think to get started as a trader or investor. So you can start off by taking it easy. It really is quite straightforward.

Here's all you need to deal online:

- a computer, with internet access (I know that might come as a shock!)
- execution-only broker(s) (easy)
- access to share prices and market info (really easy)
- a notebook and pen (steal one from the bookies)
- lots of tea and toast (try Yorkshire tea, it's the best!)

And that really is it – told you not to worry! I am sure you already have the computer.

The toolkit

We're going to look at five essential things in this section:

1. Computer with broadband

2. Online stock broker

3. Real-time prices

4. How to find the share price of a company

5. Your notebook

Let's get started ...

1. Computer with broadband

The computer's the easy bit. You've probably already got one, and it will almost certainly do. A standard desktop should be fine. Likewise a normal laptop, especially if you intend your trading desk to sometimes consist of your bed and several pillows. Probably not an iPad, though – but perhaps sufficient apps will appear in future.

I find having an additional laptop quite handy, so I can monitor share prices on one computer and trade on the other – but it's not necessary, especially if you are just starting out. You do not need loads of screens!

2. Online stock broker

There are now countless ways to make money from trading without even having to open an account with an ordinary stock broker. There's spread betting, fixed-odds betting, CFDs, betting exchanges, binary betting, options and futures, and direct market access. It's never been easier to play the markets. However, even with all these exciting-sounding ways of trading, I still believe new investors should start with a basic online stock-broking account.

All the new ways of trading shares can be pretty dangerous if you don't know what you're doing, so I think the best way to begin is via one or two online execution-only stockbrokers. Once you are up and running with that you can move onto more advanced accounts like spread betting.

Why?

Because it's straightforward. And you can only lose whatever you put in.

With a conventional online broker account you can get used to investing or trading the markets for a while before getting into anything more complicated.

I will get to the other methods later in the book, but for now don't worry about them.

So which kind of broker should you go for?

There are two types out there.

1. *Advisory brokers*

    These brokers will give you advice on what stocks to buy and sell, and even trade on your behalf if you want (this latter type are called discretionary brokers). **My view: some of them are absolute rubbish.**

2. *Execution-only brokers*

    As the name suggests, no advice is given at all. You're on your own. They're just the means by which you buy and sell whatever shares you want whenever you want.

My advice is, forget about the advisory ones – they take loads of money from you and often make big mistakes.

This book is about how to trade for yourself, so you should be looking for an execution-only one. I'm sure the reason you bought this book was to make your own decisions. So, from now on, when talking of brokers, I am writing about execution-only ones. Which is good, as they're cheap.

Selecting a broker

It's difficult to recommend specific brokers, as their services and charges are changing all the time. These days, though, the top ones are really much of a muchness.

Generally speaking they will all provide a similar service. Which is, quite simply, you choose to buy or sell a share over the internet, and they enact the trade for you. Your trade is usually recorded on your account which you can access anytime. And that's it.

Occasionally, brokers' internet services freeze or don't work. In my experience it happens to them all at some point.

So in the end it comes down to the price you're charged per trade. The dreaded commission.

The average is about £12.50 per trade. You can get cheaper; if you trade a lot the price will get lowered. Watch out for firms offering anything lower than around £8, though, as they will try and get the money back off you in other ways – e.g. spam inundation or being a bit crap.

Just go through a few brokers' sites (some are listed in a second) and check their price lists.

> **Q.** How many stockbrokers does it take to change a light bulb?
>
> **A.** Two. One to take out the bulb and drop it, and the other to try and sell it before it crashes.

Watch the small print. Some charge an 'inactivity fee' if you don't trade much.

Quite honestly, I have three accounts (being a completely greedy sod) and I don't find an awful lot of difference between them. They're all easy to use.

My accounts are with Selftrade and Barclays, and my pension is with TD Waterhouse. I have no complaints about any of them and they get me the same prices. I hardly ever have to contact them.

As it doesn't cost anything to set up an account, I would initially open two accounts. I'll explain a bit later why this can be a good tactic.

Be a bit wary if you find a very cheap deal with a company you've never heard of. If a broker goes bust, despite being supposed to have your money segregated, the bottom line of compensation rules means that officially you might only get a max of £50k back. I'd rather trade with the bigger names.

Broker checklist

A checklist when looking for a broker:

1. Check the **broker's website**.

2. Trades should cost **no more than £12.50**.

3. Watch out for **hidden charges**.

4. Consider opening **multiple accounts** with two or more brokers and compare their services directly.

5. Watch out for prices that are too good to be true.

Here is a list of some of the top online brokers. Check through their sites and see what they have to offer you:

- Barclays Stockbrokers – **www.stockbrokers.barclays.co.uk**

- Hargreaves Lansdown – **www.h-l.co.uk**

- Selftrade – **tinyurl.com/57hp4n**

- The Share Centre – **www.share.co.uk**

- TD Waterhouse – **www.tdwaterhouse.co.uk**

You may find I've got the odd special deal on my site so do check it out when broker-hunting: **www.nakedtrader.co.uk**.

Share certificates

Share certificates are a thing of the past – forget about them. Most online brokers use *nominee accounts*. This means you don't get a certificate; you are the electronic owner of the shares. In fact, getting certificates is next to impossible. So don't bother.

When you buy shares they simply go straight into your online account and when you sell them they leave your online account – wonderful! If you have any certificated shares you can transfer them into a nominee account with your broker. Call them for details of how to do this.

Show me the money

You need to put some money in!

Sorry, but … well, you need to put some money in your account or else you won't be able to buy any shares. D'oh!

The best and quickest way is simply to fund your account with a debit card, or you can send the broker a cheque. Sending cheques takes some time, so a debit card is best. Because of the new money laundering rules (why people want to clean their cash is beyond me), some brokers may ask you to send proof of who you are, so you might need to send in a copy of a driving licence or passport. Don't get annoyed with them. Blame the government or the money launderers – take your pick, as they're both thieves!

Brokers do pay some interest on cash in your account, but not a lot. You generally should be using the money for trading. That's the way you'll make more money!

Use an ISA, don't pay tax

You *must* consider putting as much of your trading money under an ISA (Individual Savings Account) umbrella as you can. (At the time of writing, you can put in up to £10,680 a year.) Why? You can trade the money inside self-select ISAs without *any* liability to capital gains tax. Every profit you make, you keep.

How do you do this? Simple. When you sign up to a broker, make sure you click the link for the ISA self-select shares account.

What makes this so important?

Under the current rules, if you make more than £10,100 profit in any one tax year you get stung for capital gains tax (CGT) and the government can legally grab part of the profit you made (however unfair that might seem).

Capital gains tax as I write is 18% or 28% depending on your income. A number of politicians have expressed ambitions to raise this to 40% in the future. Boo! Why give that away if you are making nice profits?

I have saved thousands upon thousands of pounds in taxes that I would otherwise have had to pay if I hadn't put all my share money into an ISA.

As the years go by, and you build your portfolio, the ISA tax advantage becomes more and more apparent.

Let's say you have a few good years and manage to build up £150,000 of capital inside your ISA. All tax-free. Now say you have a *very* good year and turn that £150,000 into £250,000. That's a profit of £100,000. Outside an ISA that profit could get nastily cut by over £25,000 in CGT. Inside, it's untouchable.

It is worth checking to see if your broker will make any standing charges to look after your ISA. Most do – expect to pay around £15 a quarter.

There is no maximum amount you can build in your ISA through stock market profits, only a limit on how much cash you can deposit in it from outside every year (currently £10,680 – it goes up a little bit annually).

Withdrawals from ISAs can be made anytime, but once cash is taken out, it cannot be replaced except within your annual allowance. But the great thing is there is *no limit* to profits you can make.

People do get confused about the benefits of ISAs, so here is a basic recap for anyone whose eyes have glazed over at all this HMRC-speak (I don't blame you):

- They're brilliant.

- You can add £10,680 of external cash into them in a year. (This is expected to rise with inflation.)

- You can make as much profit as you want inside them and everything you withdraw is tax free. But once you take money out, you can still only add back in the annual allowance each tax year. (Still no limit on profits, though.) If you've used that allowance, you have to wait till next year.

- You can buy and sell as many shares in them as often as you like.

- You don't have to report any of this to the taxman.

3. Real-time prices (and some extra stuff)

A broker provides you with the ability to buy and sell shares. Once you have set up your account, you'll also need a website that provides live buy and sell prices, news and information.

Plus you need to know some other stuff too:

- how to keep an eye on news about shares and what companies are announcing

- the dividends a company will pay

- when their next results are announced

- a chart of how a share price has been behaving

- what a company is worth

- how much profit it makes.

It's known as *research* and is something a lot of people can't be bothered with. But please be bothered.

Because, really, you ought to keep yourself informed – especially once you are the proud owner of a few shares and can idly mention to your mates:

"I have a portfolio ... "

On the other hand, maybe best not to mention it, as they may suddenly expect you to buy all the drinks.

Now, onto the sexy bit ...

Real-time prices

Where do you find real-time prices and other stuff like news about shares?

Well, there are quite a few websites and the good news is most of the stuff you need is free.

So you can look up real-time prices for nothing, though the 'real-time' service itself may only last a minute or so – you'll need to keep manually refreshing your screen. If you want 'always on' access to real-time prices you usually have to pay (not that much). Hey, the websites have to make some money!

I personally use a site called ADVFN.com. However, there are a number of similar sites you can use instead if you want to.

For the purposes of this book, I'm going to use ADVFN as the basic information supplier. They've not paid me a bean to do this, by the way. It just makes it far easier for me to describe how to look for things if I use the one site. I write a column for them, but do so for a number of other sites too. Once you've understood how to find what you need on ADVFN, you can easily move to another site if you want. You just need to know what you're looking for.

The following six sites are the main online sources for real-time prices and share-research tools:

- ADVFN –
  www.ADVFN.com

- Interactive Investor –
  www.iii.co.uk

- MoneyAM – **www.moneyam.com**

- Proquote – **www.proquote.net**

- Hemscott – **www.hemscott.net**

- Digital Look – **www.digitallook.com**

When you're up and trading properly, it may be worth opening accounts with two or three real-time price companies as a back-up in case your favourite breaks down – it could prove cheaper than the therapy bills!

All these sites offer some free services, so you can get a good taster before paying for any extra services. Don't do any blind, blanket sign-ups.

Right – wakey up, you beginners!

In case you've switched off, missed stuff or been sneaking looks at *Heat* or *Nuts* instead of paying attention … here's a summary of our trading journey so far:

1. Get some online broking accounts set up.

2. Think about sticking some of your money in an ISA to avoid tax.

3. Find a place where you can access real-time prices and other info.

Now, what other info do you need before you get cracking?

4. Finding information on share prices

How do you find the share price of a company, or monitor the share prices of a bunch of companies? It's easy! Let's dive in properly now to the ADVFN website (remember, other websites will be quite similar).

How to use ADVFN (and other similar sites)

Best place to start? I guess it's the home page. You'll need to register (it's free with ADVFN).

Obviously you may be reading this book on the train, or even on the loo. But for the next bit it may be worthwhile you reading it while you're by a computer or laptop so you can follow along.

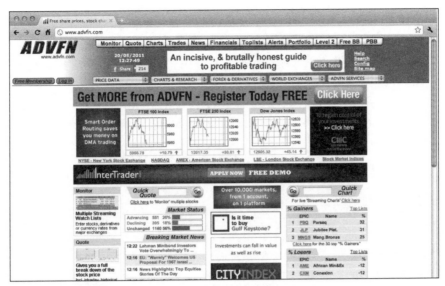

ADVFN home page

The main thing you need to focus on is the navigation menu near the top of the page (see the screenshot above). I'll go through the sections you need to be interested in initially.

1. *Monitor:* this is the most useful page! This is the basic list of shares that you are interested in and may want to follow on a day-to-day basis. I'll explain how to add shares to this later in this chapter.

2. *Quote:* gets you a quote on the current price for any share.

3. *Trades:* brings up data on buys and sells that have taken place in the share of your choice.

4. *News:* obvious ... it's, er, financial news!

5. *Financials:* info to help you research a share.

6. *Toplists:* one of my favourite pages. Contains rankings of stocks by all sorts of criteria, such as top movers of the day. Basically, a great place to find out where the action is happening.

7. *Free BB* and *P[remium]BB:* these are the bulletin boards that investors use to gossip.

The other buttons you'll want to use in time, but these should get you going.

Let's look at the information you get when you ask for a quote on a share, using the quote page.

Stock codes

You'll quickly realise that everything on the ADVFN website (as with most other stock market websites) revolves around what are called *stock symbols*. These are short (three or four letter) symbols used to represent shares.

For example, the following table lists the symbols for the ten largest companies (by value) listed on the London Stock Exchange at the time of writing.

Top ten largest companies on the London Stock Exchange

Company	Code
BHP Billiton	BLT
Royal Dutch Shell	RDSB
HSBC Holdings	HSBA
Vodafone Group	VOD
BP	BP.
Rio Tinto	RIO
GlaxoSmithKline	GSK
Unilever	ULVR
British American Tobacco	BATS
BG Group	BG

Note: Be careful, the code for BP is 'BP.' – including the stop!

These symbols are also – rather confusingly – sometimes called EPIC, or TIDM, or RIC codes. Or *tickers*. It doesn't really matter: throughout this book I'll refer to them simply as codes. (I hope you're not falling asleep at the back there – this is important stuff!)

If you don't know the symbol of the company you are interested in, you need to find out what it is. The best way to explain this is by way of an example.

Example – finding the stock code for a company

You've come across a company called Avon Rubber, and you want to find its current share price and start doing some research on the stock.

On the ADVFN website, click the 'Quote' button in the top menu bar:

The tabs at the top

On the next page, if you knew the stock's symbol already, you could at this point simply input it into the box (to the right of where it says 'Symbol:'), click the 'OK' button, and you'd be off:

The box where you type your stuff

However, if you don't know the symbol, type 'Avon Rubber' in the box. DON'T click 'Search or 'OK', though, just wait a second for the site to do its magic. You should find that suggested results appear below the box now:

Suggested results appearing

Sometimes life is simple and you get just the one stock listed, or the correct one is obvious. In this case, there are a few Avons listed. Most times we'll be interested in the share listed on the London Stock Exchange (which is indicated by 'LSE'), for which we can see the code is 'AVON'.

Likewise, on the easily accessible Yahoo! Finance both Avon Rubber PLC (AVON.L) and AVON RUBBER PLC (AVNBF.PK) pop up. Hmm ... bugger! But not to worry. We're looking for the one on the London Stock Exchange (LSE), and that is always indicated by '.L' after the code. So the symbol for Avon Rubber is AVON. (The L isn't actually part of the code.)

At this point on ADVFN you can return to the main quote page and input 'AVON' as the symbol (ADVFN also make it easy for you, as clicking on the symbol itself jumps straight to the relevant quote page).

If you don't fancy using the search functions, you can, of course, just use the A–Z list to manually search for stock codes.

You'll see that there's quite a bit happening on the ADVFN quote page. It's worth spending some time finding your way around this page.

So let's have a look at the quote for AVON.

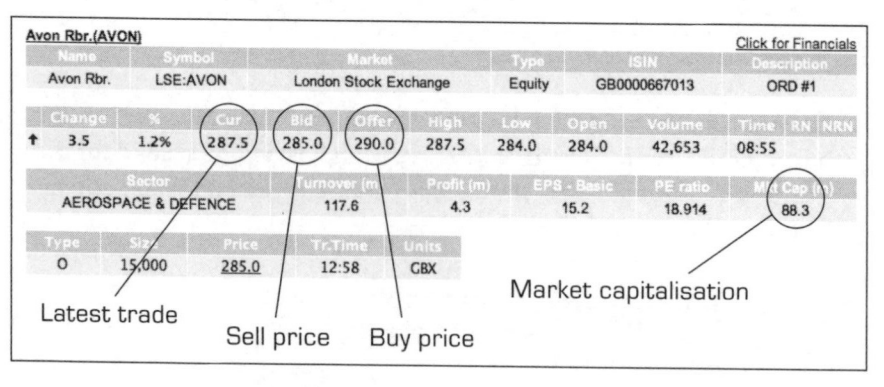

ADVFN quote for Avon Rubber

Here you can see price information: the current sell price is 285p, and the buy price is 290p (the jargon for these, as you can see, is: *bid* and *offer*). So you can sell at about 285p and buy at about 290p.

The buy price is always more than the sell price, so remember you are already losing a little just by buying a share.

'Mkt Cap (m)' is an important piece of info on this page. It stands for market capitalisation, which means the value of the entire company in the market. (As worked out by multiplying the total number of shares of the company by the current share price – which gives, in this case, £76 million).

The latest price at which it traded is there too (under the label 'Cur', short for 'current').

A word of warning: don't necessarily trust the profit and turnover figures – under 'Turnover (m)' and 'Profit (m)'– as these can be out of date. Always check these directly from the company's latest results, which you can find down in the news stories listed below the quote.

Scroll down a bit further and you will see the share price chart for the last year.

You'll also find the box for 'Recent news' stories, which is where you can begin research, as I'll show you later.

Perhaps when you're next at your computer press 'Quote' on ADVFN to see the latest, and check you understand this in the flesh. It's ridiculously simple, I swear. Unfortunately the ADVFN.com free service will dump you out unceremoniously after around 30 seconds, so I would also recommend running through it on, for example, **uk.finance.yahoo.com** where you will find things pretty similar (just not live).

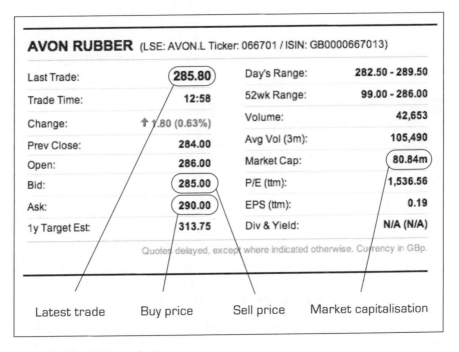

Yahoo!'s delayed free service

Using the ADVFN monitor

You may decide you want to start watching Avon Rubber regularly. In this case, you should add it to your 'Monitor' page on ADVFN. You'll be able to track its real-time buy and sell prices, amounts traded, highs and lows of the day and the latest news stories about it.

To start this monitor or watchlist of shares, just click the 'Monitor' tab, then 'Edit monitor lists':

Edit monitor lists

Give a name to your monitor, then tap in "AVON", and click 'Create new monitor':

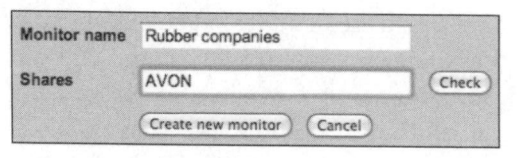

Creating a new monitor

You can add as many shares as you like to your monitor section. Remember, first find the code, then just add it in the same way. You can add a bunch all at once by separating the codes with a comma as you enter them in the box:

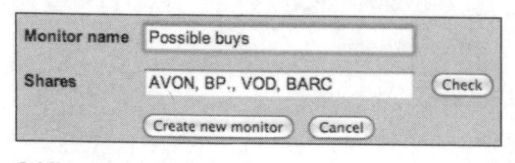

Adding multiple shares

Best of all, you can have any number of different monitor lists going, and this allows you to separately group and monitor shares of different kinds. For example, you could call one monitor 'FTSE 100' to keep an eye on FTSE 100 companies, and call another 'Small companies' to track the smaller sector. You could lump your 'maybes' together in one list, and the shares you actually hold together in another.

Possibilities: endless. And much better than just reading off a single huge list. Access all this functionality through the magical 'Edit monitor lists' button. I use ten or so monitors for different areas of the market.

ADVFN also has cracking research facilities, too. I'll show you later how to use these to your best advantage.

The cost of real-time prices

- When you look up a share price during market hours (0800–1630), ADVFN will quote you a real-time price for a few seconds before it times out. You can do that as often as you like.

- If you want always-on real-time prices, it costs around £10 to £15 a month via most sites. Money worth spending, I reckon. It's usually given to you for free if you pay for Level 2. On ADVFN, real-time prices come under its 'silver' service – and no, sadly it doesn't involve expertly trained butlers. But it *is* good. More on it soon.

5. Notebook

So, computer sorted? Broker account on the way? Access to real-time prices set up? Vaguely understand that quote page? Can you see where the news stories are? Still awake?

Good, we're nearly there. Final thing: I also recommend keeping a notebook handy. It's always good for jotting down ideas, share prices and bits of info. It's also obviously handy for jotting down phone numbers and losing them.

In fact, I strongly recommend you go one step further and keep a trading diary: write down everything you buy and sell, the prices transacted and *the reasons for buying or selling*. This will come in handy later on when you analyse why you made money, or lost it.

Similarly, next to each share on your monitor on ADVFN is a memo button. You can click on that and add notes about a share which you can come back to at a later time.

Your trading environment

Stay clutter free!

Keeping a clear head is very important when it comes to share trading – and it's just not possible if you're surrounded by clutter. I think it can seriously affect trading decisions if you're sitting in the midst of hundreds of old fag butts, empty bags of crisps, loads of bits of paper, newspapers and empty beer cans. Clutter will subconsciously put you under more pressure when making trading decisions.

Keep a clear desk and a tidy office and your head will feel clear too. And this will help your trading. Tea and toast is also vitally important to good trading. (Oh bugger, just spilled crumbs all over the desk. Fine example I set.)

KISS – Keep It Simple Stupid

Don't make trading too difficult for yourself. What I mean is: don't overburden yourself with dozens of trading monitors and a bank of TV screens in every corner of the room.

That's just to impress the girlfriend/wife/friends, right?

Keep it simple. You don't need to start buying chart systems and complicated software to start trading. All you need is access to news stories, fundamentals, charts and real-time prices. You can get this from free websites, or you might need to pay a small amount to access them. That's fine.

You don't need to be buying multi-thousand-pound systems to display this information on. All that will do is confuse things. You need to keep your mind free to concentrate on just one thing: is a share a good buy or not? I promise you, your expensive systems are just dumb computers and won't be any help. Stay with the simple stuff. One day, when you've made your first million, by all means fill your office with impressive, flashing machines. But not for starters.

The other silly thing that might tempt you around about now is to drop a small fortune on a trading system. No! Anytime you catch yourself drooling over a glossy ad for a trading system promising to make you millions, walk away very fast. Just think of Baloo Bear from *The Jungle Book* – it's all about the 'bear necessities'!

What You Need to Know to Start Trading

Beginners: things you need to know about shares!

Let's look at some of the things you really need to know about shares. These are:

1. Spreads

2. Trading costs

3. Exchange market size

4. Trading hours

5. Why shares move up or down

6. Market makers and the crowd

7. Dividends

I'll accept that some of this may not be immediately fascinating, and having read the above list you may well yawn and decide to stop reading for the moment.

Well, thanks a lot! I'm sitting here working hard (and definitely *not* watching *Deal or No Deal* at the same time) and all you can do is get bored.

But these bits and pieces are essential to understand before making that first trade. Many new traders lose money in the market because they don't understand what's going on. So you've got to get your head around these things!

1. Spreads

If you're a woman reading this, when I say spreads I am *not* talking about those woolly things you buy to put over a sofa to hide the stains if someone is coming round. (Men are less likely to be confused, as when it comes to stains we are neanderthals and don't notice.) I *am* talking about the difference between a sell price and a buy price, which is known as the *spread*.

Although you will often come across references to the 'share price', the idea of the price of a share is actually a little more complicated than that, and people new to the market can get confused over this. First, we need to define some terms:

- *Bid price:* the price at which you can sell shares.

- *Offer price:* the price at which you can buy shares.

- *Spread:* the difference between sell and buy price (bid and offer).

- *Mid price:* the price halfway between the bid and offer prices.

A key point we can see from the above is that, at any one time, the price for buying a share and selling a share is always going to be different.

Let's look at an example.

Avon Rbr.(AVON)									Click for Financials		
Name	**Symbol**		**Market**			**Type**		**ISIN**		**Description**	
Avon Rbr.	LSE:AVON		London Stock Exchange			Equity		GB0000667013		ORD #1	

	Change	**%**	**Cur**	**Bid**	**Offer**	**High**	**Low**	**Open**	**Volume**	**Time**	**RN**	**NRN**
↑	3.5	1.2%	287.5	285.0	290.0	287.5	284.0	284.0	42,653	08:55		

Sector		**Turnover (m)**	**Profit (m)**	**EPS - Basic**	**PE ratio**	**Mkt Cap (m)**
AEROSPACE & DEFENCE		117.6	4.3	15.2	18.914	88.3

Type	**Size**	**Price**	**Tr.Time**	**Units**
O	15,000	285.0	12:58	GBX

ADVFN quote for Avon Rubber

In this screenshot we can see that Avon Rubber has a bid price of 285p and an offer price of 290p. That means if you want to sell the stock you'll get around 285p a share, and if you want to buy the stock you'll have to pay 290p.

Say you buy 1,000 shares at 290p, costing £2,900. If you changed your mind immediately after having bought the shares and wanted to sell them, you'd have to sell at 285p. That's £2,850, so you would be down £50 (before even taking into account the commission cost and stamp duty). So add £12.50 for the buy, £12.50 to sell and stamp duty at 0.5% – that's another £40 or so.

The *spread* is the difference between the offer and bid price and, as can be seen in this example, is a real and significant cost of trading. Why are spreads there? It's how the market makers take their cut (these are the people that make shares available for you to buy or sell – explained more later).

Be aware of the importance of the spread, and realise that as soon as you buy a share, you're down on the deal until (or unless) the sell price rises above what you bought the share for.

Spread size

You'll soon find spreads can be wide or narrow.

Obviously the narrower the spread, the better for us – the less work our investments have to do to get into profit. Spreads will be very narrow on heavily traded stocks, like those in the FTSE 100, and wider on the smaller stocks. On some stocks, especially in the junior AIM market, spreads can be ridiculously wide.

For example:

- Look at the bid–offer spread for a large company like Vodafone. The bid–offer prices quoted could be 169.75–169.80. That's a spread of next to nothing – 0.05p – it's tiny.

- But for a small stock on AIM, where much smaller companies are listed, the bid–offer price could be 10–12. That's a spread of 20%! If you bought at 12, the shares would have to go up 20% just to break even!

A spread of 3% is about as much as I'll allow. 4% max. If the spread is more than that, I would seriously have to consider not buying, even if I like the look of the company.

Always work out what percentage of the price the spread is. If you're rubbish at percentages, ADVFN will tell you it under 'Financials'.

Spread headlines – the news tonight is:

- Remember: you're losing money as soon as you buy a share.

- Work out the percentage of the spread.

- Be cautious about trading a share with a spread over 3%, and never trade one with a spread over 5% unless it is a minor punt.

- The wider the spread, the bigger the risk.

2. Trading costs

The costs of buying and selling shares can add up quickly, so here's a rough guide to possible costs.

There are generally three elements to the cost of trading shares:

1. the **commission** charged by your broker, *plus*

2. (said through gritted teeth) a nasty and horrid tax on buying shares called **stamp duty**, *plus*

3. **the spread**.

If you're buying less than £1,000-worth of shares, rejoice! Since 2008 there's been no stamp duty for such trades. If you're buying more than £1,000-worth of shares, recoil! Stamp duty is set at 0.5% for such trades. And that's 0.5% on the *whole* trade – even on the first £1,000. So if you buy £5,000-worth of a share, the government will take £25.

Of course this tax is outrageous. Why we should have to pay a tax to buy shares in companies, I will never know. But there is no point bleating about it – we have to pay. Maybe not for much longer, but for now.

> *Note*: You only pay stamp duty on a **buy**, not when you sell a share.

To illustrate the costs of all the elements together – the commission and the spread as well – let's take a look at a simple example.

Example – trading costs

You buy 1,000 shares in a company at 500p per share. Total value: £5,000.

Costs:

- Broker commission: £12.50 (average)

- Stamp duty: £25

Having bought the shares, you decide to sell them immediately, but because of the bid–offer spread, you may only be able to sell them at 495p. Total value: £4,950.

Costs:

- Broker commission: £12.50 (average)

- Stamp duty: £0 (only applies on buys)

So:

- Total direct costs (commission + stamp duty): £50

- Indirect cost (a result of the spread): £50

And a complete cost of:

£100

That's 2% of your original investment. When you become a full-time trader, regularly dealing with substantial investments, you cannot afford to pretend costs don't matter. Let's not get all mopey, though, as there's a dead simple strategy for covering this. And we'll look at that when we look at dividends in a few pages.

Beginner investors sometimes forget to factor in the cost of the spread, but – please – don't. It is a real cost. Even if you were selling, in this case, for a luscious price rise to 800p, you'd still be down £50 from that original spread. There's no escaping it. It's a persistent little bastard, a kind of midget T-1000 of the trading world. You can never get away from it, though it's painful rather than lethal.

Of course, it could be worse – because it once was. Now we're in the age of the internet, discount brokerages and efficient trading platforms.

Imagine what it was like before, when broker commissions were a cool £50 or more!

Over-trade at your peril

As you can also see, the more you trade, the more the costs will stack up. In the previous example, trade five times, and you've knocked up total costs of £500. I probably pay around £3,000 a year to trade.

It means that if your mind is set on becoming a *day trader* – that is, buying and selling shares on the same day for lots of quick little profits – you have to be almost supernaturally good to cover the costs. And that's one of the reasons 90%+ of would-be day traders fail.

A key lesson here is: don't over-trade. It means a lot of money wasted on costs.

3. Exchange market size

You may think you can buy as many shares as you like in any company, but it doesn't always work like that. It might be true for FTSE 100 stocks, as you're more likely to run out of available money before the market runs out of available shares, but one has to be very careful when buying a smaller company.

Exchange market size, or EMS, is the number of shares that market makers guarantee to sell or buy at quoted prices. If you want to buy or sell shares in a quantity above the EMS it can lead to problems. When you are more advanced, you can check Level 2 to see the number of shares you can readily buy or sell.

Till then, how do you check EMS for free? You need to head to **www.londonstockexchange.com**. Put the code of your share – say, AVON – into the quotes search box at the top right. Click on the quote and then scroll down the box called 'Trading information' till you get to 'Exchange market size'. In this case it is 2,000 shares.

That means you can safely deal in 2,000 shares – or about £5,000-worth. If you buy more, you take the risk you might be charged a bigger spread.

In practice you can pretty much deal in three to four times the EMS without being charged extra.

But if the market suddenly tanks, the market makers can shut down and only offer you quotes strictly in EMS size.

Trading Information	
13-May-2011	
FTSE index	FTSE Fledgling (ex IT),FTSE Fledgling
FTSE sector	Aerospace & Defense
FTSE sub-sector	Defense
Country of share register	GB
Segment	SSQ3
MiFID Status	Regulated Market
Exchange market size	2,000
SEDOL	0066701
ISIN number	GB0000667013

Here's the blighter.

Finding the EMS – easy-peasy and free!

A particular danger is that, over time, you might build up a sizeable position in one company's shares – say 15,000 shares in Avon Rubber. If a time then came when you wanted to sell all those shares quickly, you would have a problem if the EMS was 2,000. You might only be able to sell some at the market price – and if you want rid of the lot, you might have to take a very low price.

So bear this in mind before building up a really substantial number of shares in one company.

I am very careful and make sure the shares I buy have a decent EMS. I usually ensure the EMS is at least £2,000-worth of shares – though I prefer £5,000. To work out the EMS in cash terms, simply multiply the EMS by the share price.

If you are dealing in a FTSE 100 share, unless you are trading in millions, don't worry about the EMS. You can buy and sell as much as your heart desires.

Summary

- Always check the EMS of a share before buying if it is a smaller share.

- You may pay more to deal in quantities larger than the EMS.

- Don't deal in shares with an EMS equivalent to less than £2,000.

4. Trading hours

The London Stock Exchange opens for trading shares between the hours of 08.00–16.30, Monday to Friday.

For a few minutes before the market opens and for a few minutes after it shuts, there are auctions of shares, but these are generally only for institutions. The opening auctions tend to decide the 8am opening price for most shares.

Be careful of dealing in the bigger stocks between 8am and 9am – the spreads can be huge because there is no depth to the market and you could get caught out.

You need to beware if you are looking at a share price *outside* market hours. The bid–offer spread may be much wider than normal because the market makers have gone home and there is only one left quoted. **Only believe prices you see during market hours.**

5. Why shares move up or down

Before we go any further, here's something you must get your head around:

What makes shares move up or down?

Not an unimportant question, no?

You might think that it would be an easy question to answer. But the factors affecting shares prices are quite complex. I get emails all the time from investors very puzzled by the movements of shares. They get very frustrated when shares shift and they can't see the reason why.

A classic example is when a share price falls following the release of good news (perhaps strong annual results). What a perverse market, people wail. But the explanation, in this case, can be found in the old stock market maxim:

'*Buy on the rumour, sell on the news.*'

By the time the news is actually announced, all the information has *already* been factored into the price – just look at the share price behaviour in the short period leading up to the announcement. So when the news is actually announced, the smart money (having bought previously in the run-up) is looking to sell and bank profits. The price therefore promptly goes down.

There are many reasons why a share might move. I'll examine some of the reasons in greater depth later. But for now, and to show how difficult it can be to know why your shares are doing well or badly, here are some of the reasons:

Broker upgrade/downgrade

Brokers regularly put out recommendations to their clients, and a buy or sell recommendation can temporarily affect a share. You'll usually find your news feed will reveal which broker and what their recommendation is. Sometimes this can move the market a lot. In my experience the broker comment usually only affects the share for a day or two, sometimes only for an hour or two.

General market move

The whole market may move up or down – for whatever reason – and your share can move in line with the market. If it is a FTSE 100 share, it might be affected by, say, economic gloom from the US and move in tandem with other FTSE shares. Small cap shares are less prone to a general move.

Sector move

Say your favourite stock is a telecoms share. A different telecoms company may have put out a profit warning, and your share could be dragged down along with all telecoms stocks.

Institution move

An institution has bought or sold stock. (Big trades – such as those made by large institutions – are usually notified on the news wires one or two days after the event.) Look for the phrase 'holdings in company' on the news service to check them.

Director buying/selling

Directors have bought or sold shares in their own company. Investors often follow movements by directors, so more shares may be bought or sold than normal, moving the price.

Results/news story

If the price is moving quickly, check the news wire for any story. It could be a price-moving statement from the company or another news story.

Dividend dates

The price will always move lower on a share's 'ex-dividend' date, i.e. the day the company pays out some of its profits to shareholders. These are usually twice-yearly, but do vary – some shares don't have dividends at all. So if the dividend paid out to shareholders is 10p per share (and it's always done on a per-share basis), the share price will move down by around 10p.

Tipped

The share has been tipped by a newspaper, magazine or one of the many tipsters out there. Especially on weekend tips, the market marks up a share before the open in expectation of ready buyers.

Bulletin board manipulation

A tiny stock could soar because a group have got together to make it sound irresistible on the BBs.

Market-maker manipulation

Market makers are moving the price to encourage buyers or sellers, and are doing so just to suit their own ends.

Tree shake

Market makers push the price down quickly and drastically to encourage sellers, then move the price back up again. Often because they have a big buyer who will then take all those recently sold shares off their hands!

Surprise events

Something major happens like a terrorist strike – all shares could be hit. Or some political drama unfolds somewhere.

Rights issue

A company decides to raise money by offering more shares at a lower price. This usually lowers the existing price.

Takeover/merger

Companies announce a takeover or merger. Expect a big rise!

Stake building

Someone is building a stake in the company.

> My brief summary shows just how on the ball you must be. Always know why a share you might want to buy or sell is moving. There is more coming on why shares move later in the book.

6. Market makers and the crowd

We now need to talk about liquidity (no, this is nothing to do with what you fill a paddling pool with).

If you want to sell some shares on the stock market you need someone in the market willing to buy those shares. If there isn't anyone, you'd think it was a pretty rubbish market. But this can be a problem for small companies with few investors; at any one time (or even for a whole day) there may only be one or two investors interested in buying or selling the shares in a company. In these cases, the market in these small company shares is said to have *poor liquidity* (in other words, poor tradability).

For large companies (e.g. all FTSE 100 companies) this is not a problem. At any one moment there may be hundreds or thousands of investors wanting to buy or sell shares in, say, Vodafone. Anytime you want to buy (or sell) shares in Vodafone you can be sure there will lots of people willing to sell to (or buy from) you. Therefore, the market for large company shares is said to have *good liquidity* (good tradability).

But we still have a problem with small companies – a problem of poor liquidity.

What can be done?

The answer the stock exchange came up with was to assign one or more financial companies to guarantee that they would always be willing to buy or sell shares in a designated company. And this was done for all small companies. This guarantees that there is always someone in the market willing to buy and sell shares in any small company that is listed on the stock exchange. The financial companies that provide this guarantee are called *market makers*. In technical terms, market makers ensure that small company shares have liquidity (i.e. they can be traded anytime).

A quick glance at bulletin boards will reveal that market makers are not popular with traders. According to some traders, they are masters of spin – a kind of hideous lovechild of Gordon Gekko and Tony Blair Esq.

Why is this?

Mainly due to the way they make their money. It can put them in direct opposition to traders. Here's how.

Remember, market makers make their money from a share's spread. The more that traders buy and sell, the more money that market makers make. Therefore, **it is in the interests of market makers to move their prices around a bit to encourage active buying and selling of shares.**

So, the market makers may move a price up to encourage you to sell your shares, or move it down to encourage you to buy. Or even the other way round. The result is that share prices can move in odd ways, sometimes with little seeming relation to the actual situation of a company.

This can be very confusing to new traders who see a price moving, but can't understand why it's moving. It drives a lot of investors crackers – especially if it makes you sell your shares at the wrong time.

Try and relax a bit with price movements and try not to watch every tiny penny move. **If you have a good company, value will out eventually.**

Tree shaking

All sorts of 'tricks' are employed by the market makers. For example, when they drop a share for no reason, it's known by investors as a *tree shake*.

One morning you'll roll out of bed, switch on your computer and see your favourite share is down 2p, then 3p, 5p and 6p … ! You'll start to scream, sweat, swear and panic – that's exactly what they want you to do. In a panic, you'll sell immediately at any price because something terrible must be happening.

What's really happening is a tree shake.

It's designed to make you very afraid. Afraid enough to think that the share's going down further so you should get out. But once you and a few others have sold out, the price will gradually start to go back up. This will also make you scream and sweat, and probably swear. At least the panic will have gone!

You've been shaken out!

So why do they try and shake you out?

It may be because the market makers have a big buy order to fill, and they need your shares to fill it. Or perhaps the company is doing well, results are due and they want to get some cheap shares into their 'bank'. They hope they will get your shares by dropping the price, especially by doing it one pence at a time.

Tree-shake antidote

Instead of panicking and swearing, here's what you do: check to see if there is anything on the news wires regarding the share. Maybe check the bulletin boards, too. If there is no obvious and well-publicised reason for the fall, it's 90% certain that it's a tree shake.

So instead of selling, go and make a cup of tea and some toast and relax. Later in the day you can pat yourself on the back – you weren't shaken!

A tree shake will also usually only last a few hours. If the share continues to go down over a day or two, it could be more than a shake. Click the 'Trades' button at the top of ADVFN.com and see if there has been any serious selling.

A final point: if you do get shaken out of a share and it goes back up, sometimes it's best to swear a bit at the computer but then leave it alone. Otherwise you will go back in with a bit too much emotional involvement, and that can complicate things with a share. It may make you less ruthless than you need to be in future. As we have discussed, you do need to be as cool and calm as possible.

There is always another share, another day.

The general point is, if you are happy with your share, there is no bad news about and it still looks cheap to you – and the main market itself is not in meltdown – it's best to ride out the fall and sit tight.

7. Dividends

Dividends are cash that you receive, usually twice a year, from a company in which you've invested. Most decent shares pay dividends.

The money comes from the company's profits, and the amount you get will depend on the number of shares you hold. It's always on a per-share basis.

Dividends may at first glance seem to be quite small amounts, but I can promise you that over the years they add up to an awful lot of money. A good number of companies pay out more in payments than you'd get in a building society. So not only are you getting a capital gain (as the share price increases), but income too!

As at the time of writing interest rates are so low that they might as well not exist, and some companies' dividends will return you several per cent (a few as high as 5% or 6%) on your investment, this is rather attractive! And remember the 2% or so that every trade costs? Dividends are a beautifully neat way of covering that, and that's what I use them for. A very good idea for full-time traders if you ask me.

So how do you find out when the company is likely to send you some money, and how much will it be?

It couldn't be easier.

Example – finding out about dividends

Let's take one company as an example – say one of the big FTSE chaps from earlier: Vodafone Group (VOD).

First, bring up ADVFN (or equivalent) in your web browser. Click on the 'Quote' tab at the top, and type in the code for Vodafone (VOD). Once it's brought up the summary quote page, click on the 'Financials' tab at the top of the website. This should bring up a detailed page full of lots of mildly baffling numbers and tables about Vodafone.

Vodafone Grp Key Figures		
(at previous day's close)		
Market Cap.	86,156.43	m
Shares In Issue	51,375.33	m
Prev. Close	167.55	
PE Ratio	10.20	
Dividend Yield	4.96	%
EPS - basic	16.44	p
Dividend PS	8.31	p
Dividend Cover	1.98	
Cash Flow PS	25.43	p
Return On Equity (ROE)	9.57	%
Operating Margin	19.50	%
PEG Factor	0.06	
EPS Growth Rate	181.51	%
Dividends PS Growth Rate	6.95	%

The key figures panel

Panic not. They're actually very direct ways of seeing how the company is doing and judging the value of the share. But we're not interested in all that yet. The only one worth noting in passing is 'Yield' on the main table, or 'Dividend Yield' in the Key Figures section. In this case it is a building-society-shaming 4.96%! Gotta love that current account 0.0001%, eh?

So in other words, for every £1 you invest in a share of Vodafone you will get 4.96p back in dividends – only twice yearly, of course, and if performance remains on course. And of course you have to be actually holding the share still, and prepared to suffer a fall in value immediately after the dividend is paid. But if you're in for the long term, you're fine.

Now, just scroll down a little way till you get to the dividends table – in this case 'Vodafone Grp Dividends'. Here you can see all the details of the dividends that have been paid out over the years.

Vodafone Grp Dividends

Announcement Date	Type	Curr.	Dividend Amount	Period Start	Period End	Ex Date	Record Date	Payment Date	Total Dividend Amount
09 Nov 2010	Interim	GBP	2.85	30/03/2010	30/09/2010	17/11/2010	19/11/2010	04/02/2011	-
18 May 2010	Final	GBP	5.65	31/03/2009	31/03/2010	02/06/2010	04/06/2010	06/08/2010	8.31
10 Nov 2009	Interim	GBP	2.66	30/03/2009	30/09/2009	18/11/2009	20/11/2009	05/02/2010	-
19 May 2009	Final	GBP	5.20	31/03/2008	31/03/2009	03/06/2009	05/06/2009	07/08/2009	7.77
11 Nov 2008	Interim	GBP	2.57	30/03/2008	30/09/2008	19/11/2008	21/11/2008	06/02/2009	-
27 May 2008	Final	GBP	5.02	31/03/2007	31/03/2008	04/06/2008	06/06/2008	01/08/2008	7.51
13 Nov 2007	Interim	GBP	2.49	30/03/2007	30/09/2007	21/11/2007	23/11/2007	01/02/2008	-
29 May 2007	Final	GBP	4.41	31/03/2006	31/03/2007	06/06/2007	08/06/2007	03/08/2007	6.76
14 Nov 2006	Interim	GBP	2.35	30/03/2006	30/09/2006	22/11/2006	24/11/2006	02/02/2007	-
24 May 2006	Final	GBP	3.87	31/03/2005	31/03/2006	07/06/2006	09/06/2006	04/08/2006	6.07
15 Nov 2005	Interim	GBP	2.20	30/03/2005	30/09/2005	23/11/2005	25/11/2005	03/02/2006	-
24 May 2005	Final	GBP	2.16	31/03/2004	31/03/2005	01/06/2005	03/06/2005	05/08/2005	4.07
16 Nov 2004	Interim	GBP	1.91	30/03/2004	30/09/2004	24/11/2004	26/11/2004	04/02/2005	-
25 Feb 2004	Final	GBP	1.08	31/03/2003	31/03/2004	02/06/2004	04/06/2004	06/08/2004	2.03
18 Nov 2003	Interim	GBP	0.95	30/03/2003	30/09/2003	26/11/2003	28/11/2003	06/02/2004	-
27 May 2003	Final	GBP	0.90	31/03/2002	31/03/2003	04/06/2003	06/06/2003	08/08/2003	1.69
12 Nov 2002	Interim	GBP	0.79	30/03/2002	30/09/2002	20/11/2002	22/11/2002	07/02/2003	-
28 May 2002	Final	GBP	0.75	31/03/2001	31/03/2002	05/06/2002	07/06/2002	09/08/2002	1.47
13 Nov 2001	Interim	GBP	0.72	30/03/2001	30/09/2001	21/11/2001	23/11/2001	08/02/2002	-

The full details of dividends over the years

Dividends generally get paid twice a year in varying amounts – the final dividend is usually bigger than the interim dividend.

Ex-dates

Here's a question that must be in the top ten questions I get asked about shares:

When do you have to be holding a share to get its dividend?

It's quite easy. It's the day *before* what's called the 'ex-date'.

Say the ex-date is 21 March. This means that, on 21 March, the share will be trading 'ex' – or without – the dividend. So if you held the share up to and including the close of play on 20 March, *the day before the ex-date*, you would be entitled to the dividend.

But if you buy the shares on 21 March, which is the ex-date, you would *not* be entitled to it.

You may also come across something called the record date – just ignore this one, it doesn't really matter. The ex-date is the big one.

Now, often new investors say to themselves:

"Aha! I'll just buy a company late on the day before the ex-dividend date, and sell early on the ex-dividend date – picking up the dividend for nothing!"

Nice try, clever dick! Don't you think the market has thought of this not-so-cunning ploy!

Well, it has – so there goes your nice little earner.

Sadly, what happens on the ex-date is that the share price will invariably start the day lower by the amount of the dividend. So if you bought the day before 'ex', and sell the day after, what you make on the dividend payment you'll lose on the fall in the share price.

 You should definitely know the dates of ex-dividends for your shares.

For example, if a dividend on your fave share is 10p per share, your share will start the ex-date 10p lower! If you aren't aware that it's the ex-date, you might panic and sell because you think the share is being sold off, or it has dropped through your stop loss. **So pay attention to these dates.**

Is it worth buying shares just for the dividends?

Is it worth buying shares just for the dividends? It really depends on your market strategy:

- **Low-risk investor**

  The answer is yes, if you are an older investor and are looking for very steady shares and prioritise income over capital gains. For example, utility companies pay big dividends, but their actual share prices don't move much, so you won't get quick capital growth. But say you're 60 years old, and want to grow your money slowly but surely and with minimum risk. You could just go for an income portfolio of high-yielding shares (the slightly agricultural name for shares with big juicy dividends).

- **Medium-risk investor**

A medium-risk investor might look on dividends as a bit of a bonus.

- **High-risk investor**

This investor doesn't care about dividends because he only wants big growth, and the kinds of shares he invests in generally don't pay dividends.

What do I think?

I love dividends but don't worry too much about them. They are beautiful things indeed, and pay pretty much all my costs, but my trading isn't built around them. Nothing wrong with building your trading around them, of course, but don't expect to make a fortune from share price rises in the near term if you do so.

How do you buy and sell a share?

How do you buy a share online?

Dead easy! Each broker's website is slightly different but generally they operate along similar lines.

After you've registered an account, logged into their website and put some money in (preferably into an ISA account) look for a tab or button labelled: 'Deal', 'Invest', 'Dealing' or 'Trade' – they usually use one of these words.

The 'Trade' button on Selftrade

If the only button you can find is labelled something like 'Cha-ching!!' or 'Show me the money!!!', it's probably worth reconsidering your choice of broker.

Next you type the code of the share you want to buy into the box that comes up (e.g. 'DXNS' for Dixons):

Type the share's code in here on Selftrade

After confirming you've chosen the right share, you then get a choice of whether to buy or sell. Select the relevant button. Then you'll be asked to enter the quantity of shares you want to deal in or the amount of money you wish to deploy:

Where you enter the number of shares or amount of money

Finally – nearly there, honest! – you get a choice of the type of order you want to make:

The types of order

At the current best price

If you just want to buy it at the current price then click 'At best'. On Barclays you'd click 'Quote and deal'.

Others have different names for it. Play around with your broker's site till you are confident you've found the right button for this!

A 15-second countdown usually comes up and you haven't bought the shares till you finally press the 'Accept' button (or similar). Check you are happy with the price offered. If you are, press the button:

Tick-tock – the 15-second countdown and the 'Accept' button on Selftrade

Don't worry about the 15-second countdown making you feel under pressure; you can always get a quote again if you let it expire!

At the price you want – if it becomes possible

If you want to be a clever clogs and try to get a lower price at some point, you could put in a 'limit order' by clicking 'At limit' rather than 'At best'.

A limit order means you won't pay more than the price you want, as long as shares become available at the price you specify (if they don't, nothing gets exchanged).

For example, say the bid–offer price of Petrofac is 1472–1474. If you wanted to buy Petrofac shares immediately, at the current best price, you would pay 1474p.

But perhaps you don't want to pay 1474p. Let's say you think 1465p is more reasonable. In this case, you would place a limit order with your broker, setting the limit at 1465p.

Once the limit order is placed, your broker will hold onto your order and watch the market (while you have a snooze in the garden). Your broker will watch to see if the offer price falls to 1465p (in other words, if there is anyone in the market willing to sell Petrofac shares at 1465p). If this does happen then your broker will nip into the market and buy your shares at 1465p.

He may sometimes be able to buy the shares even cheaper – but the key thing is that you won't pay more than your limit price (1465p). If your limit order is executed at 1465p, then you may feel very chuffed with yourself – instead of paying 1474p, you've ended up paying only 1465p. Very clever.

You might be thinking: if these limit orders are such a wheeze, why not use them all the time?

The reason is that they do not guarantee any trade will take place.

In the previous example, you bought shares at 1465p because the price in the market fell to that level – but the price may not have fallen to 1465p. Instead, from the time the shares were offered at 1474p the price might have just risen steadily; for the sake of saving a few pennies on the price, you might have missed the shares taking off upwards.

All the above is also true when it comes to selling a share, except obviously you press sell not buy. (In the heat of the moment, it's easy to make a mistake here and press the wrong button – we've all done it. So be careful!)

If when buying or selling you don't get a 15-second countdown it means the share you want can't be dealt with online in the amount you want and the deal will have to go through a dealer. So instead of a countdown, your order goes through to a dealer. The site will shortly tell you if your buy or sell was successfully done.

If this happens, you will not be sure of the price you are going to get. *So do set a limit price before pressing 'Send order to dealer'.* This is a price you do not want to pay more than. Otherwise if the share is fast-moving you could end up paying a silly price. So if you are buying a share which is 100 to buy, you might want to put a limit on of 102.

If you're a complete beginner, practise a lot before you press the accept button for real.

A bit later in the book we'll look at more complicated matters such as setting a stop loss when you place the trade.

THE NAKED TRADER GUIDE TO MARKET JARGON

- *Bull market* – A random market movement causing an investor to mistake himself for a financial genius.

- *Market correction* – The day after you buy shares.

- *Stock split* – When your ex-wife and her lawyer split all your assets equally between them.

- *Stock analyst* – The twit who just downgraded your favourite share.

- *Momentum investing* – The fine art of buying high and selling low.

- *Value investing* – The art of buying low and selling lower.

- *Long-term investing* – The short-term trade that kept going down.

- *Head and shoulders formation* – That bloody dandruff is back.

- *Breakdown* – What you'll have when you hold onto one loser too many.

- *Profits* – What you used to make before you started share trading.

- *Moving averages* – You'll be moved all right, as they keep going down.

 # The Mental Side of the Markets

I hate to be the bearer of bad news – but don't think for a second that the market is a nice place. There are NO nice people out there, okay? The moment you make your first trade, you are into battle.

You need your shields up (that was for *Star Trek* fans – you know you love it, resistance is futile), and your sword ready for action. It's you against other people – you are a seller of something and someone else will be a buyer; or you are a buyer and someone else will be opposing you. And you need to be on the right side more often than the wrong one.

Who are your opponents?

Anyone and everyone. You'll be up against short-term traders just wanting to grab a couple of points. You may be up against a market maker. Market makers are clever and devious. You've got to be good! And, indeed, you may not even be up against a human being at all! It may be an unemotional robot taking the opposite end of your trade. But who or whatever it is, if you win, someone else loses.

And to win, you have got to be focused and disciplined.

Oh, and also a bit competitive!

I can hardly believe how many people I have met or who have emailed me since the first edition came out who find it next to impossible to do what I kept banging on about in this chapter.

TAKE YOUR BLEEDING LOSSES QUICKLY BEFORE THEY BUILD INTO BIG LOSSES!!!

PLEASE!!!!!

I cannot stress that enough. [Please, Robbie, think of your blood pressure! You need to be alive to finish this book. – Ed.]

The most important lesson

The most important lesson I can teach you about trading or investing is: *make money by making losses!*

You heard what I said. Don't pretend you didn't.

Before you start trading, I want you to bear this in mind – taking lots of losses will make you a lot of money.

Sounds crazy, right? But really, taking losses will make you a lot of money.

In fact I should say it in capitals for emphasis. Why don't I?

TAKING LOTS OF LOSSES WILL MAKE YOU A LOT OF MONEY!

I have not just knocked back six pints, and this isn't being written three sheets to the wind. I am not pulling your leg (or any other body part). It really is true.

Let me expand on it a little. I should add the crucial word 'small' – taking lots of *small* losses will make you a lot of money.

And further to this I must add: take lots of small losses and one or two big gains and you will make a lot of money.

There. It's all about getting rid of losses while they're little, and holding onto profits while they grow. What I look to do is to take losses of no more than 10%-ish when a share turns bad, but hold on tight to the really good risers and look for 30% and upwards from those going into profit.

So a really good trader's banked losses and profits could look something like this:

Last ten closed trades
-7%
-5%
+25%
-10%
-3%
+40%
-7%
-6%
-9%
+32%

At first glance, this trader looks like he's losing money. He's taken a lot of losses: seven, in fact, and only three winners. *But!* He has made a lot of money.

In fact, if each trade had been £5,000 of shares, the trader would be up by £2,500.

So it's really a percentages game. It's not the number of wins or losses that matters.

If the trader above had taken his profits too quickly, despite cutting his losses, he wouldn't have made much. He may have been tempted to take profits at just 10% instead of the 25%, 40% and 32%. And that would have spelled disaster.

You need the courage to sell losers fast and hold winners for a while.

If the losers start to fall more than 10–15%, I cut them immediately. No matter what. The art of treating gains correctly is an opposite one: you mustn't be ruthless with a gradually expanding number. Don't get giddy and grab them. And don't get out if they reverse a little. I have let my winners run and run. (I explain the rule of thumb for this on pages 242 and 308 – it's dead simple.) The biggest percentages among the winners have been held for a couple of years. And I think they still have further to go.

Of course I have picked some decent shares. However, I have also picked my fair share of losers but cut them before they started to eat away at the profits.

It is one of the hardest concepts in share trading – to sell at a loss.
And blokes are really bad at it. Just as hard a concept as resisting taking
profits too early.

Some traders find taking losses next to impossible. So you have to steel
yourself into thinking that taking a loss is a *good* thing.

Remember, if you're aiming for at least 30% as a
reasonable gain, if a share starts going down by more than 10% and
you're still holding, you'd have to think it will actually be a far better
buy than you originally anticipated: now you're expecting at least a
40% gain! Even though it's done nothing so far but tank. Crazy!
Especially if you let it tank by 20, 30, 40, 50% (and I know people
who have). So you think that share you bought, and reckoned might
give you a 30% gain, and which has done nothing but lose its value,
is actually going to be an *80% gain*?

It will be – around about the same time the devil has put his skis on.

I have met so many people since I started writing trading books who just can't take their losses.

It's all down to our emotions. If you can conquer those when you're trading, you'll be a winner. You need strength and courage to sell those losers and hold onto the winners.

Example – waiting for the comeback

"It's going to come back."

This is the perennial claim of traders who have a big losing position. In fact it was once said directly to me by someone who had bought a share. He'd bought it at 1200p. It had gone down and he'd then bought more at 800p. It kept going down.

"I've just bought some more at 400," he told me very confidently. "It's going to come back," he added.

"It might go down some more," I suggested. "Shouldn't you have set a stop loss with each trade? Then you wouldn't have lost so much money."

He got annoyed. "I haven't lost anything," he said. "I only lose if I sell. But I won't. This is a great company, it's just been caught out by the oversold market."

"How much have you got in it now?" I asked.

"About 20 grand," he said. "It'll go back up to 1200p and I'll have made a fortune!"

There was no point in me arguing that the fact it was down so much already meant that something was badly wrong. Nor was it worth telling him it wouldn't do his trading any good if, every time he opened his broking account, he had to stare at a massive losing trade.

Or that he had made the classic mistake of letting a losing position run away.

He was fixated.

As said, I always cut anything that's gone over the 10–15% loss level. The thing is, you can always buy back lower if, in the long run, you think things will eventually turn round. **You don't need to be along for the expensive ride downwards for that.**

But it is amazing the number of shares that go down 15% and just *carry on going down*. And if you carry on holding them, you're risking some serious damage.

I've met people who STILL have a 70% loser and have had it for YEARS. They can't bear to sell it. I suspect they never will.

I ought to end by telling you what the company was my acquaintance had bought.

Northern Rock.

(And he never sold.)

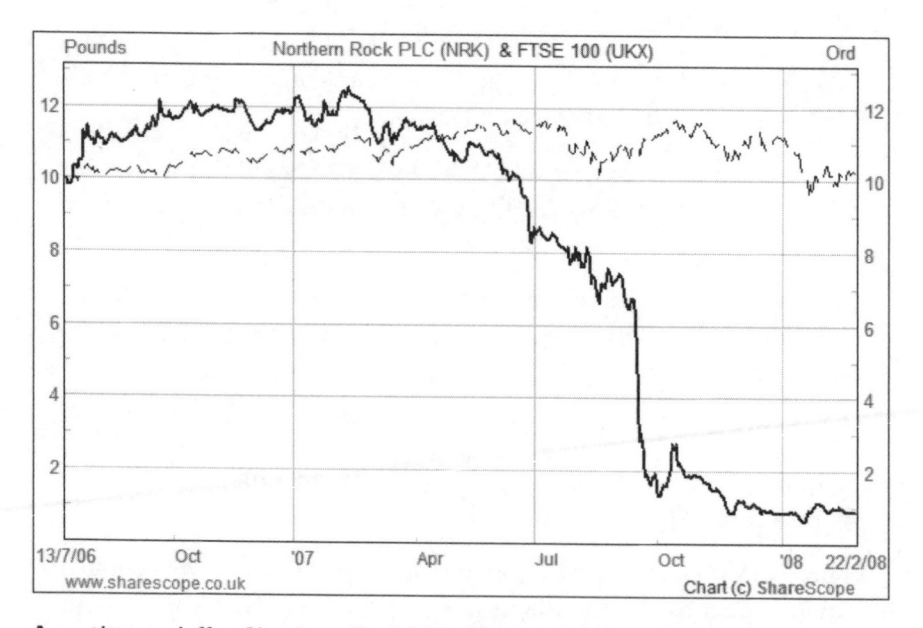

A cautionary duffer: Northern Rock (July 2006 – February 2008)

Emotions

You do have to get to know yourself and your own emotional strengths and weaknesses.

Because **however cool you think you are, your buy and sell decisions will end up being affected in various ways by your emotions**. And, being humans, we are very emotional creatures. We let emotions rule various aspects of our lives (which can often be fun); and it's just the same with investing (where it is usually disastrous).

Emotions, quite simply, get in the way of making good investment decisions.

So, imagine you're Mr Spock ... traders need to be logical! Never emotional!

Why?

Emotions lead to taking quick profits ...

We all want to feel good about ourselves, and selling for a quick profit makes us feel *very* good. The trouble is, our feel-good emotions harm long-term investment gains because it stops us sticking with the winners.

Many investors even take profits if a share has only gone up two or three per cent. That's because they can proudly boast to themselves and others: "I banked a profit."

... and hanging onto losers

Emotion is also the main reason for hanging on to losers for far too long.

We hate feelings of regret, and selling a losing share definitely makes us regretful – maybe even a bit mad at ourselves. We want to avoid that. So we'd rather watch a share continue to decline, in the vain hope it might recover, than take the loss and feel bad about it. It's stupid, really, because eventually when we sell even lower we feel even worse!

I've met people who have bought shares at something like a tenner and watched them sink all the way to 20p – *without selling them*!

Arrrrgggh!

It's almost unbelievable. It sometimes seems that the worse the loss, the less likely investors are to take it. You may not think you've made a loss till you close your trade, but that's just not true in any remotely meaningful or comforting way – believe me! Take the loss early.

Revenge on the market

There's another psychological problem when it comes to taking too long to sell at a loss: feelings of revenge! When we've taken a particularly big loss, we want to get our money back and that causes us to be emotional and start taking too many risks. If we've lost half our money, we might be tempted to go for a big stake in a small stock we think might double to get the money back – or some other dodgy trading behaviour.

This is where the unemotional stop loss (discussed shortly) comes into its own and will ensure we sell shares before we lose too much. That way a stock is sold without bringing in the emotions of regret and getting even. And that means you are less likely to make an overly-risky trade next.

Ego issues

Our inability to sell something at a loss is mainly due to ego. Taking a loss is very difficult to do. I used to find it difficult too – now I love it. Mmmmm, taking a loss … delicious!

Taking a loss means accepting you have got it wrong. If we just stick with the share, we believe it'll go back up, we might even make a profit and – hey presto – we were right all along. But usually the opposite is the case – the share keeps sinking and we lose more money. And absolutely every investor has done this and you will do it too!

I did this a few times in my early trading career. The worst I remember was Hartstone, where I bought at 450p and allowed it to sink all the way to 250p before bailing out.

Another good example is when I bought Coffee Republic. When I bought the shares for 28p, if I had set a stop loss of 22p, and acted on it, I would have sold without emotion at 22p and lost only £500. As it was, with no stop loss, I eventually lost around £7,000.

Let's look at an example.

You want to buy a new share but you have to sell one you currently hold to raise the cash. The choice for selling is between two shares:

1. Stock A is showing a loss of 20%

2. Stock B is showing a gain of 20%

Which share should be sold?

I would bet that, nine times out of ten, the investor would sell the stock that has gone up 20%, rather than sell the loser.

That's because selling the winner shows what a good decision it was to buy it and validates that decision. There's also an element of pride involved and it feels good to lock in the profit. It affects all of us. Personally, I feel pretty good when I lock in a profit and extremely irritated when I have to take a loss!

You can also tell your best friend: "I just made 20% profit" – while you keep the loser to yourself! Bad move, buster, guess who's going to have to buy all the drinks tonight!

You really have to learn not to postpone the feelings of regret. Avoidance of regret is one of the main reasons investors lose money.

 So you have to love to take losses and hate to take gains.

To a beginner investor, this will sound odd and counter-intuitive; and until you understand this saying, you will remain a beginner investor.

Over-trading

As well as not taking losses, another error often made is, quite simply, over-trading.

People simply press the buy and sell button too often – they feel like they should be making a trade every day – or most days. And this is quite common with new traders starting out. They get the bug and want to chase every stock that moves.

This is okay if you're a really hot day trader, but sadly there are hardly any of them around. I've had it said to me time and time again (especially from people I've met who work for spread betting firms):

"Our losing accounts are those which make too many trades."

The desire to over-trade probably again stems from our emotions. We want to make money quickly and we think if we keep trading, the money will come pouring in. Wrong! It's more likely to go pouring out.

The more trades you have running, the more time you have to spend monitoring them, the more stress you'll feel and the poorer your decisions will be.

And on commissions alone you'll waste a small fortune.

So don't go bananas and have a whole raft of open trades everywhere. Stick to a sensible number that you can keep control of.

Gambling or investing?

For a couple of years in the 1990s, I was a professional gambler on the horses. I even owned a couple, so I had access to a bit of inside info on form and the like. But even with that info, I didn't make a lot of money – just about enough to get by. Never anything big.

It's next to impossible to make a living on the horses. However, the stock market is different because if you stay disciplined and calm you can definitely make big money.

It's not about who crosses the line first, but about picking businesses whose performance will keep getting better – and, happily, there can be plenty of winners in that race.

But you have to invest and not gamble to become a stock market winner that makes real regular money.

What's the difference between a stock market gambler who loses and a stock market investor who wins?

Quite simple: a market gambler is itching to trade and press that exciting deal button almost for the sake of it alone. And gamblers make up 90% of spread betting accounts that lose.

- **Gambling** is putting money on shares that you know nothing about. Buying something for a punt – with no trading plan in place.

- **Investing** is buying into a company you've done your research on and trying to get your timing right.

I get so many emails starting:

'I am going to have a punt on … '

Don't have 'punts'. Invest. Make money. If you have punts you will lose, maybe not right now but eventually. Punts are just lazy gambling.

So there – have I made myself clear?

Fear and greed

It's a stock market cliché, but fear and greed are prevalent in all traders and investors.

The fear as shares fall, and fall again, then the greed as they start to rise. We all want to be out when shares are falling and back in when they are rising – there's nothing worse than being frightened out of the market and then feeling irritated when you see it rise back up and you're missing out.

The main thing you must consider is your capital – above all else that must be protected.

As a general rule:

- **Buy shares** trending upwards and breaking new highs.
- **Don't buy shares** trending downwards and breaking new lows.

This may sound obvious, but so many people make the mistake of doing it the wrong way round.

Downtrends

When it comes to investing, the human reaction is generally to want to buy a share that is a bargain. In particular, investors are attracted to shares that have fallen – they think that's the definition of good value:

" ... you see, it's come down a long way, so look at how far it could go up. "

Take a look at the following chart.

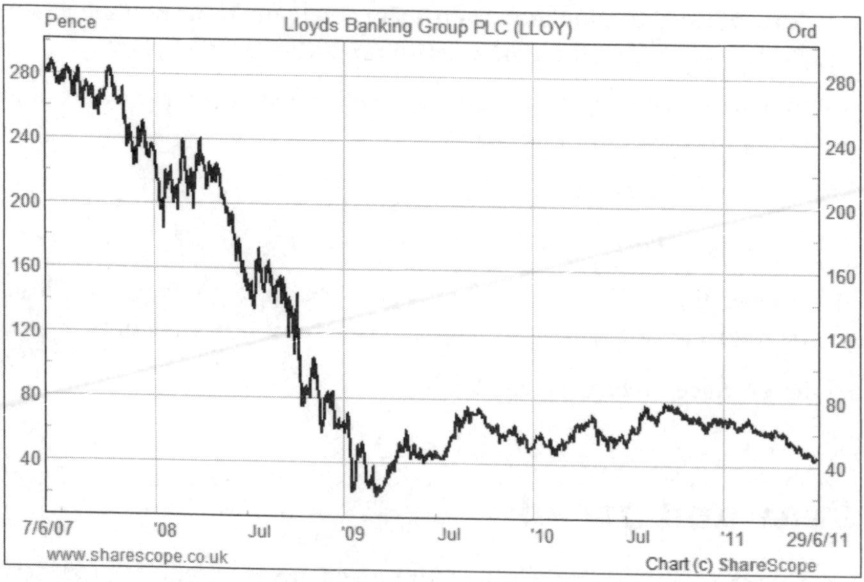

Lloyds (June 2007 – June 2011)

As can be seen, Lloyds Bank did very little but go down from 2007 to 2011, but it did so in a slightly higgledy-piggledy way.

Have you ever wondered why share price charts don't simply move down in straight lines? Well, I'll tell you! Bottom pickers (not a nice topic, I know – but we have to face the truth). Look again at the chart: at multiple points throughout the five years, investors thought:

The share price is going to bounce off this level, and I'm going to make a packet in double quick time – easy money …

and then a little later when the downward trend has reasserted itself:

Ooh-err, whoops.

The share price then falls some more until another would-be 'support level' is hit, and the cycle repeats itself. All the way to the bottom. Over the five years, Lloyds fell over 85%, and investors would have been buying it all the way down, thinking at each point it was 'cheap'.

And because this point is so important … take a look at the following chart:

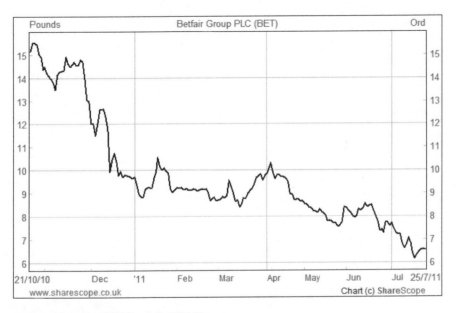

Betfair (October 2010 – July 2011)

Again this is the sort of chart beloved by wayward investors. Betfair just kept falling but punters kept coming in for it, thinking it had to turnaround. Well, I guess Betfair is a company all about gambling!

The moral is:

Don't try to bottom pick – it's a nasty habit, stop it!

Uptrends

Conversely, investors can be terrified of buying shares that have gone up a lot. Their reaction is:

> *"That share's gone up a long way … it'll never go up any more and it could easily go back down again … definitely a bit dangerous!"*

This is what I used to think when I first started trading. I did what a lot of newer investors do: I looked for the shares that had fallen and were 'showing' signs of imminent recovery.

Take a look at the following chart.

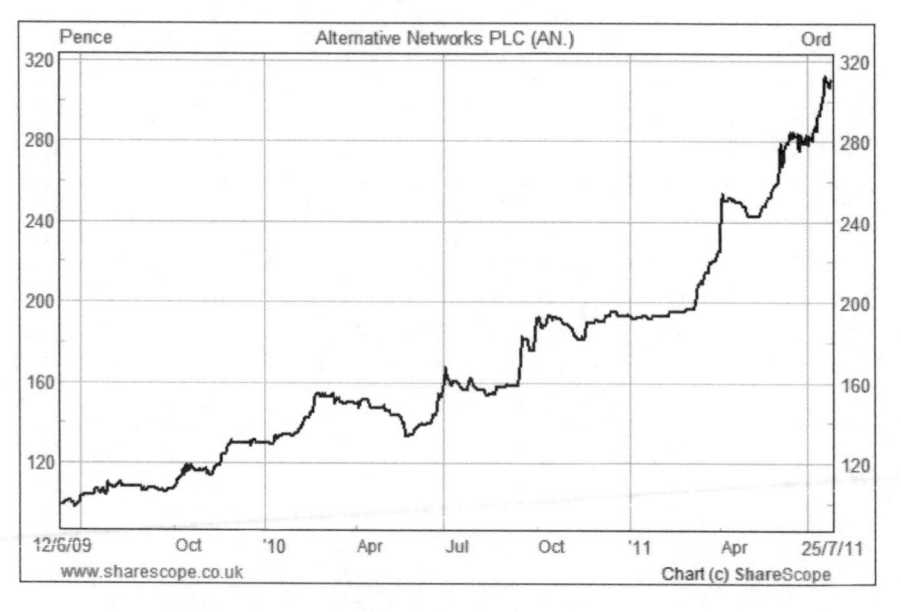

Alternative Networks (June 2009 to June 2011)

Alternative Networks (one of my favourite shares) was in a steady uptrend from 2009. Again, the share price is not a straight line, but this time the cause was not due to bottom pickers but their mirror images: Chicken Littles. At every stage the Chicken Littles were crying:

> *"Ooooh, help, it's too high, it's going to fall."*

Then the share would go up a little further, and some more Chicken Littles would shout louder:

> *"Ooooh, help, it's too high, it's going to fall."* [Repeat, *ad nauseam*.]

You have to learn to buy shares that are in an uptrend. Get to learn to love and buy into uptrends such as this one:

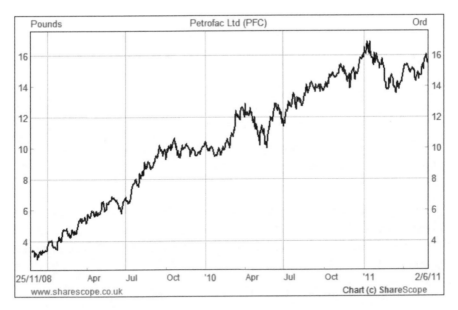

Petrofac (November 2008 – July 2011)

Lovely share this one. I was in from the mid 300s and bought all the way up. If you can add as the uptrend continues, this is the way to make money. NOT by adding as it goes down – a basic mistake made by so many beginners.

Confidence and handling pressure

If you're going to win at trading, I'm afraid you're going to need some confidence – and you'll have to be able to manage a little pressure. (I know, I know, it sounds like a job interview: *where do you see yourself in five years' time?*, etc.)

But you really have to stay cool when the markets aren't doing what you expect, or your money will start to disappear. Of course, some anxiety will always be present – it still is in me. In fact, I'm feeling scared right now: I think I'm out of choc bars!

You have to cope with it somehow (the pressure, not the lack of chocs). The fact is you *will* make losses on some trades and that's inevitable. But it isn't the end of the world. The first company I bought into went bust!

You either give up or plough on. And those who have the guts and determination to plough on through adversity often become the big winners.

> You really have to stay cool when the markets aren't doing what you expect or your money will start to disappear.

Remember the Chumbawumba song:

"I get knocked down but I get up again ... "

You don't? Look, those were the lyrics. You *are* going to get knocked down. But you just need that confidence to get up again, and the resilience to keep going.

There have been many times in my trading career when the market was going down and I thought: do I need this stress? Shall I just jack it all in? No! I got up and fought on, and every time I'm glad I did. Learn from the pressure.

Mark Douglas in his book, *Trading in the Zone*, says:

"Winning in any endeavour is mostly a function of attitude. "

And he's right. It's a question of staying positive. Keep a good attitude and you're much more likely to make money.

Reader spot – share traffic control

"I'm an air traffic controller, and it seems that back in the wild days of the late '80s some bright spark in the City figured that people who can handle the stress of air traffic control would be ideal traders. An approach was made to several controllers from the old London air traffic control centre in West Drayton, and talks went fine until the controllers started asking questions ... 'How often do we get breaks?' 'Is there a roster for late starts and early goes?' 'I'll still get four days off at a time, right?' Project cancelled."

What beginners always do

It's classic: overconfidence causes them to load up with tons of shares under 20p, thinking they will be multi-baggers. They get into all kinds of small oil, mining or drugs companies, or ones with an 'amazing' product that will do all kinds of things like cure cancer. Fear then sees them stay in denial for some weeks or even months as the shares slump.

Then they end up losing a big amount and give up.

Don't fall for this trap.

Tiredness

A quick final note here. You should try not to make any, or too many, trading decisions when you're tired. If you've had a few drinks the night before and you wake up with a sore head, watch what you do. Or if you feel generally in a bad mood, be wary of trading. If you don't have a clear head, don't expect to be able to stay unemotional and make good trades!

All of which brings me to ...

A typical three years in the life of a wayward trader

A mystery share! (April 2008 – April 2011)

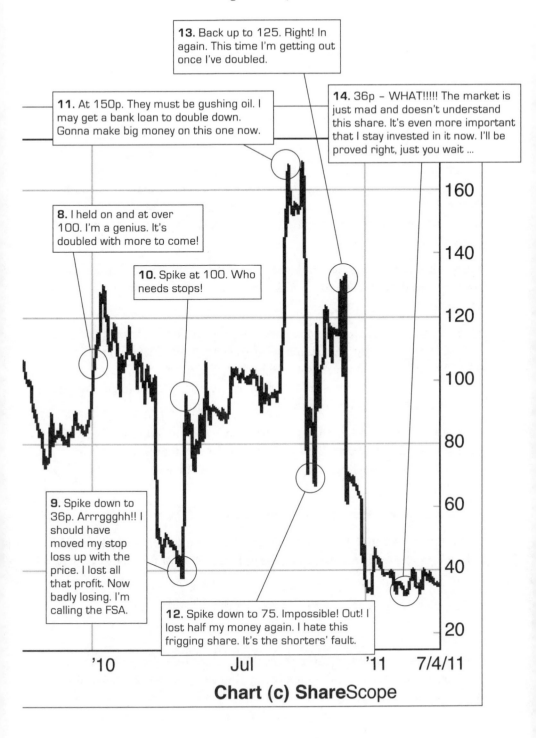

Chart (c) Share Scope

The share, by the way, was Desire Petroleum – and the three years of pain just described were a true tale for some traders. I have met so many people that lost money on that one. It said it had found oil, and then announced that it was actually water.

The picture painted here is a bit dramatic, but it's true to life. You'd be surprised how easy it is to combine almost all of the worst trading habits in a single bout of out-of-control trading. It isn't inevitable, though: you just have to be disciplined. If need be, don't just get out, but get out, close the laptop down, stop trading for a space and pledge to abandon forever a particular share that's caused you problems. There's no point obsessing over one when there are so many others out there that you can make money from.

On this point there are two traders I've met that stand out. Both sat in the front row at different seminars and told their stories. Both stories are very interesting.

One chap told us how he had nearly lost his house, marriage and everything by punting on just one oil share using CFDs. You'll find his full story in the Traders' Tales chapter (Chapter 27). He was very happy to get his story off his chest – he was keen to warn newcomers not to get into the terrible state of mind he got into.

The other one is another chap who was in a real state. He had a basketful of really awful penny dreadfuls and he was down a significant amount on them. But I had a feeling that, despite the losses, he was never ever going to sell them.

"I'll sell each one when it gets to, say, break even," he suggested.

I knew there and then he would never make it as a trader. Unless you can take a loss you really are doomed. I expect he will have the shares forever.

Well, I guess you realised, throughout this chapter we've really been sitting back on something of a therapist's couch (Frasier's, not a masseuse's, thank you!). We've been talking about psychology – yours and the markets. And it is important. What goes on in your mind will affect every trade you ever make.

Okay, time to move on.

Part III
Picking Shares

"Select stocks the way porcupines make love – very carefully."

– Bob Dinda

How Do I Find Shares Worth Looking At?

You want to know, do you?

Oh, all right, if you insist. The best way to explain this is to tell you how I look for them. Usually I try the kitchen first, then the living room but I typically find them under the bed. [Robbie! Shares, shares – not keys. Concentrate please. – Ed.]

Well. There are many ways. A good summary, I think, would be that I am looking for shares where *something seems to be happening*.

And preferably the shares are rising.

My first stage is to simply try to find shares that *might* be of interest. I'm not saying I'll buy any of them right away – I'm on the hunt for shares I might buy soon, or I might buy next year.

Here's how I try to find shares at least worth adding to my daily watchlist.

Where I don't look for ideas

First, however, these are the places I *avoid* looking at to get ideas:

- internet tipsters/tipsheets
- bulletin boards
- columns from gurus.

Where I look for ideas

These are my favourite places for looking for ideas:

1. national newspaper round-ups
2. investment publications
3. ADVFN news (especially at 7am)
4. ADVFN Toplists.

Why do I use these particular sources?

Well, they have all served me well in the past, and shares usually appear in these sources because there is a story to tell or the share is moving. Of course, if you read about a share rising in a paper or a magazine it doesn't mean it'll carry on going up: it might well fall.

But when I say these are places that I look for ideas, I don't mean these are places where I will just copy ideas from. **They provide good starting points for putting on the old deerstalker and playing detective.** This is where I start my research, Watson.

Let's look at these sources in more depth.

1. Newspapers

I get *The Times* every day and, erm, the *The Sun*. Mrs NT gets the *Mail*.

I find the *The Times* very good. I have a proper read through and see if any share is mentioned in there and make a note to research them if they sound interesting. The *Mail* is worth a gander, too.

It might sound strange, but I don't bother with the *Financial Times* – I find it too dry and heavy-going. It's more of an international, business-oriented paper. What I might buy is the weekend edition of the *FT*, which has some thoughtful coverage of shares.

Within the newspapers, I'll take a look at the daily stock market round-up – reporting on the shares that have gone up or down and why. I'll also have a scan of the news stories.

Once or twice a week I'll see something that looks interesting. I'll make a note of the share and why it might be one to buy.

2. Investment publications

There are two main magazines that I regularly check out:

- ***Investors Chronicle***

    The *IC* is as sober as a judge and has a large circulation – it's been around for a long time. It has some good analysis of company results, some good trading input and some interesting in-depth pullouts which are well worth reading.

    (Published: weekly, on Fridays.)

- *Shares*

  Appears to be aimed at a younger readership more inclined to the 'have-a-punt approach' to trading. It's heavy on oil exploration and riskier stuff. But it has some sensible stuff too.

  (Published: weekly, on Thursdays.)

I think both magazines do a reasonable job, so I rate both as 'buy'! [Shameful pun. – Ed.]

But I would NEVER be tempted to buy into the tips of either magazine (especially as these would already have been marked up by market makers on the morning of publication). You should look at the comments made by the magazines as a guideline and not just buy something because a company is recommended.

Sometimes a story they've written about a company might intrigue me, so I'll have a look at it. I especially like the round-up both mags do of recent company results statements. It's interesting to read their comments; they get some right and some wrong. Occasionally I'll notice a company I hadn't spotted before and pop it in my notebook to look at in detail.

A word of warning: don't get fooled by any magazine that boasts about producing winning tips. Some of their tips will turn out to be epic stinkers! Also, note that judging the performance of tips is not always straightforward:

- Was the broker's commission and stamp duty taken into account?

- Was it actually possible to deal in the market at the prices used in the calculation?

- Often the aggregate tips performance will be heavily influenced by the stellar performance of one flukey share – if you'd missed buying that one share, the aggregate performance of the remaining tips might be nowhere near as good.

However, it is important to know which shares are being tipped (even if you don't buy them). Tipped shares will often increase in price before the market opens, and it's important to know why they rose (i.e. they were up on a tip). Otherwise you might buy them thinking there was more to the rise than just a tip!

My tip is: by all means buy good quality magazines, but use them for reference and as prompts for trading ideas, not as a source of sure-fire tips.

International Business Times research

I don't really bother with any other investment publications. However, I do subscribe to a daily email from the *International Business Times* research department.

This is my main source of news for a whole range of things. It covers broker upgrades, main news items, analysis of stocks and markets, forthcoming company statements and events, stock recommendations and targets from the top brokers, what kind of earnings are expected from companies and a whole heap of other useful stuff.

It costs me £7.99 a month at the time of writing (I take the yearly option, which gives a 20% discount). Emails usually arrive around 5ish every day.

I also sometimes get ideas from this for companies to watch or monitor or even buy.

I contacted the people behind it and they have put together a free 14-day trial for my readers – so you can try it out and cancel after 14 days if you don't feel it's useful enough. Access this at: **bit.ly/eBPXuG**

I hope you find it useful like I do. It's one of the few paid-for news services that has really impressed me.

3. ADVFN newswire

ADVFN has a streaming newswire (i.e. it continually refreshes itself, without you having to reload the page). I always keep it running in the background on one of my computers. It covers pretty much everything that's happening. It includes company statements, directors' dealings, market reports – all you need! Just click 'News' on the top menu bar, and then 'Streaming News' from the page menu.

Most company reports are published between 7am and 8am, so I usually pay more attention to the newswire early on.

Again, sometimes I'll find a company worth looking at, especially if a company report looks very positive. I make a note of anything that catches my eye, from a company reporting to directors buying – often waiting till the evening to check out the company concerned.

There are plenty of other newswires and websites out there if you are interested in following the latest news.

The majority of the most interesting stuff is released just after 7am. I read through what the various companies are reporting and take notes if there are things I like the look of. Make sure you get up early if you don't want to miss this! (Hey, there's nothing wrong with going back to bed afterwards – if you're your own boss, you can make it company policy. Oh yes.)

But my favourite way to find shares worth looking at is ...

4. ADVFN Toplists

ADVFN Toplists are a great way to look out for shares on the move. The lists are compiled by a computer which has been given certain criteria:

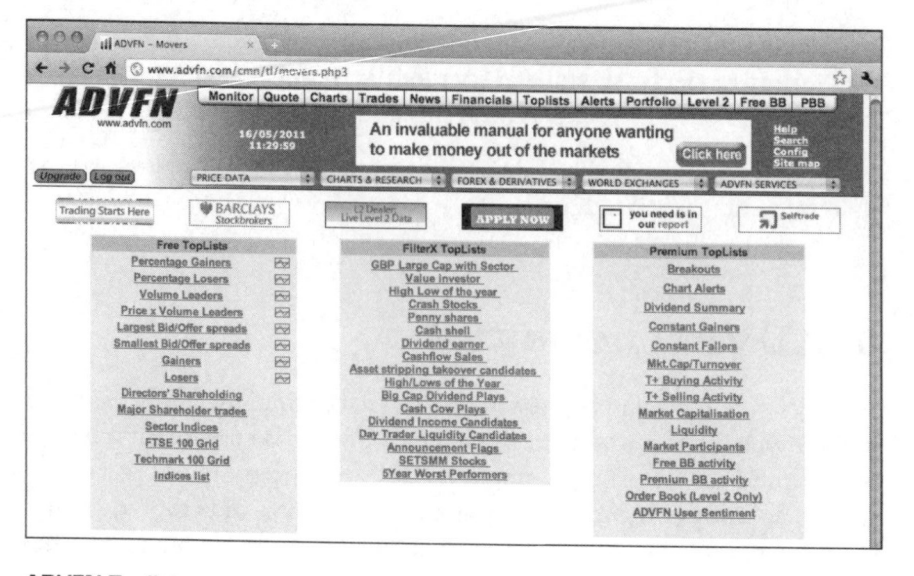

ADVFN Toplists menus

As you can see, on the left are the lists you can have for free and on the right are premium lists that cost £60 a year to access (£5 per month). That's money well worth spending.

> I'm glad to say ADVFN offers *Naked Trader* readers access to the lists for just £41 for the first year, saving you a decent £19. If you want to take up the offer, just email me at **robbiethetrader@aol.com** with 'Cheap Bronze' in the subject line and I will email you back with the details.

Bronze also gives you access to the premium bulletin board on ADVFN, where serious investors discuss shares. Oh, and if you want bronze PLUS real-time prices, ADVFN offers a decent discount on that too! Mail me with 'Cheap Silver' in the subject line.

The lists I particularly like are:

Percentage gainers and losers (free)

In other words: the biggest movers of the day. These lists give an excellent snapshot of what is moving.

To find out why the share is soaring up or plunging down, there may be a '1' or '2' by the share in the list's news column. Click on that to get a reasonable idea. It means there are one or two related news stories.

I'm interested in shares going both down and up, because the ones going down this year could be the recovery play of next year. And the ones going up could have a lot further to climb.

Breakouts (premium)

This is probably my favourite share-finding method. This lists the shares breaking out of previously established price ranges. A breakout is often significant.

ADVFN allows you to search for 52-week, 12-week and 4-week breakouts. My preference is for 52-week breakouts. A 52-week upward breakout often means a share is about to rise steadily higher.

Why is looking at breakouts potentially so rewarding?

Because you are finding share prices breaking out of previously established ranges, and this often points out that something interesting is happening with a share. Probably more people are buying in. Volumes will be up, something good may be going on and there are fewer sellers around.

When you click on the breakout list you will often find 20–30 shares on there to have a look at. I do my usual initial screening process at this stage, and generally don't bother to investigate further with AIM shares, illiquid shares, etc.

But I don't particularly look at the big boys either.

I tend to favour shares that have a market cap of between £50m and £900m because they have a lot more room for growth than, say, a FTSE 100 share. These can be found on the FTSE 250 and FTSE Small Cap indices.

Most of the ones you will find on the ADVFN Premium TopLists will be similar. The computer is just telling you a share has gone up through an old resistance area.

Once you've found a share that's broken out, of course, the real work begins: it is then time to do the research to check it's dependable.

Sometimes you will get what is termed a *false breakout*: the share breaks away for a short time and then goes back to where it was. So sometimes it is worth missing a point or two by not jumping on immediately, and checking it really is breaking out.

Tons of examples of profitable shares I found using a whole variety of methods are coming up a bit later in the book, in the bumper chapter on 20 trading strategies ... but no skipping ahead just yet. I'm watching!

How to Select Shares

My research involves finding out everything I can about a company before I consider buying in. And so should yours. The lazier you are about research, the less money you'll make. And really, it's not even that difficult.

For the moment I will assume you have already found a share you are interested in (there's even more on how to find ones to look at later in the book).

I want *the whole story* about a share. *I want it* and *I want it now*! (Sorry – the last bit is a coded message to the Mrs.)

I look at everything I can, and much of the research involves trying to pick out the negative things – I guess I'm trying to put myself off! I use every scrap of info I have to come to a decision – and so should you.

> Good research means if you reach a decision to buy a share you are really sure it is worth buying.

Don't skip the research

It's only human nature to try and skip research. After all, it can be pretty boring, and it's more exciting to just press the buy button on a whim.

Much more fun to buy a penny share because a bulletin board punter has posted up some pretty charts and posted something about "amazing news" on the way. Don't!

I urge you to get down and dirty: do your research. Don't skip it, and be serious about it. Find out anything you can, however you can. This is your money you're playing with, and if you really want to make a profit there's no such thing as enough research.

And whatever you do, don't see a share and think "I fancy that one", then do research that only looks at the positive stuff and ignores the negative. That's not research!

Reader spot – skipping research, losing money

"I bought £15k of African Eagle at 10p, and it's currently trading at 4.75p! Never ever buy a share on impulse because someone tells you it's going to rocket. Proper research beforehand is so important!"

What's the story?

What I do is build up the 'story' of a share.

Do I want to buy the story?

I want to share with you some of the questions that I try and answer in my research. And I don't buy a share until I have found the answers. What I'm trying to do is build a clear picture in my head about what a share is all about. Where's it been, what is it doing and does it hang around outside the fish and chip shop causing trouble?

First let me highlight one major point.

I am looking for a share that has everything going for it, with no question marks.

I am also trying to keep things simple. Perhaps what I'm trying to say is: you need to cut through the bullshit. I'm looking for good things and trying to avoid shares with the bad – or with question marks.

Keep it simple

Let me give you an example.

You've probably seen two TV shows that feature no-nonsense bosses: Lord/Baron/Sir/Darth Sugar ("You're fired!"), and millionaire chef Gordon 'F***' Ramsay.

You haven't? Oh right, I forgot, you spend your time watching *EastEnders*, *Emmerdale* and *Neighbours*. Don't try to deny it – I've got your number!

Well, that Baron Alan is as sympathetic towards BS as he is tall: not very. Now imagine what he'd want to know if he was thinking about buying a share in a company. He'd cut through the crap like a light saber through ice cream, which is exactly what I try to do. I can imagine him collaring the chairman, and barking in his gruff Hackney tones:

> **66** Don't give me no bloody crap about Fibonacci Bollinger hatstands, resistance stars, bleedin' double negatives and roving averages.
>
> What I wanna know is: how much is your bleeding company worth, how much are the bloody profits, and how much do you owe? Don't give me nothing else, I don't need it. **99**

And if he got the reply:

> **66** But Lord Sugar, the company has EBITDA of £5.3 million, our reorganisation is going well and we've hired some consultants ... **99**

The mighty Sugar would say:

> **66** Right! I've bloody had enough. You talk and talk but don't give me no real answers – it's all complete rubbish, I can't make head or tails of it. You. Are. Fired! **99**

This is exactly what is needed. And in this spirit, I always try to be a bit Sugarish when I'm looking at potential share purchases. I don't quite go to the length of making all my potential shares live in a house in Richmond and perform weekly tasks in order to winnow them down. But I do keep it bloody simple.

Similarly, on one of his numerous shows, chef Gordon Ramsay goes into failing restaurants and tries to rescue them whilst swearing loudly. He generally finds out that everything they do is too complicated and that's why they're losing money. Their sauces are too over-thought, their menus don't make any sense unless you've got a PhD, they spend money on the wrong things. It's exactly the same with share traders who try and over-analyse situations. Simplicity is best.

I know just what he'd say if he visited a share trader losing money:

"F*** me!"

Yeah, I know he says that about everything. (From now on I'll just put (f) when he talks to represent his favourite word.)

66 Look at all those (f) screens on your desk. What have you got all those (f) chart packages for? (f) me you've got hundreds of stock analyser tools – no wonder you're losing (f) money, you haven't even got (f) time to buy a (f) share. 99

And I really believe both these successful people would approach share trading in the same way I have.

Lord S would be right. You just need to ask a few direct questions about a company to know if it is worth investing in or not. And Ramsay would be on the money too: you don't need to get bogged down in too much detail. You should find all the answers on ADVFN or an equivalent service.

There are so many traders out there with so many systems. Yet my simple methods have always worked and made me lots of money.

The questions

Okay, best thing for me to do here is take you through some of the simple steps I use to build up my research.

As Lord Sugar might say, the first two things I want to know are:

"What's your bloody company worth and what are your profits?"

But here is the full list of questions I want to know the answers to when looking at a share.

These are the kind of questions you should be finding out the answers to as well. Write them down if you want and use them whenever you look at a share.

Questions to ask about a company

- What is it worth? (Market cap)

- What are its full-year pre-tax profits?

- Are profits rising?

- Are dividends rising?

- Is the outlook positive?

- Are there any negative things happening?

- What is the net debt?

- What kind of dividend does it pay?

- What does it do and what sector is it in?

- Are its markets likely to improve or get worse?

- When's the next statement due?

- Is the share price on the way up?

All the answers to these questions can be found online. I use the following pages to get them:

1. The quote on the share to get the market cap. (Quote tab of ADVFN.)

2. Then the last full or half-year results to check the company's figures for myself.

I don't use ADVFN's 'Financials' tab or any financial website to check things like profit and debt because they can be wrong or out of date. The most recent officially published results are the place for that. So I click 'News' on ADVFN for the share and scroll down till I come to the last full or half-year results. This also means my highlighter system will work (coming later in this chapter!).

I want the answers to all these questions, and only when I'm satisfied with all my answers will I be tempted to buy – then it's down to timing, which I'll discuss later (if I get my timing right).

Now, let's look at how to interpret any answers we get.

The answers

Perhaps a hazy mist is coming over you now and you're thinking:

> *'Yeah, yeah, research – all a bit boring, isn't it? Sod that, I know Robbie's right but I can't be bothered and I'll take a chance and trust to luck.'*

Well, not if you want to make good money and avoid losing it. It doesn't even take much time!

1. Market cap

Okay, market cap first. Remember, this is what the market thinks the company is worth. It's not a special hat that traders have to wear.

The cap stands for capitalisation, and it is worked out by multiplying the current share price by the number of shares a company has.

For example, at the time of writing Dixons has a share price of 17.75p and 3610m shares in issue, so its market capitalisation is £639.4m (17.75p x 3610m). If the market thought Dixons was worth £1bn, then investors would buy the shares until the shares had risen to 27.7p (£1bn/3610m); but the market at the moment doesn't think it is worth £1bn, it thinks it is worth £639.4m and that is why the share price is 17.75p.

A quick guide:

- **Up to £50m:** is considered very small.

- **£50m to £140m:** smallish.

- **£140m to £450m:** small–medium company.

- **Above £450m:** the company is in the top 350 in the UK.

- **Above £3bn:** the company is probably in the FTSE 100 index.

As we saw earlier, the market cap info can be found on the far right of the ADVFN quote page.

I personally prefer to look for companies in the £50m to £950m size range – they often have better growth prospects than, say, FTSE 100 stocks. But I do buy FTSE stocks sometimes too.

2. Company report

The next thing I want to do is find out the health of the company. So, as we looked at earlier, having brought up a company on ADVFN, click on the 'News' tab and then scroll down till you see 'Full year, preliminary or interim results'.

Two things in particular I'm after: finding out the negatives and looking for the positives.

Reading company reports

Every few months, companies have to put out a financial report. These sometimes come in the form of a full report, which includes in-depth figures. Sometimes it's a trading statement, which gives an indication of how things are going.

The statements are usually quite long and often complicated. And it doesn't seem to matter how badly the company concerned is doing, there will almost always be some kind of positive spin applied to the report – so knowing what it actually means is never completely straightforward.

If you're like me, you won't want to trawl through a company report: they're pretty boring. Fortunately, there are one or two key things to watch out for when reading a report that mean you don't have to sit there carefully weighing every sentence only to find out, four hours later, that the company's a duffer and you wasted your time.

I came up with a system which works through a company report in a few seconds and lets me know in a matter of moments whether it's worth getting into or not.

So, let me present …

The secret Naked Trader traffic lights system!

I call it my 'traffic lights' system: red for sell, amber for hold and green for buy.

It enables me to quickly tell from a results report or an AGM (annual general meeting) statement what the state of play is. I can tell in just a few seconds whether to carry on looking at a company or to forget it immediately. Once you have set this little system up you will wonder how you ever did without it.

How does it work?

It uses a neat tool which is available at ADVFN. The tool can be set up by clicking on the 'News' tab in the top menu bar, and then clicking 'Highlight Phrases' on the next page:

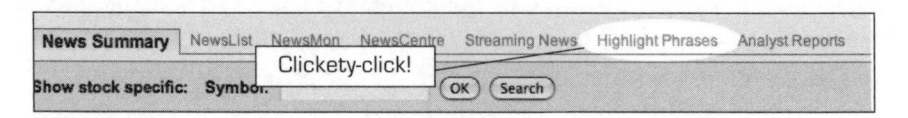

'Highlight phrases' – second in from right, after clicking on News

This allows you to arrange for up to 20 words or phrases to be highlighted in the colours of your choice in any news text that you read on ADVFN:

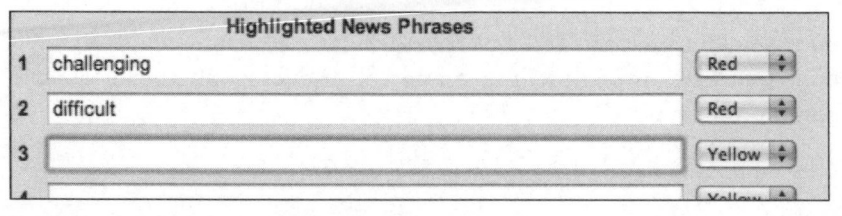

Entering the phrases to be highlighted

With the right words and colours, you'll be able to instantly pick out the negatives and positives about any company in any report or news item.

Here's what I do – and what you should do as well:

- Put 'challenging' into the first box, in **red**.

- Then 'difficult' into the second box in **red**.

And continue inputting all the other words and phrases from the following table, selecting the colour indicated as you do so:

Colour	Word/phrase
Red	challenging, difficult, down by, unpredictable, lower, poor, difficult trading, tough, below expectations, deficit
Yellow	in line with expectations, cash
Green	exceeding expectations, positive, favourable, profit up, excellent
Blue	debt, covenants, borrowings

Finally, click 'Ok' at the bottom to store all the phrases.

Now look on ADVFN news at the latest company report of any share you're interested in or hold in your portfolio. Where any of those key words or phrases occur, they will be highlighted in their respective colours. The same will happen in any news item you look at. You won't see the highlighting until you click through to the articles themselves, nor anywhere else on ADVFN.com, but then you don't really need to.

Now what this tells you about companies is really rather simple:

Any company report that you see with lots of **red** is a probable sell or, at least, not a buy.

Any with lots of **yellow** is a hold.

Any with lots of **green** is a potential buy.

The more greens the more positive, the more reds the more negative.

Now you may scoff at what might seem an over-simplistic technique. And, of course, my system is only the basis to start some more in-depth research.

But I don't think you can beat it for a quick judgement!

I'm not saying for a minute that you should buy every company which has loads of greens or sell every one that's red, but it should give you an instant 'flavour' of the report. As you get used to the system, you could add your own words or phrases that bring out things you're really looking for.

What about the blue highlighted words?

Well, that's all to do with working out whether the company's got too much debt or could even go bust. More on that shortly. 'Cash' is in yellow, as if it hasn't got debt it might have net cash.

So after discarding any shares with too many red negative words, the next thing is to weed out some more. This is the second stage of my quick but stern filtering process.

And the number one tool to discard a share at this point?

Net debt!

Net debt! This is what I'm now looking for. And the traffic lights system makes it dead easy to find!

Companies don't exactly like to boast about their debt, so you will often find it hidden away in their reports. But 'debt' should now be a bright blue colour throughout reports you read, and pretty simple to find.

Remember, I am not an accountant but I reckon net debt gives you a pretty good idea of the finances. Net debt is basically a company's debt minus its cash. In other words, it's probably the most accurate possible figure you can put on a company's total debts.

I believe if I rule out companies with a big net debt I can avoid a company going bust on me. So far it's worked.

Quite early on as a trader I looked at various companies which had gone bust in the past and discovered something rather interesting. Their net debt was in each case more than five times the size of their full-year profit. So I give myself a massive safety margin: my rule of thumb is not to buy anything with net debt more than three times the full-year pre tax profit, or what the likely pre-tax profit might be next year.

So, at this point in the weeding out I simply go to the profit figure and then to the net debt. And if, for example, profits are £50m, I just times this by three – and won't buy if net debt is over £150m. Simple!

The only exceptions to this rule of mine are oil, mining and property companies. Oil companies often have big debts but they are rated on their oil finds. Property companies get rated more on their net asset values (the value of all their assets minus any liabilities). So, houses. A different game.

> If you cannot find net debt using the blue highlighter on 'debt', keep an eye out for 'borrowings', which should also show up in blue. Also, try finding net cash (cash should come up in yellow). A good sign: it means they have cash. And that's great!

The final test of the first stage

Having made my potential shares run like Indiana Jones through a sequence of hellish trials and poison-dart fire, there remains one final set of hurdles for them to pass at this first stage. I pull the trap-door on them and say goodbye without further investigation if:

- they are a very small AIM listed company, or have an EMS below £2,000 worth (too illiquid and dangerous)

- they are losing money or haven't made any yet ('jam tomorrow')

- they have a big spread (more than 5%).

This eliminates the high-risk stocks that are left. There's nothing wrong *per se* in having the odd high-risk stock for small stakes once you're experienced. But if you're newish it's best to stay safe.

When I say AIM, there are some okay AIM stocks, but because I trade mainly in my ISA (and AIM stocks aren't allowed in ISAs), I don't go for them unless I think they are very special. And then they'll probably end up in my pension fund or as a spread bet.

3. Dividend check

Now we're going into greater depth. The next step is to check dividend payouts.

- **Rising dividends** put a big tick in my book.

- If I see a **falling, or cut dividend**, I would probably end my research there – it's not a good sign.

If a company always increases its dividend year after year, that's a very good sign!

4. Chart check

Next is a look at the chart for the last year – that's at the bottom of the 'Quote' page on ADVFN.

Is the line higher once it reaches the right-hand side, or lower than when it started? The former is a good sign – the share is in an uptrend. If it's lower, I'd have to look into it further, but it puts it in dodgier territory.

I'd also take a look at the three-year performance chart. I'll come back to charts a bit later, but for now I want to see a share in a good-looking uptrend.

5. Company background check

The next step is to find out more about what the company does, and to look back through the last couple of years' news stories connected with them.

I like to see reports of rising profits and turnover, and a gradually improving share price. I look to see when it reports next. Is it next week or in three months? If it's next week, could there be a nasty shock on the way or will those already in the stock be ready to take profits?

To check when it might report next, scroll down and see when it reported last year; report dates are usually about the same. Also, companies tend to put out a 'notice of results' with the date a couple of weeks beforehand.

Any big share movements reported? Any institutional buys? I check all this out. ADVFN makes it rather easy, as you can click through all the news stories going back over a long time.

What I'm doing is trying to build up a picture of the company concerned, and this is what you should be doing. Keep clicking, keep reading.

Just because you see one thing you like about a company, don't just buy it on an impulse.

> Don't ignore things you don't like the look of because you suddenly fancy buying a share anyway. Stay objective and searching.

Reader spot – always hoover up research

"I'd been reading over the years about how successful Dyson had become. One day I was looking for new opportunities and saw Dyson mentioned again in an article. Without doing any further research – after all, I felt I already knew the company well enough now – I went off and bought a load of shares at 18p. They'd come down a bit so it felt like a good buying opportunity.

"A few weeks later I saw they were suspended. I never bothered to look into the reason why; I just assumed it was a restructuring or perhaps even a takeover.

"After about six months, and fed up now with seeing how well James Dyson was doing, I picked up the phone to speak to him to find out when the shares would come back. I can still hear the laughter as I learnt that Dyson was never quoted [i.e. made publicly available to trade on a stock exchange], and I'd bought a company that had nothing at all to do with hoovers. It was a small engineering company called Dyson Group, based in Sheffield.

"And I'm a very experienced trader, who's been at this for years. Yes, we really are just as human as everyone else! Skimping on research can be terribly expensive, not to mention embarrassing."

6. Directors' dealings

Many investors believe it's worth keeping an eye on directors buying and selling shares in their own companies.

The reason is: if a director is buying a lot of shares, it's assumed he or she has some confidence in the future of the company – and that no one should know a company better than its directors.

Conversely, if a director is dumping shares, perhaps the confidence is simply not there and one has to be careful.

Generally, directors are allowed to buy and sell shares in their own companies, but they are not allowed to trade in shares of their company in the six weeks preceding a results announcement (this is known as the *closed period*). So you will often find directors buying or selling shares on the day of results or one or two days afterwards.

Many investors believe that by following buys or sales by directors they can make money – i.e. by buying into companies when directors are buying, and selling (or shorting) when directors are selling.

Interpreting directors' dealings

Of course, just because a director buys, it does not necessarily mean the shares are going to rise. You have to examine the buys and sells in tandem with doing proper research into the companies. In my opinion, following directors' dealings slavishly will *not* lead you to stock market millions.

Why do directors buy their shares?

Sometimes they buy because they think their company is doing well. Sometimes it's simply to give a vote of confidence and encourage investors to back the company (heads of credit-crunched banks did this in 2007–8 but the freefall continued). And often it's simply because they think they will make a lot of money and they have to do something with their money.

Why do they sell?

It could be because they feel the company's future for the moment is not all that bright. But it could simply be because they need the money to pay school fees or buy a house.

The problem, as you can see, is that without the wider context of additional share research, directors' dealings can easily be over-interpreted. And directors know that any purchase they make of their company's shares will be publicly announced, and that this could cause investors to buy in. So things are actually a bit foggy!

But it'd be just as damaging to ignore them altogether as to follow them blindly. There's a simple way of getting the most out of them.

> In my experience, the key to working out whether a director buy or sell is worth following or not is the *amount* of shares being bought or sold.

If they are buying a huge amount then I am more interested. But much more so if they are buying a lot of shares in relation to their current holding. The key measurement is always: how many shares they are buying/selling compared with how many they own?

For example, if a CEO of a company sells one million shares, does that mean it is time to follow suit?

Not necessarily – if the director still owns 15 million shares. He might just have needed the money to buy a better house! But if he'd sold half his stake, I might get a bit worried.

It's the same with buys. **The proportion of shares bought compared to the amount owned is what you should look at carefully.**

It can sometimes be a good sign if a director buys, say, £20,000 worth of shares if they only currently hold a small amount. Not all directors are wealthy, and £20,000 might be quite a big investment for a director of a smaller company.

Summary – directors' dealings

To sum up, watching directors' dealings is something every investor should do. And sometimes seeing a deal can lead you to examine a new company that you haven't come across before.

But you should never slavishly follow a deal. There is no substitute for doing your own research into a company – and just using a director's deal as good bonus information.

Directors' dealings can be found for free on ADVFN.com – click the 'Toplists' tab and find 'Directors' Shareholding' in the 'Free TopLists' table.

7. Check the company website

I always check the website of any company that I'm thinking about buying.

This might seem obvious, but I bet most investors don't bother. A company's website can tell you an awful lot. It should also help you to confirm that you know exactly what the company does to make its money! By the time I've finished reading a site, I try to make sure I can say what the company does in a sentence.

And if the website is crap, one has to wonder if the company is able to compete in the 21st century.

If the company uses the website to offer goods to the public, how good is the presentation? Would *you* consider buying goods from its website and, if not, why not? If the site doesn't tempt you to purchase anything, it could have the same effect on others.

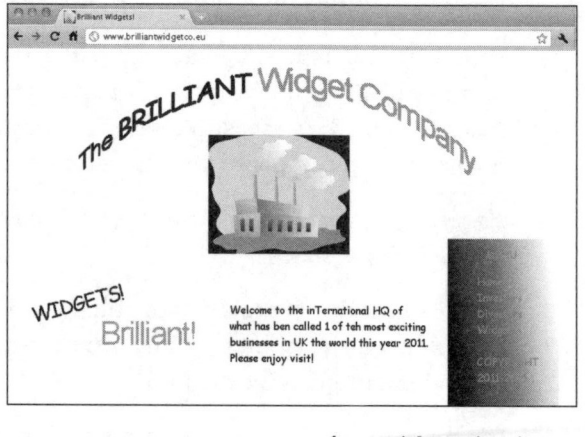

A potential warning sign

Google, of course, will find you a company's site in no time. It's also worth putting in the company name and the word 'reviews' and Googling that too.

Are customers getting their goods on time or are they slagging the company off?

All bloody good research!

If the company doesn't use its website to sell, you can still directly test its service levels in one crucial area – how does it treat its shareholders? Does it have a good news service and does it contain up-to-date news about the company? It ought to at least have a copy of its latest financial report, which you should be able to download. You should be able to send an email to the company as a shareholder, too.

Simple test: send an email stating you are a shareholder and you want to know the date of the next AGM.

See how long it takes them to reply. The quicker the better. If they don't reply, what does that say about how they regard their shareholders?

8. P/E ratios

You'll hear a lot about P/E ratios and you may be surprised to learn that I don't take an awful lot of notice of them. Also, I just know the moment I mention them you'll close the book and go off and do something else. Have you gone? For those of you left:

What the hell is a P/E ratio and why do people go on about them?

It means price-earnings ratio and it is calculated as the share price divided by the earnings per share.

But forget about the formula, it's what it really means that's important. The P/E ratio represents the number of years it will take for the earnings of the company to cover the share price.

Interpreting P/E ratios

1. *Company A* has a share price of 10p, and earnings per share of 2p. The P/E ratio will therefore be 5 (10/2). So, with earnings of 2p, it would take five years for those earnings to cumulatively match the share price.

2. *Company B* has a share price of 90p, and earnings per share of 3p. The P/E ratio will therefore be 30 (90/3). It would take 30 years, with earnings of 3p, to cover the share price of 90p.

One can safely say that the investors in Company B are more optimistic than those in Company A. Company B investors are willing to pay 90p for the shares and wait 30 years (on current earnings) for the share price to be covered by the cumulative earnings. If they weren't confident, the investors would sell their shares, the share price would fall, and the P/E ratio would therefore also fall.

> *Note*: I say that investors are willing to wait 30 years *on current earnings*. But the point is that the investors believe that the company's earnings will actually increase quickly and that they won't have to wait for so long.

By contrast, Company A investors are not so confident. They're only willing to give the benefit of the doubt for earnings to cover the share price in five years' time. They presumably don't think earnings will be going up any time soon.

In general, high-growth companies (e.g. tech stocks) tend to have high P/E ratios, whereas low-growth companies (e.g. utility companies) have low P/E ratios.

If a company has a high P/E ratio, then investors have bid the share price up because they are bullish on the company and expect it to perform well.

You might therefore think that it's better to invest in a company with a high P/E ratio – it could do really well.

Sadly, it's not that simple.

The market could be overvaluing the high P/E company and it could come down to earth with a bump.

Personally, I quite like lower P/E ratios (provided all the other signs on a share are good). That's because the market isn't expecting much, so if the company can beat expectations, the share price could soar. I like my P/Es to be in the region of 12–20.

A comparative measure

The main use of P/E ratios, though, is not as an absolute measure. If a company has a P/E ratio of say 20, that isn't very meaningful in isolation. The power of P/E ratios is when you use them to compare one company's share price with another.

For example, if Company A has a share price of 400p, and Company B has a share price of 14p, nothing can be said about their relative values. Is Company B better value than Company A? We don't know. However, if we know that Company A has a P/E of 12, and Company B a P/E of 32, we *can* say that the market values Company B more highly than it does Company A.

P/Es are most useful when comparing companies within the same sector, as different sectors tend to have different P/Es. As I mentioned above, tech stocks tend to have high P/Es while utility stocks have low P/Es. Because of this, it is not very useful to compare the P/Es of, say, ARM Holdings (260) with that of BHP Billiton (20).

If a retailing company has a P/E of 15, while the average P/E ratio of all companies in the retail sector is 20, one could say that the company is undervalued relative to the sector. There may be a very good reason for this. But if there isn't, then the company may merit further attention as a buy.

My view

Personally, I find P/Es too abstract and only give them a passing glance.

A problem with P/Es is that publications differ on the P/E. So the *FT* might quote a different one to ADVFN. This is because some use historical earnings, some use forward earnings ... blah, blah, blah. Quite honestly, the whole thing washes over me – which doesn't seem to matter, as I still make money!

Picking undervalued shares – my secret

All the best things in life are simple, and I think the system I use to pick out undervalued shares is simplicity itself.

Here's what I do.

I am a billionaire

I use this system after researching any company that looks of interest. I pretend that I am a multi-billionaire and can buy up any company or as many companies as I want to.

But of course, as I'm a billionaire, not only do I want to acquire them on the cheap to get good value for my hard-earned cash – I also want that cash to give me a return. And the only way to do that is to buy companies that are *making profits*, enough profits to ultimately pay me back what I paid to buy them, and to make plenty of money on top of this. Why else would I be interested?

If a company satisfies these billionaire criteria, I decide that I should buy shares in them because, if I'm right, sooner or later someone big *will* buy the company or the share price will go up anyway.

So, how can I work out whether to splash out a small part of my billions on snapping up a company?

The first thing to look at is the profit the company makes; the second is the market capitalisation. In my billionaire role, the figure for how much the company might cost me to buy is the market capitalisation. So if a company's market cap is £50 million, that's how much the market currently thinks the company is worth altogether.

ADVFN provides the market cap and the profit on its 'Quote' page on the same line, so they are easy to find.

As a billionaire, I don't really care about complicated financial ratios and all that twaddle. What I want to know is: how much do you want for your company and what are the profits? How soon will I get my money back, and make some more on that? There's no other reason for me to spend the capital amassed in my glistening dungeon of gold coins.

Putting it simply: if a company is making profits of £10 million, and its market cap is £100 million, that would interest me.

But if a company makes a £10 million profit and is capitalised at £200 million, then I'm not so interested – even if it has some kind of stupendous product that is about to dramatically raise profits. I don't want to spend £200 million to get profits of £10 million, whatever the prospects.

In other words, my rule of thumb is a max of around 15 times market cap to profits.

Let's go back to the company making £10 million. The most I want to see the market cap at is around £150 million. That's 15 times. Any more than that and it starts to look expensive – so why would I buy the shares?

15-times market cap is my personal rule of thumb – something I've arrived at after years of experience in the market. It's not an industry-wide standard, just my own threshold. This metric can't be used with oil or mining companies; they are a different ball game, as we shall discuss later.

Some of my loose change.

Summary – selecting shares

This is a good point at which to sum up what will make me put a share on a to-buy shortlist:

- There is still growth to come.

- It has a full listing.

- Dividends, profits and turnover are rising.

- There are tons of positives.

- There are no question marks.

- It is liquid.

- I understand what the company does.

- It is priced at under 15x profits to market cap.

- It looks cheap.

- It is in a good market.

- Demand for its products is likely to grow.

- The chart looks positive and is in an upward trend.

- Debt is under three times its full-year profits.

Once all my boxes are ticked, the share goes in my shortlist and then it's down to timing. And we'll come onto that shortly.

As you can see, it takes quite a bit to get a share onto the shortlist. And quite right too!

I think at this point it's time to look at some examples of shares I bought and why. And maybe a good time for you to have a break.

Reading the book in bed?

Have a sleep and come back tomorrow. You've earned it.

Part IV
Trading Strategies

"Never invest in any idea you can't illustrate with a crayon."

– Peter Lynch

20 Winning Strategies

Here's a chapter of new and improved strategies. In the last book there were ten. This time I've done 20. Talk about value for money!

These are all tried-and-tested strategies of mine for making money out of the stock market. Things I've picked up over the years. No one taught me these. I got them from the street, check it. Word! (Sorry.)

I also think most of them will work for a long time in the years to come. Perhaps even if you are buying this in 2030, and I'm in a home somewhere trying to find my teeth. Nurse, the screens!

It goes without saying that any shares I would trade using these strategies would have to also pass muster with the research outlined in the last couple of chapters. So don't think you can ignore the research side of things (I saw you thinking about it!).

Okay, without further ado, let me unveil ... *Naked Trader's TOP 20 STRATEGIES!*

STRATEGY 1: Buy shares just before they get into the FTSE 100

A great time to buy into a share is when it is getting close to a market cap of £3 billion. At just over this level, stocks can gain promotion from the FTSE 250 and entry onto the FTSE 100. Funds track the FTSE 100 and this usually gives a lift to the shares, as they will buy into it as soon as it hits the FTSE 100. Also, you may have found a good share anyway – it must have been doing something right to rise so nicely.

So I look for shares around the £2.7–3 billion mark that have been steadily going up. I do my usual research as well (*always do the research, please!*) but a steadily increasing share price heading towards £3bn market cap is a great sign.

For example, I spotted John Wood Group in October 2010. It was gradually rising nicely towards the £3bn mark, so it looked like it had a very good chance of getting into the FTSE 100 within three to six months. (Shares get promoted and demoted from the FTSE 100 index every three months, in mid-March, June, September and December.) I bought in at 520 when I saw it in October '10.

It got its promotion to the main index in March and rocketed up to near the 700 mark!

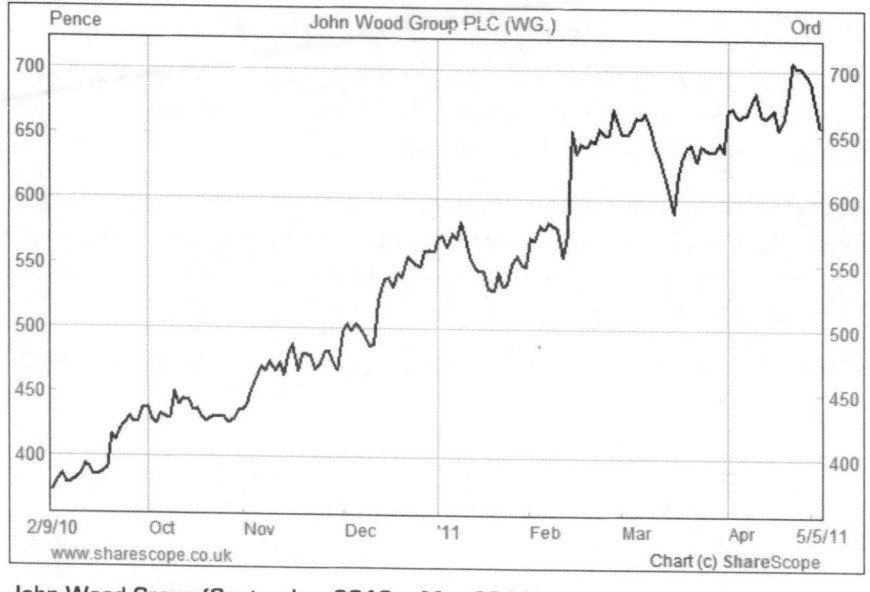

John Wood Group (September 2010 – May 2011)

I also managed the same trick with ITV in March 2011, making decent money out of a spread bet before it got promoted – though I sold it a few days later as I didn't like the fundamentals.

Sometimes it can be a good move to take profits a few days after a share gains promotion, as promoted shares can often slide for a bit once the funds have bought in.

You can get a list of FTSE 250 stocks at **www.londonstockexchange.com**.

Summary

- Check for shares in an uptrend heading towards £3bn.

- Look at high-ranked FTSE 250 shares at the London Stock Exchange site.

- Think about taking profits a few days after promotion.

STRATEGY 2: Get to love the phrase 'ahead of expectations'

I really love buying companies which put out a trading update stating that their current trading is 'ahead of expectations', or 'ahead of market expectations' or 'better than expected' – or which is generally extremely upbeat in a similar way. This is because you know pretty much for sure that the next results are going to be really good.

Time and time again I've seen share prices of companies issuing short but good updates in-between results go markedly higher for weeks after such a brief statement. Often they then go higher still as the good results come in, especially if good trading has continued.

I've made some lovely profits from buying into these. Here's one I bought called Treatt. This is the paragraph from their trading update that I liked:

> ❝ It is pleasing to announce that the positive news reported in the Interim Management Statement issued on 15 February 2011 has continued, and in some parts of the Group has accelerated. Consequently, trading for the half year has significantly exceeded expectations and with order books remaining strong, full year results are now likely to be materially higher than previously anticipated. ❞

> Note that 'positive' was caught by our nifty traffic-light highlighter system: that box around it, on ADVFN, was a healthy green colour!

Well, okay, this statement didn't say 'ahead of expectations' – but "materially higher" is the same thing, if not even nicer.

I now know Treatt's results should be, erm, well a Treatt.

I already had some of their shares when the statement came out, but on reading it I immediately bought more. The shares have continued to motor nicely higher as this lovely chart shows.

Of course, if I hadn't already done my research, I would definitely have looked into the share a bit more – especially its debt levels – before buying in, but having done that, "materially higher" is good enough for me!

The best place to find such statements is simply to check the share-related news reports that come out at 7am each day. You can find them by clicking news on ADVFN or other such services. Keep checking through till you find one. Might be worth the time and effort spent!

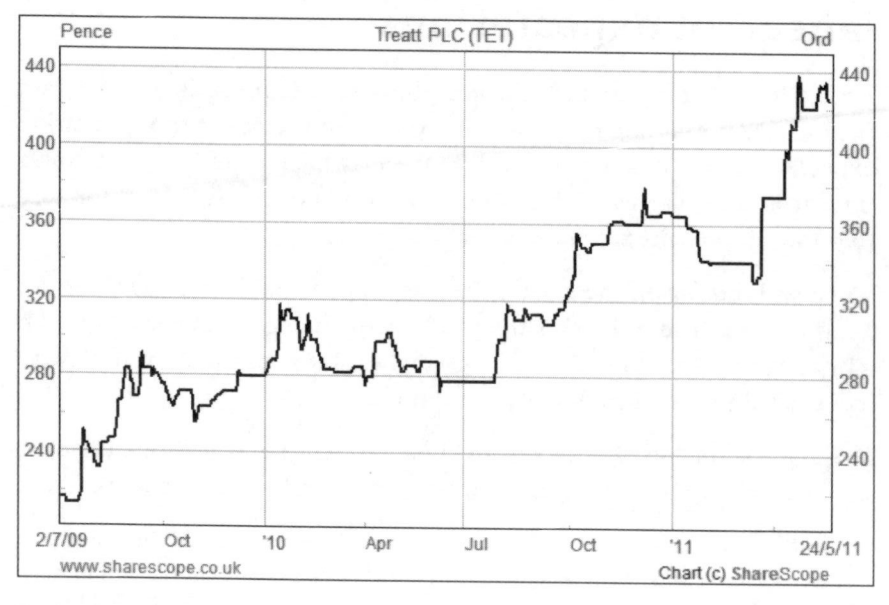

Treatt (July 2009 – May 2011)

Summary

- Look for good news.

- Cherish phrases like 'ahead of' or 'better than'.

- Make the effort to find good news stories by clicking through news from 7am.

STRATEGY 3: Buy retailers your partner or friends rate

If you are looking to buy shares in a retailer, check with everyone you know. Where are they shopping? Where are their partners shopping? Where is your partner shopping?

I've found a number of great trades this way over the years, including Supergroup (which trebled in value in just a few months). Even better was Mulberry, the high-end handbag makers. The following chart tells all you need to know about how that pick went! (I'll get into the story of how I chanced upon it in a moment.)

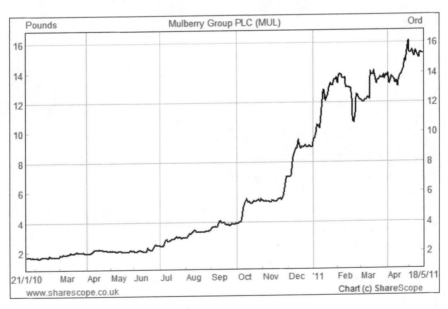

Mulberry (January 2010 – May 2011)

In particular, look around your richer friends with disposable income, well, er, if you have any! Find out what they are spending their money on. And especially anything they are buying that might have high margins. Like boots and handbags!

But whoever your mates are, it's worth checking the names on most of the bags that they come back from the shops with.

It's also worth finding out which shops they don't like or which are being shunned. Then you could consider shorting them, or betting on them to go down (more on this when we discuss spread betting later). One great short I got this way was Mothercare. My wife knows lots of women who buy the kind of products Mothercare sell. And they were all shopping elsewhere.

I shorted, and Mothercare just carried on slumping.

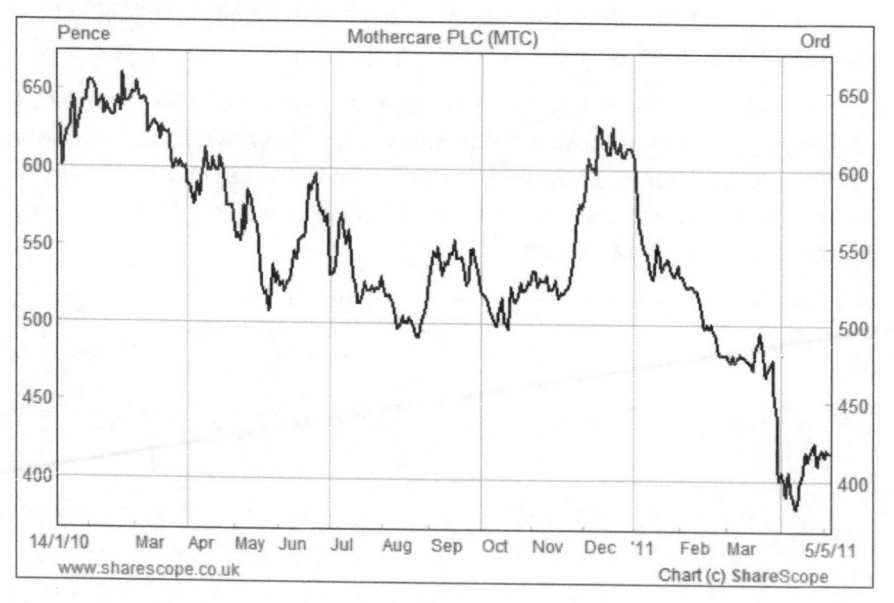

Mothercare (January 2011 – May 2011)

Also consider that retailers can be in fashion for a year or two but then fall from grace. So keep an eye on your friends' changing habits and get ready to take profits!

Summary

- Which stores do your partner/friends like?

- Buy if many praise the same store.

- But don't hold onto them forever, as fashions and trends change.

Example – round and round the Mulberry bush (but not on a Halfords bicycle)

I have made a packet from quizzing my wife, her friends, my friends and others as to what and where they are buying. This started a long time ago when Mrs NT pointed out how great Ted Baker was and how much she shopped there. I bought the shares and doubled my money.

You might think this kind of anecdotal evidence is nonsense and should be ignored. Well, you couldn't be more wrong. Recently I have made more than I could have dreamed of by buying retailers which kept being mentioned by Mrs NT, friends and those that came to my seminars.

I kept seeing various pictures of bags and boots come up on Mrs NT's computer. On quizzing her she told me something called 'Mulberry' was the big thing.

Mulberry, she explained, was where any woman with a spot of spare cash was buying her bags and boots.

Apparently they were all ridiculously expensive. Over a grand for a handbag! Sometimes a lot more than that. Same for boots.

Now I know guys reading this – myself included – would never ever pay a grand for a bag or a boot. My gym bag is currently a Waitrose cooling bag I got for free. But women do and that's a fact. Blokes of course spend their money buying yet another laptop. Women laugh at them. A fair exchange, I suppose.

"Mulberry bags are to die for," explained Mrs NT. "Ask any woman – they are great quality, look fantastic and are a must own!"

By chance the very next day I was holding a seminar. I asked the women in the audience what they thought of Mulberry. Every single one rated Mulberry very highly. And all bar one had bought something expensive from them.

That was enough for me.

Now, while I personally do not drool over Mulberry bags, I did drool over the share price chart after I bought the shares! (It's the one we saw on page 137.)

I bought quite a few between 200p and 300p. A year later they hit 1300! More than six times the price when I made my initial investment. This netted me more than £20,000. Enough to buy ... oooh, at least two Mulberry bags and a boot.

Halfords is an opposite example. One evening I walked into one of their stores with my young son to buy him a bike. We knew the one he wanted. I had the cash in my hand. We were ready to get us some wheels.

I pointed out the desired bike. The sales guy looked at me as if I was insane.

"Oh no. You can't buy that now."

"Er ... "

"It's on display – I might miss a sale. Come back tomorrow if you really want it."

"Really?"

"Yes."

"Wait a second ... " I said. "I have cash and want to buy. But you think that, in selling this to me in the last 15 minutes of opening hours, you might miss a sale in the last 15 minutes of opening hours?"

"Yes," he said.

"Right. It's just that–"

"You can't buy it now."

"Okay. Well, don't go in for *The Apprentice*," I sighed, "If I was Lord Sugar, you would be well and truly fired now."

He didn't care whether he got a sale or not – from me or anyone else. The store was closing soon and he just wanted to cash up and go home. After all, it wasn't really his business and he'd get paid whatever.

Then I looked around the store more carefully. Hmm ... stock seemed low. Demotivated staff members loafed variously about the place. Not many customers.

The very next day I went one better than Lord Sugar. I logged into my spread betting account and shorted the shares at 550p. Over the next year, the share price collapsed and I had made £6,000.

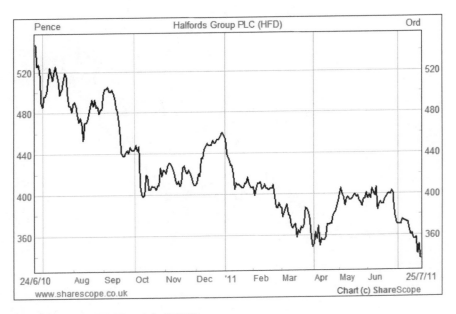

Halfords (June 2010 – July 2011)

STRATEGY 4: Seek game-changing changes

When you are reading through company reports (after subjecting them to the good old traffic lights) ask yourself:

Is this company doing anything new? Is it getting into a new area of business which could be a game changer and start an upward surge in the share price?

I'm looking for companies in the doldrums that are beginning to go through a transformation. I especially like ones that at the same time state they are shutting down loss-making divisions and putting resources into profit-making areas, or indeed finding new revenue streams.

The best example of one of these I bought into is Carclo. This company was a safe, solid but perhaps a little dull engineering company. But all of a sudden the company started talking about being involved in developing an exciting new technology called CIT, which could be used for all kinds of gadgets. That got me interested. This was a solid engineering company which looked like it could turn into a more highly-rated tech company. I bought in at the low 100s and the share nearly trebled for me up to 300. And there could be more to come if the technology takes off.

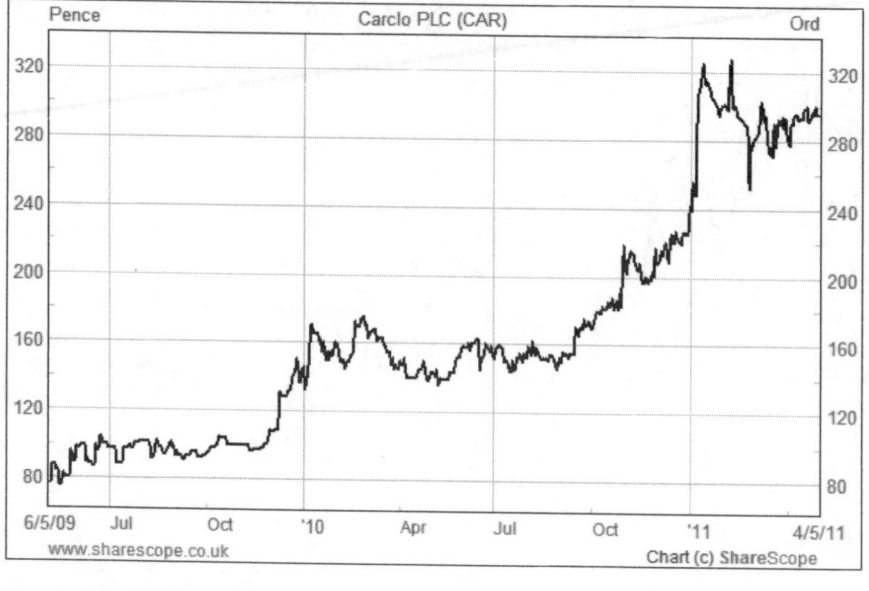

Carclo (May 2009 – May 2011)

How do you come across something like this? Again, it is simply a matter of clicking on company reports every day when they get published at 7am or looking at them when you get home in the evening.

Look for the word 'transformational'. Look for anything where it appears they have a new line of business or revenue stream. You could also look at a company that has bought another company. Could that purchase transform it? One little bit of research could pay back big time like it has for me here …

Summary

- Look for any new line a company has.

- Look for the word 'transformational'.

- Any company that is changing tack is worth checking out.

STRATEGY 5: Find something cheap!

I know what you're thinking:

Hey, Robbie, that's easy enough for you to say. How do you find cheap shares?

What I'm looking for is a market cap that looks very low compared to full-year profits or the likely full-year profits that are on the way.

Remember my rule of thumb: if a company has a market cap of, say, £100m and is making £10m profits, that looks cheap. (Trading at only ten times profits to market cap.) If it was over 15 that would start to look more expensive. Again, this is just my personal rule, fine-tuned over the years. I'm really looking for something perhaps trading at eight times, where the outlook is good. *That's* cheap.

Alternative Networks came up when I was idly checking through company results in July 2010. I really liked what I saw. Its market value was £70 million. But it reported in the half-year results that profits were up a massive 30% to £4.5 million. I doubled that for the full year, figuring a full-year profit of more than £9m. That showed the share trading at under eight times the value of its annual profits. And on top of that it reported net cash of more than £7m, which made it even more of a bargain. I had little hesitation and bought in at 154p.

When full-year results came out in December it showed a profit of £9.2m and even more cash! This time £11m! With market cap now at £90m it was still trading at under ten times its yearly profits. Plus it had all that cash. I then thought what the next full-year results could be if it kept going at the same rate: another 30% up on its profits next time would put them at around £12m. That would place the share at less than eight times its profits again, and that's not counting the cash. So I bought more!

Not long after this they were trading at 250! A very nice 70% increase thanks very much!

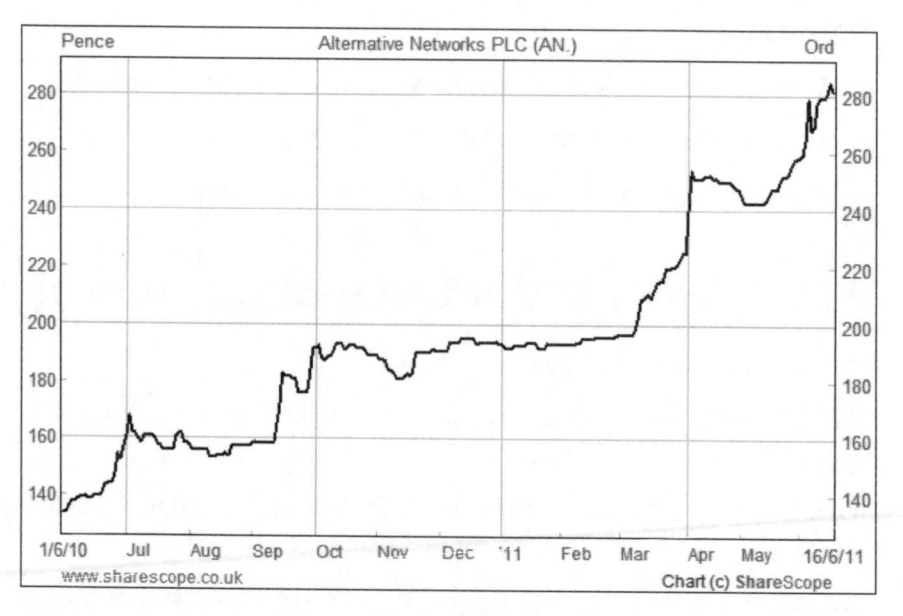

Alternative Networks (June 2010 – June 2011)

Summary

- Look for companies that have a low market cap compared to their annual profits (no more than eight to ten times is good).

- When you find it, think about buying in, unless it fails the strict tests you should apply to every share purchase.

- Check again that debt is not an issue.

STRATEGY 6: Look for investment in new facilities

A great way to find a company that's going to grow is when you see in a set of results that they are so confident that they have decided to prepare for growth by building themselves new production facilities.

This often happens with companies that make things. Orders have been coming in which they cannot fulfil, so they announce they are increasing capacity in order to meet them.

In February 2009 a statement came out from XP Power. It looked good: profits and its dividend were up and it had seemingly survived the recession. But it was this particular part of the statement that got me very interested:

> 66 Construction of new 70,000 sq ft manufacturing facility started in June 2008. Upon completion, the new facility will increase XP Power's manufacturing capacity by 400%. 99

Interesting! That's bold. If they think they need to increase capacity by 400%, they must be pretty confident the orders are coming in! So I bought the shares at 150 and a couple of months later bought more in the 160s.

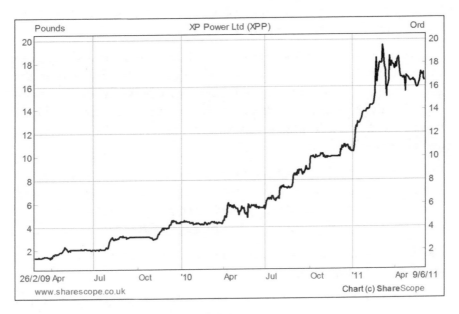

XP Power (February 2009 – June 2011)

Oh boy, do I feel lucky I saw this?

Very lucky. I should be so lucky, lucky, lucky – to quote the great philosopher Kylie.

Why? Amazingly the shares went up from there and never stopped. And I made a fortune from them. They went all the way up to 1800 in just two years! I still hold them as I write the book. A great profit of more than £20,000.

Summary

- If a healthy-looking company announces it's increasing capacity, and everything else about it checks out, it could prove a great buy indeed.

STRATEGY 7: What's the hot sector (and its close relatives)?

Sometimes you'll find that one sector of the market is hot.

How do you know it's a hot sector?

Well, it's partly down to common sense and partly down to looking for sectors where the share prices in that sector are rising.

One sector in particular has been 'hot' for a long time, a sector still ignored by a lot of people (at least at the time of writing): oil services. That is, the people who provide the equipment needed by the booming oil companies. Over the last few years, of course, oil itself has been a hot sector and I have made a lot of money buying oil exploration companies like Burren Energy and Heritage Oil.

But of course with the continued boom in oil exploration, the oil services sector also continues to be a great ride. And I suspect for a while longer. In particular, I've bought three oil services companies that have made me a fortune between them: Sondex, Hunting and Petrofac.

My favourite one of all is Petrofac: bought at 350, it has hit 1500 and shows no sign of slowing.

Of course, a hot sector isn't going to be hot forever, but usually I try and carry on riding the waves of a hot sector for as long as I can until it enters an obvious downturn.

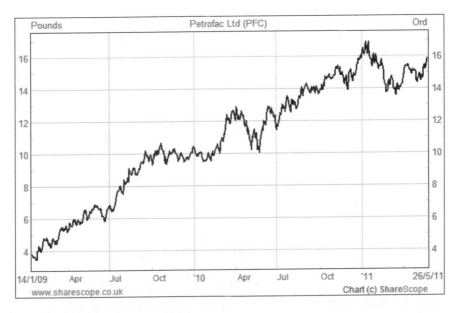

Petrofac (Jan 2009 - May 2011)

If you find a share you like, check out others in the same sector – they might be doing well for similar reasons.

Having brought up the quote for a share, click 'Financials' on ADVFN – and near the top of the page there will be a clickable link, next to the name of the sector, named 'more like this'. Click on that to find other shares in the sector. Maybe you found a hot sector!

Vodafone Company Financial Information

FREE

Vodafone share price | Vodafone company information | Vodafone Share Charts | Vodafone Share New

Company name:	Vodafone Grp.					
Company Description:	A group engaged in the supply of communications services and products					
EPIC:	VOD			Trading Currency:		GBX
Market Sector:	FE00	Click here!		ISIN:		GB00B16
Market Segment:	SET0			Share Type:		DE
WWW Address:	http://www.vodafone.com/			Description:		ORD USD
Industry Sector:	MOBILE TELECOMMUNICATIONS - more like this					

Price	Price Change [%]	Bid	Offer	Open	High	Low
159.30	↓ -0.3 [-0.19]	159.30	159.35	159.00	159.85	158.75

Market Cap. [m]	Shares In Issue [m]	Beta	EPS	DPS	PE Ratio	Yield
81,394.28	51,094.96	0.81	15.20	8.90	10.48	5.59

I don't know what the next hot sector is going to be, but I will probably find it in the course of researching shares in my usual way. When you do find it, don't be afraid to really go for it and buy well.

Summary

- If you can find a hot sector, it can stay hot for quite a long time. At some point it'll lose its shine, but it's worth riding a hot sector for as long as possible.

- Ensure you still do normal research into the particular share you are interested in.

STRATEGY 8: Recovery plays

A recovery-play strategy is all about finding a share that was once doing well, has had a terrible time but is now starting to rise again.

The trouble here is finding the right share: one that is actually recovering and not still in the dumps and likely to get further in the dumps!

You *must* have worked out a reason *why* the company is going to/is recovering and not just jump into a share that's gone down a lot. I'm usually trying to find a company that has got something wrong but is putting it right – meaning there's plenty of potential in the share price.

But whatever you do, ensure you are not just buying a dog that may not recover. **You must have your reasons why it will recover.**

One successful recovery play for me has been London Capital Group. This one runs lots of spread betting sites for companies like Betfair and PaddyPower.

It was riding high in early 2008 as everyone was spread betting like crazy – but then the recession hit and scared punters stopped betting. The shares tumbled all the way down to 58p in 2011, which is where I bought some. Why?

Because the company took action regarding its decline. It raised £8m in a placing (selling new shares directly to institutions), and its directors showed confidence by picking up shed loads of shares at the same time. It also reported increasing revenues and strong cash flows. With a lowly market cap of £30m, whilst it held £13m in cash, it looked an excellent recovery-play candidate.

Time will have to tell with this one, but I'm pretty confident.

London Capital Group (July 2008 – May 2011)

Summary

- Have the reasons why the share will recover clear in your head.

- Don't buy if the share price is still going down and it could go bust. Check the debt.

- There must be a tangible reason for recovery.

STRATEGY 9: Get trendy for short-term gains

Sometimes I come across a share and notice something peculiar about its price performance: over a year or two it doesn't do much and moves sideways. But it moves sideways in a repetitive up-and-down pattern, because the market struggles to know how it should be rated.

And here I can get some shorter-term gains: I simply keep buying, selling and then shorting the same share time after time as it carries on doing the same thing.

My best example of this is with a company called Dignity. Which, erm, well specialises in ... death. No, not like those seedy Swiss suicide shops –

I draw the line somewhere! Its business is funeral services. Well, it has to be someone's business!

Given that we all have to peg it sometime, you would have thought that it would always go up. But it seems that death is an expensive business, and it has high debt as well as profits.

But take a look at this amazing chart for yourself!

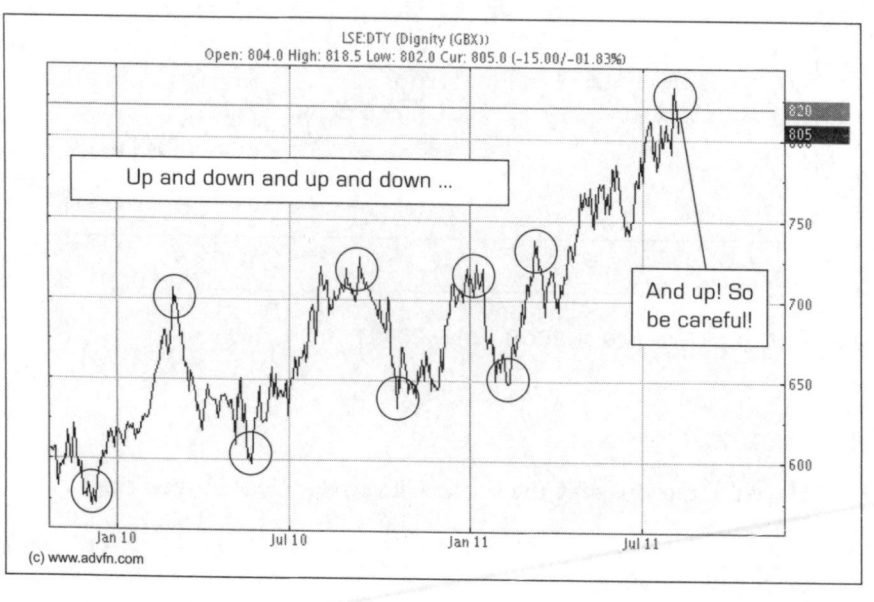

Dignity (January 2010 – August 2011)

There it goes: 600p to 700p. 700p to 600p. 600p to 730p. Then it tightens a bit. 730p to 650p. 650p to 730p. 730p to 650p. 650p to 740p ... get the message?

Each time it did this – perhaps using a spread bet for greater speed and flexibility, particularly with shorting (explained later) – you'd have made decent money on this one by playing the top and bottom. How easy was that?

Of course, you have to be careful with this kind of share. They can break out of these ranges. In this case Dignity later starts to rise fairly steadily over half a year, perhaps establishing a new range. When shares start to break out, I put this kind of strategy on hold. I might wait a bit to see where a share peaks again. Despite the rise, the history of bouncing between a high and a low can repeat itself.

So examine a few charts – FTSE 250 stocks are your best bet, in my experience – and find some trading range patterns and start to play them. You are looking for a share that has been oscillating between two levels for a few weeks or months. Each time, you want to try to buy near the bottom of the range and sell near the top.

I mention FTSE 250 stocks because they are liquid and the spreads are normally tight, ideal for short-term trading. FTSE 100 stocks, though also liquid and with tight spreads, in my experience just don't work as well – they're just different beasts. And if you tried this with smaller stocks, the bid–offer spreads would be greater, which would reduce the profit.

If you can only look in on stocks once or twice a day, it may be worth having a stop loss with your broker or spread betting firm – say around 2% below the bottom of the range, in case something happens when you are not at your desk.

Summary

- Make sure it is a strong company, and of sufficient size to allow you to buy and sell easily at the price you want.

- Confirm it is in a range, then buy at or near the bottom of the range and sell or short near the top.

- Get out fast if a range is broken either way.

STRATEGY 10: Buy boring companies!

I bet you don't want to buy boring, do you? You want excitement! I know it! You want something, ooh, that explores gold ... dreammmyy! Or oil in some place dangerous!

Well, keep it quiet (and don't tell your trading mates), but what you should really be doing is looking for boring companies. In my experience, these are the ones that can make you big money.

When I look at a company's website and see a load of boring-looking cogs and widgets I get excited!

Let's take my favourite bore, Devro. It makes the casing that goes around sausages. How boring is that? Well, not so boring if you are stuffing your face with a sausage sandwich, agreed. But other than that: yawn!

The thing is, though, people will always eat sausages. And Devro have a near monopoly in sausage casings. Even in a recession, people like a good banger.

Look at their price chart and tell me they're still boring!

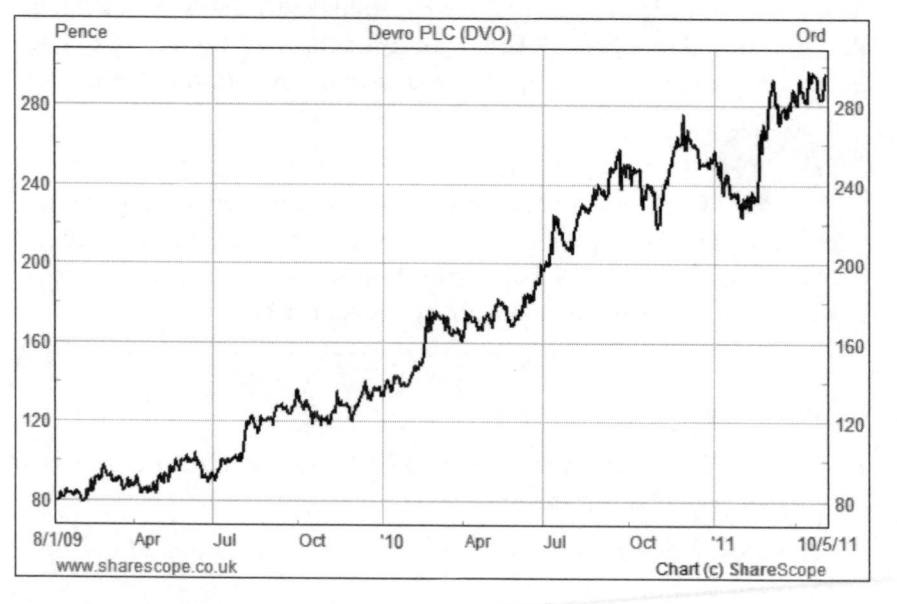

Devro (January 2009 – May 2011)

Ahhhh! Yes, as you can see, boring old Devro has more than trebled in just over a couple of years! Ruddy tedious, eh?

Engineering companies can also be brilliantly boring. Take Fenner, which makes dull things like conveyor belt components. But these dull things sell ...

The chart on the next page shows you how well this company has done.

It's amazing how these engineering companies can pay out in time. My timescale for such boring but steadily gaining companies is about three years. You'll find they can become the great bedrock of, say, a self-select ISA. They are always there, gradually increasing your wealth.

So the surprising thing to remember is: boring products often sell really well. Just because you come across a company that has a product that starts you yawning, doesn't mean you should overlook it!

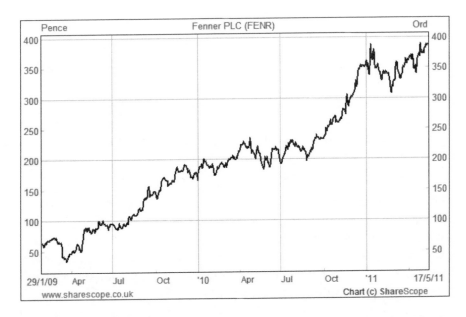

Fenner (January 2009 – May 2011)

Summary

- Think about having one of two boring companies in your portfolio – buy and hold them.

- They will keep you going during the bad times and steadily help to increase your wealth.

- They often pay good dividends too.

STRATEGY 11: Buy shares 'doing the splits'

What the hell are you talking about, Burns? Buy fit shares? Nope. I'm talking about share splits, consolidations and bonus issues.

Delightfully simple. Allow me to explain.

Companies whose share prices are under 50p or over 1000p sometimes get stuck in a rut – simply because investors don't like buying shares under 50p, as they come with a *penny share* tag, and don't like buying shares over 1000p as that is perceived as being too expensive. Also, in both cases, the spreads between the buy and sell prices tend to be a bit higher than the norm.

So what some companies do when their share prices are seen as too cheap or too dear is simply change the price of their share via a split or consolidation. It makes absolutely no difference at all to the value of the company or the amount in value held by the shareholders. It just changes the share price by increasing the number of shares. It's like instead of having a cake divided into eighths, and everyone having one slice, you cut it into sixteenths and everyone gets two slices.

The best recent example of this is Greggs. You've probably bought a sausage roll there sometime! The trouble for Greggs was that its share price was sitting at 3650p in 2009. No investor or trader wants to buy a share trading at £35! It just seems too much to pay. So, cleverly, Greggs did a share split, meaning existing shareholders got a different amount of shares but kept the same value of holding.

Instead of the share price being £35, it became 350p! (Or £3.50.) Now investors felt better about buying the shares. And boy did this work well.

As the chart shows, the shares boomed over two years from 350p to over 500p.

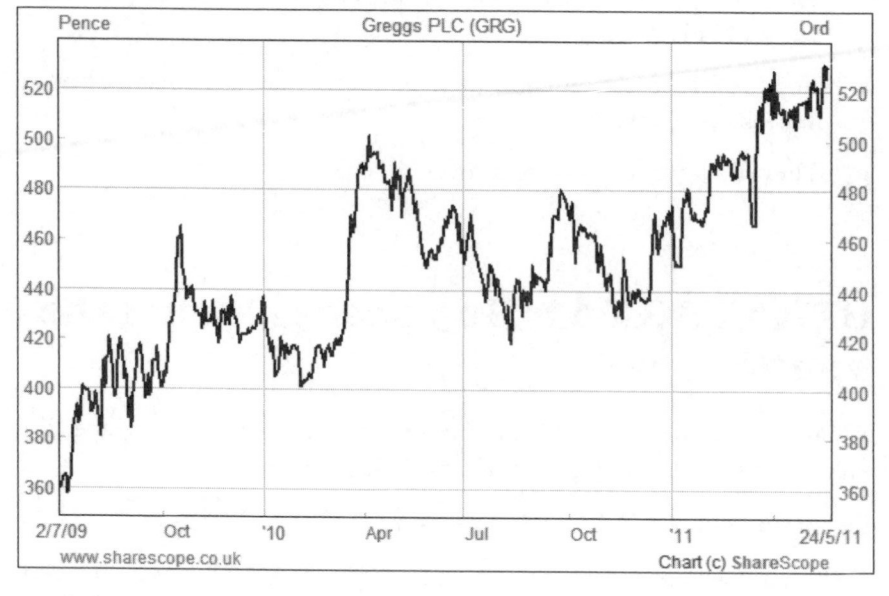

Greggs (July 2009 – May 2011)

How do you profit from a split?

I find the best thing is to buy the share before the split. Research has shown there is an average rise of over 3% in a share price on the day of a split and many shares outperform after a split or consolidation.

How do you find out about splits?

They usually get announced during a company's report, so it's a question of always doing a sift through of company reports as they come out at 7am every day. A quick look through them on ADVFN news or any other news service you might use will do the job.

> *Note:* After a share split or consolidation, charts of share prices will automatically adjust the old prices (to provide a continuous share price).

Of course, you should not buy a share just because it is splitting – you must still only buy after you've done the usual research and you're happy with the share anyway.

But I've bought a number of shares before their price has changed and found it's been well worthwhile.

Summary

- Shares that change their price often rise after the change and can be worth buying in before the price changes.

- But still research as normal, as the company needs to actually be decent.

STRATEGY 12: Find strong companies in a niche market

I like finding companies that are strongly positioned in specialised markets. There are quite a few examples around. It's especially good to find companies who specialise in areas that are growing.

So when you read through a company statement and try to understand what it does, work out if they have a nice little niche market – because often, at some point in the future, they get bought out by other companies who operate in related fields. They also have the best chance of defending profit margins in tough times.

Dialight is one that stood out for me.

I noticed LED lighting was becoming the new thing. Everywhere you looked, LEDs were coming into fashion. And this was the market Dialight specialised in. I took a look at its website and its reports and liked what I saw. In particular, it had a good foothold in the USA and supplied a lot of the LED lights used for traffic lights. Another good plus, these LED lights lasted a whole lot longer than normal lights and so saved councils and governments money. Especially with traffic and rail signals. That would make them popular.

Dialight's profits were growing and it had plenty of cash. And it had a big foothold in a niche market that was growing at a tremendous rate.

So I bought some at 150, 180, 220, 250 – and the shares simply boomed. All the way up to 800! **My profits have soared to over £100,000.** Dialightful! [I quit. – Ed.]

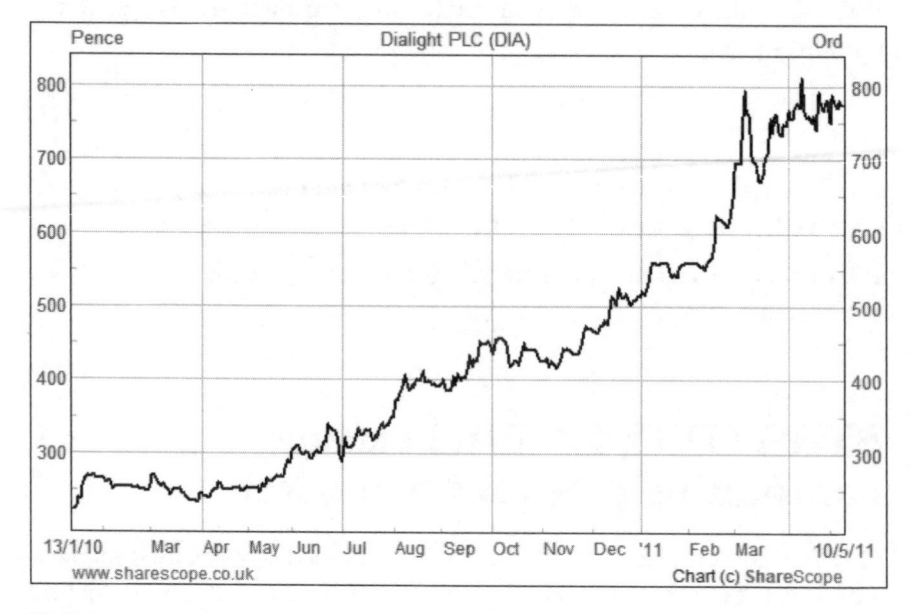

Dialight (January 2010 – May 2011)

Summary

- Look for growing companies in unusual or specialist markets.

- Buy and hold while the market grows.

STRATEGY 13: Find bid targets

I usually manage to be in a share that is bid for about five or six times a year. Why is it so good to be in a company that agrees to be taken over? Because the shares usually increase in value by 50% or more.

And I'm sure the question you're busting to ask me is:

Okay wise guy, how do you find a bid target?

There are four main ways, all of which can (and probably should) be combined:

1. Seeing increased buying activity in a share.

2. Buying into a company which common sense tells you would make a good bid target for others in the same area.

3. Quite simply, keeping your eye on bid gossip in the papers.

4. Would YOU buy this company if you were a company in the same area?

My best recent example is Nestor Healthcare.

With the population of Blighty getting older and older, this one looked ripe for a bid to me. It owned care homes and care facilities, and was pretty much the only stock-market-listed healthcare company in this field.

I thought to myself: this must make it interesting for other companies not listed who want to buy up a whole heap of care homes in one fell swoop.

So I bought Nestor all the way from 20p through to 80p. And indeed, they were taken out at 110p by Saga.

The share price rose throughout and there was good volume in the shares in the weeks before the bid. The press picked up on the bid at 80p – you could still have bought in there and made a killing.

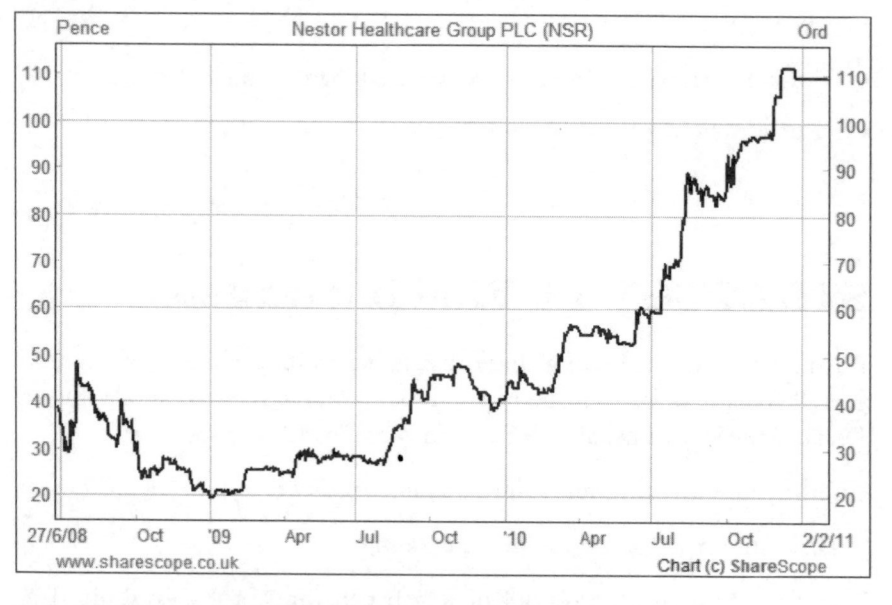

Nestor Healthcare (June 2008 – February 2011)

Something else to check when trying to identify bid targets, especially with smaller shares, is whether you are seeing quite a few small buys coming through, with a steady rise in the share price?

Although insider trading is illegal, you see time and time again lots more shares than normal in a company being traded in the run up to a bid. Because, let's face facts: those in the know gossip about it, and so the news gradually spreads.

Picking up on this activity has worked for me a few times in the past and is especially good in smaller companies. If you get to know shares on your watchlist, as time goes by and you gain experience you will, like me, develop a nose for abnormal buys or trades coming in – and it's usually worth acting fast.

Seems to me that those in the know tend to find out around six weeks before a bid is due in the smaller companies.

Of course, there are also plenty of risers in bigger companies in the run up to bids. It's worth watching for price rises and mentions in the press.

Catching a bid is often a case of picking up news and gossip from the ADVFN newswires, other websites and general bits and pieces from the newspapers.

Often when a company is mentioned in a gossipy way in the press as a possible bid target, there is still time to get on board. It's a matter of timing and a bit of guesswork.

You have to decide whether a counter bid is likely from some other party – this happens quite a lot. For example, the Boots share price was around 770 when rumours first went round about a bid. It was possible to get in then. The price rose to near a tenner and then a counter bidder came in and the price rose to 1130p.

Of course it is not all plain sailing. If you come to the story late and a bid does not materialise, the shares can come down quite a bit. If the price is already close to where a bid might come in, you may have missed the action.

Summary

- Watch for sudden buying activity in quiet shares.

- Check daily above-average volumes in the larger companies.

- If you think shares are cheap, so might a bidder.

- Keep an eye on newspaper gossip.

STRATEGY 14: Buy shares moving up to the main market from AIM

Most companies that you will come across as an investor will be listed on the London Stock Exchange. But there are other markets that companies can join, for example the AIM and PLUS markets. These other markets are usually for very small companies; often new companies joining an exchange for the very first time. The LSE is sometimes referred to as the *main market*, to distinguish it from the other markets.

> Rather confusingly, AIM is actually owned by the LSE, but it is in all regards a separate market.

A fairly common progression for a new company is to first join AIM and then once it has grown to a certain size to leave AIM and list on the main market.

One of my favourite strategies is to look for AIM shares that have just moved onto the main market, or are about to move to the main market.

You get about ten companies a year who decide to move onto the main market, which is good news for investors like me who use ISAs and can then start buying into these companies under a tax-free umbrella.

Why is it a good move and why do the prices tend to rise?

It shows the company is serious about its growth prospects and wants to be a big player.

Also, both ISA investors and fund managers can now start to invest in shares they wouldn't have wanted to get involved with before, which can help give the price a boost.

Companies with a value of £400m or so will get in the FTSE 250 – and inclusion in that index will see tracker funds buy in.

So whenever you see an announcement that an AIM share is planning to move to the main market, it's pretty much a buy signal. I would say probably one of the best buy signals there is!

Of course, again you need to make sure you do the normal research and don't just buy anything. But if you like a company, it's invariably worth getting stuck in when you hear they are going on up from the AIM.

How do you find out? A company normally announces it is going to make the leap when it announces results, so it is worth flicking through results every day.

Recently Kentz, a company I was holding in a spread bet, announced it was going to join the main market. It said it would probably do so in 2011.

I'd already bought Kentz at 200. When it said this, I bought more. And at the time of writing, it's still going up.

When it finally makes the move, it will get an automatic entry onto the FTSE 250, which will help the price gain even more!

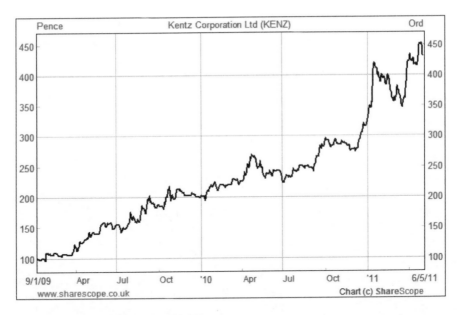

Kentz (January 2009 – May 2011)

Summary

- It's a great signal when a company goes to a main listing from AIM. Very well worth noting and thinking about buying.

- You have to keep your eyes open for these announcements. Check daily results.

STRATEGY 15: A company's division booms

Sometimes a company that has varied interests suddenly sees one of its divisions begin to do very well. And that is a great time to buy in.

A read-through of a company's report can throw this up. What you're looking for is a company that is already doing okay with its revenue streams, so you have the income coming in. It then takes just one division to begin to outperform and you get a share price uplift.

Avon Rubber is a good example of this. Its main business was in the dairy industry. It's a good business but not exactly in an exciting growth area. After all, there are only so many cows!

What caught my eye was its defence division, where it supplied equipment such as masks. The statements revealed it was finding lots of new markets for its masks, including in the US and in the Middle East. As, unfortunately, troubles in the world seemed to be multiplying, there was not much doubt to me that orders were likely to continue to come in.

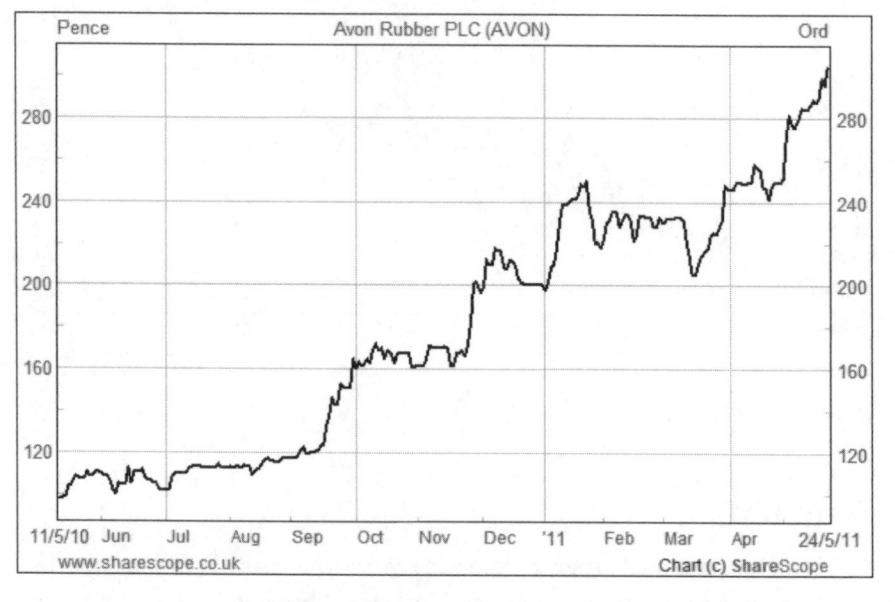

Avon Rubber (May 2010 – May 2011)

As the chart reveals, the price went from a quid to close to three quid. On top of that, the results showed profits were heading up fast and debt coming down.

Summary

- Look for companies where one division is picking up steam.

- With income coming in from other safe but dull divisions, that should help underpin the share price.

STRATEGY 16: Smaller oil exploration

Oil exploration companies – aka oilers – are going to continue to be in demand for a long time to come.

While they obviously have their risks, I have made some good money from them. Researching them is a little harder than it is exploring other companies, and I find it difficult to get my head around production rates etc. But as long as they are producing oil and the oil price stays high, they can be a decent earner for any portfolio.

In summary there are four things to look for:

- Has it already found oil?

- Has it got enough cash to keep going?

- What is the management like?

- Is the area it is in likely to produce more?

You should find the answers in the company's news stories and its website. You must beware that any investment in smaller oil companies is fraught with risk and should be a distinctly small part of any portfolio – almost for fun, if you like. The problem is that a dry well could see 50% marked off a price overnight.

Parkmead was one small oil explorer that caught my eye at 10p in November 2010.

This was a buy on the strength of the management. The main man it had got on board was Tom Cross, a seasoned oil man who had helped take Dana Petroleum from a penny share to the dizzying heights of 1800! Obviously it seemed worth taking a punt given his massive experience. He even said he was trying to do another Dana!

So a small stake was worth a go – and so far I have doubled it.

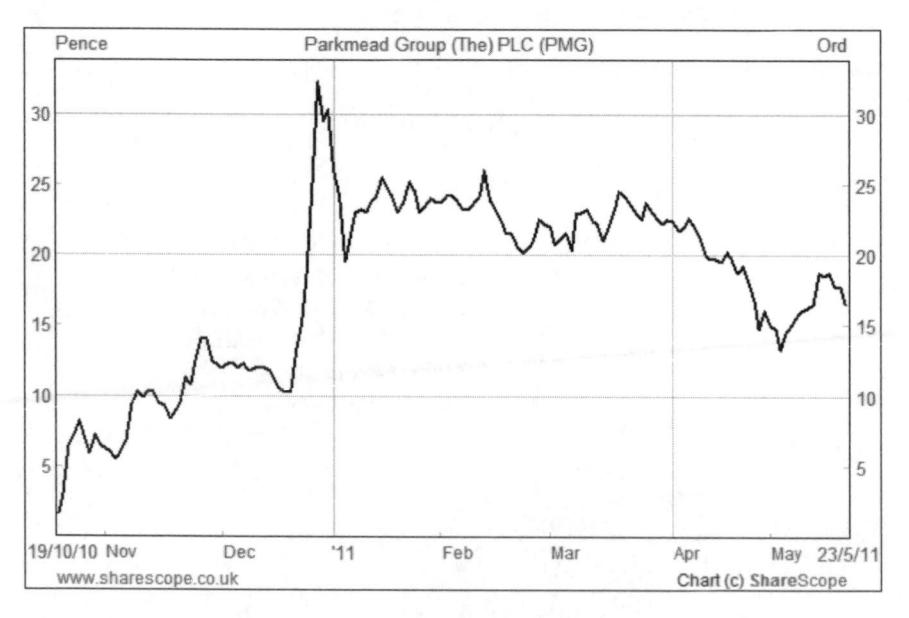

Parkmead Group (October 2010 – May 2011)

What you have to be careful with is any oiler low on cash (they will need to fund raise), as well as any that has kept disappointing. And you must remember: it is next to impossible to value an oil company, so they will always be scary and volatile!

Summary

- Oil exploration is an exciting sector, but beware of having too many oilers.

- Look for ones that have already found oil or have good cash reserves.

- Check the management team and the drill areas.

- Watch out for serial disappointers.

STRATEGY 17: A punt on metals

I have to say I know nothing about metals. Why they go up and down in value is a mystery to me, as is how to value them. It's a nightmare! So I don't get involved that much.

If I trade any metals at all, I actually tend to rely on picking up scraps from newspapers and magazines. Which metal is currently hot stuff?

Gold always seems to hit highs when there is a recession on. But bits and pieces in papers and mags kept catching my eye in 2010/11 about the strength of the price of silver.

So I set about finding companies that drilled or produced silver, came up with two, and decided to take a punt with small stakes on both. This was entirely based on what pundits were calling a longer-term bull market in metals.

Now, even more than oilers, this kind of thing should be confined to an extremely small part of your trading. There's little substantial about it – I'm just hoping to ride a bit of a wave with a very small portion of my funds. It means I won't miss out entirely on what could be a good market. But as I have no idea about when I should be taking profits, as the price of the companies rise I will just move a stop loss gradually up in line with them. When the bubble goes pop, I'll be out without damaging much of my profits.

My two choices were Arian Silver and Fresnillo.

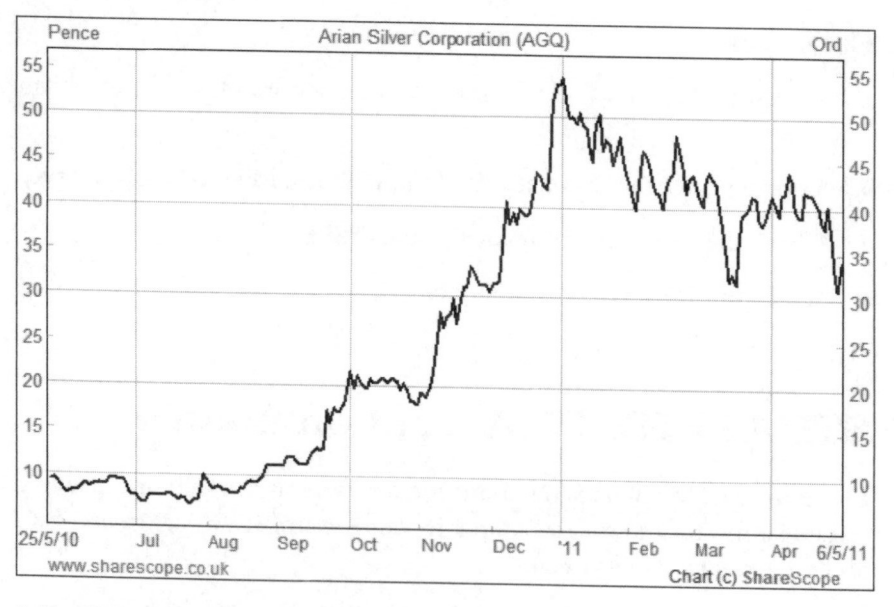

Arian Silver (May 2010 – May 2011)

Fresnillo (May 2010 – May 2011)

Arian doubled for me from 18p through 40p and Fresnillo went up 50%.

So if you fancy a little gamble on metals, keep your eyes on newspaper reports (*The Times* is good for this). Metals tend to go up in price when there is trouble in the world. Sadly there has been a lot of this in the last decade, and the problems don't seem to be going away anytime soon … Of course, such gambles are just that: gambles. You might be buying into a bubble and it might go pop! Set stops and be careful out there.

Summary

- Check news stories for metal news.

- You are taking a punt but it could pay off.

- Raise a stop under a rising price, if unsure like me.

STRATEGY 18: Think about the future

It is always worth asking the following two questions about a company. Is what it is doing going to get even more popular in the future? Is its market likely to grow, and why?

One great example of this, and one I have done nicely with already, is Aggreko.

The company's market is an easy one to explain. It provides temporary power. The more I looked into temporary power, the more I discovered how much it was not only needed now but would be in the future. On top of that, Aggreko seemed to be the market leader. It supplies all the big events such as the World Cup and the Olympics.

So many places need temporary power and power back-ups. And in the future the need for this is going to get bigger. In India and China, for example, as they grow, so does the need for temporary power. There is even talk of blackouts in the UK later in the 2010s. Indeed the more I looked into this, the bigger the market seemed likely to become.

Unfortunately the awful earthquake in Japan in early 2010 again showed the demand for this kind of service. Japan will sadly need temporary power for years to come, and Aggreko will be one of the major suppliers.

It already shows through in Aggreko's share price and profits. The company has soared onto the FTSE 100.

I bought at a tenner and some more at around 12 quid and the share price gradually keeps motoring upwards. I'd expect to keep it for many years.

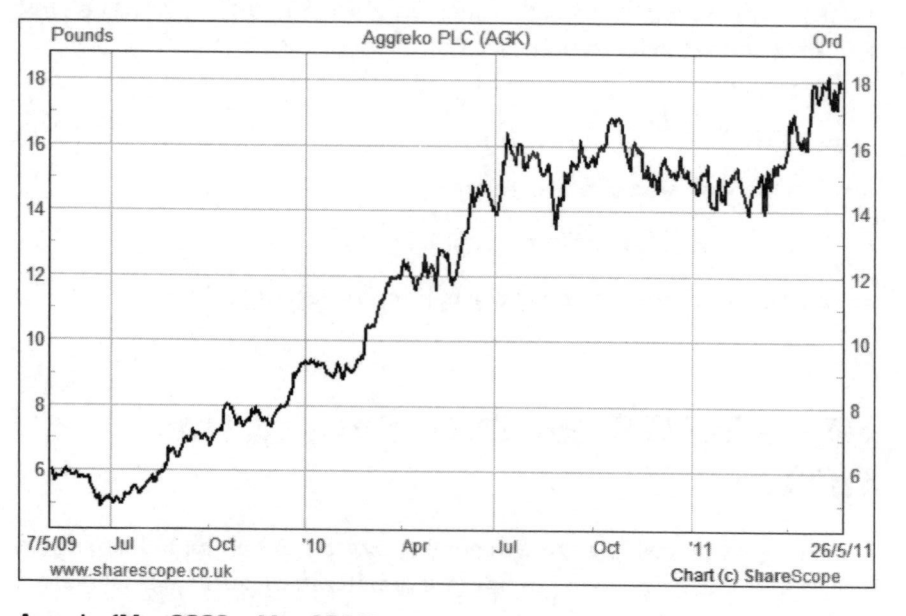

Aggreko (May 2009 – May 2011)

So when researching a company, think hard about its future markets and how they are likely to grow.

Summary

- Look for companies in a market likely to grow.

- Think hard about why a company's future may be bright.

- If it is, hold it for the long term.

STRATEGY 19: Profits and dividend rises over three years

This really is quite a simple strategy.

If a company you are interested in has managed to raise its profits and dividends every year for three years in a row, you have got to get interested. If it also has net cash, too, then that is even better.

A company that fulfilled these criteria was Microgen. This has been a terrific share for me – I bought in at 45p and have trebled on it.

The chart tells the story.

Microgen (June 2008 – May 2011)

It quite simply keeps improving its profits, dividends and its net cash. Indeed it amassed so much cash it had to give some back to shareholders. Fine by me.

And when a company continues to do this, what happens? Over time the share price simply carries on rising.

What do I do? I keep holding until a question mark creeps in. Say it suddenly says one of its divisions isn't performing as well as it has been. Or there is a problem somewhere. Or, indeed, if profits began to fall for any reason. That's when I would take my gains and sell.

So it's always a good idea when checking out a company to see how well it's done over three years. Look back over the results and see if it has maintained a consistent uplift. There cannot be a better sign!

Summary

- Has the company shown consistent profit gains?

- Has the dividend risen every year?

- Keep holding unless question marks appear.

STRATEGY 20: Buy what you know!

If you work in a particular industry, you ought to have a pretty good idea of how that industry is going. You probably have friends in the same business too.

For example, maybe you are in the house-building industry. If you keep your nose to the ground you should be able to gain good information about how your industry is doing. Make sure you chat to people in your industry. Do things look good or are there worries? If there are problems in your business there might be comparable problems in similar listed businesses.

Or if your business is going well, take a look at some comparable businesses that might be listed on the market and research them. Maybe they are doing as well as your business and for similar reasons.

I was in the media business for a long time so I was pretty clued-up in that area and that helped me make decisions as to whether to buy media companies.

Of course I haven't had a conventional job for many years, but I always ask people: What do you do and how is that business going? Sometimes it gives me ideas for new sectors to research.

As mentioned elsewhere, I do continue as an independent distributor for Telecom Plus, which under Utility Warehouse provides energy and telephony. So I meet a number of people in that industry and have an idea of how it is doing. It enables me to keep my ear to the ground on margins on phones and energy, for example.

And I've bought what I know – indeed a lot of what I know – and own a significant amount of Telecom Plus stock. And I expect to keep hold of it for a long time to come. I've quadrupled my money on it.

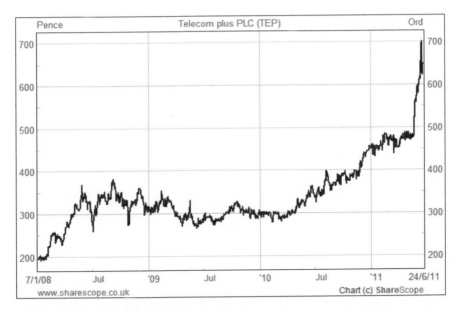

Telecom Plus (January 2008 – June 2011)

So think about your job and the industry you are in (or once were in, if you've quit the rat race). Then look at the stock market listings. Is there anything listed that is comparable? Talk to your mates and get their feedback.

Summary

- Think about your sector and the expert info you have on it.

- Talk to peers and get their views.

- But *do not deal* if you have any specific price-moving information the general market does not also have access to. That's illegal, you dodgy bastard.

Phew! That's a lot of strategies to be getting on with, but that's not the end of this bit of the book. There are some particular trading approaches that I think deserve a bit more focus, so we'll be going through the keyhole with those fellows next. I know you must be itching to go and take the markets by storm, but trust me – wait till you've read what's coming up.

IPOs – How They Can Make You Money

This is a strategy that could have been included in the previous chapter, but it deserves a chapter to itself.

Why's that Robbie?

Cos I say so, that's why!

The real reason is that, looking back over 14 years of trading, some of my biggest winners have come from buying into IPOs.

And what is an IPO?

It's basic jargon for companies coming onto the market for the first time. IPO is the abbreviation for: Initial Public Offering. Well *public* is a bit debatable, as it's not always easy to get your hands on them.

If the market is going well, there can be lots of companies debuting on the stock exchange like this. But if it's tanking, there will be fewer.

I look at all new issues coming onto the market, as I find that there can be gems amongst them that prove eventual long-term winners. Over the years I've had some massive successes with these. Some have gone up 400–500%! Many doubled.

Some new issues are launched on the junior AIM market. They are generally small and I don't like them much as I can't get them into my ISA. So in general it's the *main market* new issues that I am more interested in.

First, though: how do you keep track of what's coming onto the market and what's just been launched?

There are various ways.

- One is simply to check news stories on ADVFN or whichever news provider you use: usually along with results at 7am you will see the odd 'Intention to list' news story. Those are the ones to click on.

- Papers like *The Times* tend to keep track of them.

- If you put 'IPO' into the search engine of your fave finance site, they'll come up.

- There is also **www.allipo.com**, which keeps track of a lot of them.

The 'Intention to list' story, newspapers and other sources will usually give you the skinny on whether it's an AIM or main market listing.

To research them after this I usually just Google the company and track down recent profit figures, etc. Then I wait till they announce what the likely market value will be.

I especially like those valued at £400m or more as they'll get automatic entry into the FTSE 250 where trackers will buy. Anything over £3bn will see it get into the FTSE 100.

Buying into new issues

So you found a new issue and you want a piece of the action. Getting in on the first day just takes a bit of determination.

The thing is, your broker or spread firm probably won't have heard of it yet so there's *no chance* you'll be able to deal online.

First things first, you'll need the stock code of the company. You ought to be able to find it from around 7am on the ADVFN news service. Trawl through and it ought to say:

"Blah blah … company lists today … the code is XXX."

If you want to buy the shares in the market you may want to buy in pretty early. So call your broker and say:

"I want to buy this company. It's a new issue today."

He'll faff around a bit but then he should come back and ask you how many shares you want and you should be able to deal.

If you want to trade via a spread betting firm it might be more difficult; it's a question of which firm you use. Some might give you a price and some might not be able to straightaway. Not much you can do if they won't give you a price, it's up to them really. Sometimes they've said to me they could give me a price but needed *half an hour to set it up*.

Sometimes I wait and sometimes I dive in on the first day. It's a difficult call and something that takes a bit of experience and some luck too.

> If it starts trading on the market way higher than the issue price, you may want to consider holding off as the price could come back a bit in the days after the IPO.

But the main market new issues tend to do so well that, even if you buy in and it comes back a bit, it'll probably go up over time.

I don't simply buy *every* new issue – obviously not every one is going to be a winner. It's a matter of common sense and the same old research tools. In particular, ask yourself:

- What does it do and are its markets expanding?

- Is it the sort of company likely to be a winner?

Main market new issues are not as frequent as AIM, which is why they are so precious. But there is usually, on average, one a month. A company has to satisfy many criteria to get a main listing – the AIM market is far easier – such that it means this company is serious and wants to get somewhere. One of the many reasons I like them.

I always have a read through the statement issued. How much money are they raising and how much is the market cap going to be?

The following table summarises the types of new issues I do and don't like.

New issues I like	New issues I don't like
Oil and gas	Retailers
Oil and gas services	A business I don't understand at all
Hedge funds	Any business where I can't see the growth
Finance	
Technology	
Renewable energy	

Main market new issues

New issues I've bought

It's just amazing how well new main market issues to do with oil or energy get on. Over the years I've pretty much come not to worry about whether or not I should buy them. I'm in – generally speaking, especially if valued over £400m, I've found they tend to go up very nicely.

My biggest successes have been with Petrofac, Hunting, Sondex, and I am particularly fond of Burren Energy, which went from 200p to get bid for at 1250p!

And also, Wellstream. I saw this one coming a mile off!

In fact, do you want me to be perfectly honest?

I saw two things:

1. *Sector*: oil services

2. *Market*: main

And, well, that was enough for me. Oil services new issues have made me a fortune – take a bow Sondex, Hunting and Petrofac.

These companies were in demand and right from day one I wanted some!

So, bang, at the start of the first day I was onto my brokers and spread bet firms demanding shares! I bought a huge amount – after all, history was easily on my side here.

It wasn't too long before a stream of good announcements started to come from the companies as they began to win major contracts.

I bought into Wellstream at about 360p in April 2007. I took a huge spread bet position (£100 per point). The shares just rose and rose, climbing rapidly to over 500p – making me a quick paper profit of over £15,000.

However, I did not take profits at this level because I felt the shares had even further to go. Just as well: they went all the way to over 1500, though I ended up banking a huge profit at around 900.

Exillon Energy came up as new issue in late 2009. This one again looked a no-brainer, an energy company getting a serious full market listing with likely entry to the FTSE 250.

So I dived in at just under 200p, and by 2011 it had more than doubled! I also topped up along the way as it rose.

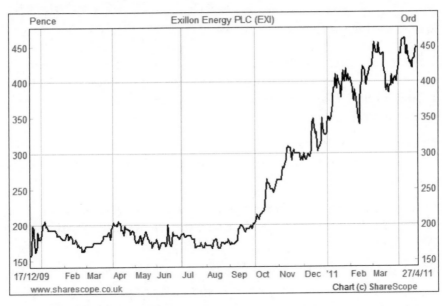

Exillon Energy (December 2009 – April 2011)

Moving away from oil and energy, I think you do have to be more cautious and the usual rules of research definitely apply.

SuperGroup is an example of a fantastic IPO in a different sector – internet and retail fashion.

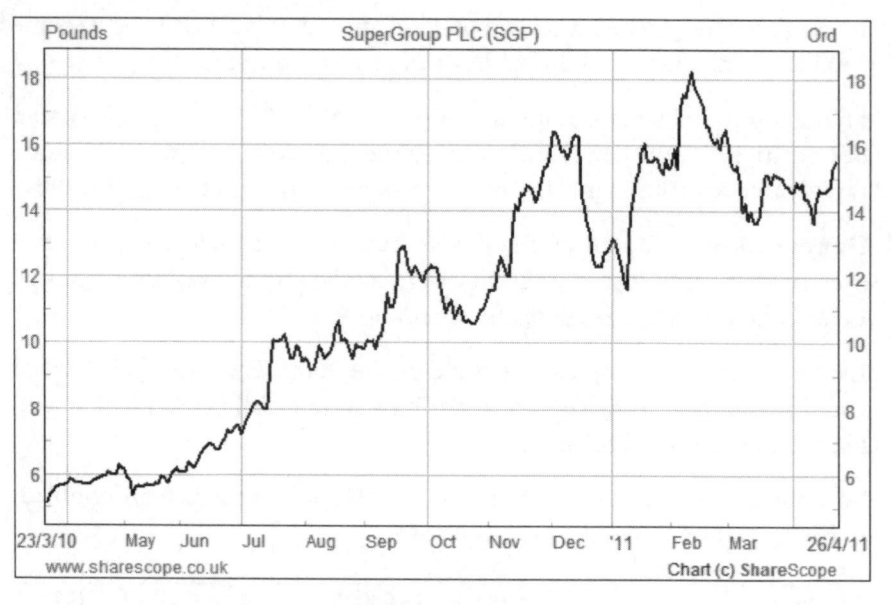

SuperGroup (March 2010 – April 2011)

I didn't quite get in at the issue price but I still more than doubled my money so I was very happy. Why did I jump in? SuperGroup's profits were simply surging away year on year. Whatever they were doing they were doing very well.

However, not all IPOs are going to hit the jackpot. By no means. In 2010 I actually made a lot of money on shorting a new issue for a change. This one was Betfair.

I actually like Betfair and use it myself, but I was shocked to discover that in October 2010 it was being placed on the market at a valuation of … £1.5 billion!

Why was I shocked? Well, I had a good look at the figures. (The best way to do this is Google the company and add the word profit in quote marks at the same time – the figures usually come up.) It was only making a profit of £18 million. And it looked forecast to get to about a £40m profit.

Even taking the £40m figure for granted, £1.5bn meant it was valued at nearly *40 times its profit*.

So I had little hesitation in betting on Betfair to go down. I shorted it when it came on the market at over 1500p and it quite rightly tanked to below 1000p, at which point I grabbed a very large profit quite quickly. Too quickly as it happens, as it went down further.

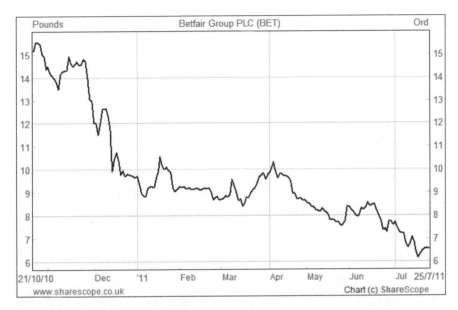

Betfair (October 2010 – July 2011)

Another stinker was Promethean – but I got it horribly, horribly wrong. I liked the look of its fundamentals when it was launched as an IPO and bought some at around 180. However, I never took into account the fact that it relied on government money – it supplied interactive whiteboards for schools – and when the recession came, money on such things in schools just dried up. However, I didn't lose too much as I was saved by a stop loss.

The point here is that, although an IPO is of itself a positive sign, it is definitely not all-sufficient: you do still have to treat IPOs like normal shares. And once they drop by more than 10% or so, you have to realise it might be a stinker and get out. Sites like ADVFN won't have the figures you need yet, so, as mentioned, Google the company, add a key word like "profit" or "debt" in double quote marks and the figures will invariably come up. Ensure they're the latest and research away.

AIM new issues

Though I'm not as keen on them as main market IPOs, I do still buy into the occasional AIM new issue. I generally do so for my pension fund as that allows me to avoid tax implications. The other tax-free alternative is getting on the phone and spread betting.

Just a reminder about the difference between the AIM and main markets. Remember, the AIM market is cheap for companies to get onto and is lightly regulated. Therefore any old rubbish can get onto it. It's different with the main market, where it's expensive and only top notch companies generally apply. Also, AIM issues are generally less liquid and far more volatile.

> You have to be very careful with AIM new issues, because unlike the main ones, you can really get your fingers badly burned. So I don't often invest, but will do occasionally.

There are usually loads of AIM new issues – so I am looking for the gold amongst a sea of dross.

What I tend to look for with AIM new issues is: *what will catch the imagination of private investors and institutions?*

I'm looking for a company with some track record and a sector that looks like it is growing.

An example is iEnergizer.

iEnergizer and their interestingly boring website

I Googled it and saw its website and got very interested because it supplied 'business process outsourcing' – in other words, helping businesses to make more money and cut costs. I figured that, especially in hard times, customers should be quite easy to find. It was also almost debt-free, with growing revenues, and it had some nice contracts with some good businesses and household names. All these things I like.

So I bought some at 140p in late 2010 and six months later it was up and over 200p. Not a bad return!

---

proactiveinvestors.co.uk

A great website that covers AIM new issues, the aftermath of their release and other stories about them, especially in the resources sector, is **www.proactiveinvestors.co.uk**. It's a free site and well worth a read. (In the interest of full disclosure, I do write an occasional column for them.)

Proactive Investors also hosts presentations from newish AIM companies in the flesh. You can attend, again for nothing, and meet the top bods from some of the companies. I've been to one or two of these presentations myself. They can be well worth going to – and you get free wine and canapés!

Summary

- You have to be wary of AIM new issues; I don't personally buy very many. But if you're careful you can make money. I would not recommend this to very new traders, as you can get your fingers incinerated if you buy the wrong one.

- Look for main market issues likely to hit the FTSE 250. Be especially interested in energy ones. However, do research and check you are not buying something overvalued already. Google their profits and prospects.

Trading Times of the Year

I tend to treat shares a bit differently at different times of the year.

Some months, the market historically tends to be strong and some months it tends to be weak. It's worth keeping an eye on the time of year and its likely effect on stocks.

Here's a look at the different months:

February – March

These tend to be middling months. After some good gains over Christmas some people take profits in February, so don't expect big advances here. I would look to have a bit of cash on the sidelines during these months.

April

Amazing how holiday times and flowers budding put people in a good mood. Around Easter the market does really well and it's often a good time for short-term gains. The market's typically stronger in April than any other month – on the basis of its performance in the last few decades, the probability of the market rising in April is 78%. So it may be worth thinking about buying in mid March to catch any April lift.

May – July

I'm sure you've heard the old saying:

'Sell in May and come back on St Leger's Day.'

(St Leger's day is in September.) There is a bit of truth in this, as May can be the start of some underperformance. In recent years it has been challenging September to become the weakest month of the year. 2006 saw a large fall in stocks, though 2007 wasn't too bad. Still, it's time to perhaps be wary, take some profits and keep cash in hand. June is pretty much as weak as May – usually it's the third weakest month. And July generally isn't that much better! So in summary, May–July ain't great. Maybe time for a holiday!

August

From the gloom of the previous few months there usually comes a great August.

Of course a lot of people are away, which for a start means there is always a lot less volume. So what happens is that shares can move much faster than normal on far fewer trades.

According to market historian David Schwartz, August is the third best trading month of the year: "Good gains can often be achieved in August. But of course with the volatility you have to get the right entry price."

I agree with David; I often find I can make a lot of money in August. However, beware too: because of the volatility August 2011 proved a disaster as shares fell a lot.

One thing to look for is companies reporting in August. There aren't many, but if you find one that produces a strong statement, you often find the share price responds very well on smaller volumes.

Also, it is worth looking at companies reporting in early September; August is a good time to get in early in the run up to the results.

September

Yuk! September has the worst record of any month – on average it falls 1.4%. Upside is usually limited but downside can be large. If you ever want to try shorting, this is the month to do it. And as things bottom out, maybe keep an eye out for bargains.

October – November

Well it's not as bad as you think. A couple of famous nasty crashes have happened in October, particularly the one in 1987. Stripping out a couple of bad years, October is actually pretty decent and it's often a good time to buy. November is middling, but buying the right shares in October and November can be a good move in the lead up to the Christmas buying spree ...

December – January

December is one of the best months for share performance. January too.

Why?

Because most years, while it's cold outside, December and January markets are hot!

The statistics support my argument: historically the strongest week of the year for the market is the 51st week. And the second strongest? The 52nd week!

The probability of positive returns in December is a high 69%. The market's only had one significant fall in December since 1981. Both mid- and large-cap stocks perform equally well.

Why are the markets so good at the most wonderful time of the year?

I suspect it is down to something as simple as human psychology. We all feel good with the approach of Christmas, then there are New Year hopes and dreams. But by the end of January we tend to be left with a bit of a hangover and that's why February isn't so good.

Also, as markets often fall somewhat in October and November, investors begin to come in now and buy what they perceive as bargains.

The period between Christmas and New Year often sees stocks squeezing higher on thin volumes. While I might well be tucking into mince pies, I'm usually also at my trading desk watching for opportunities to make money. Many stocks race higher during the holidays; there is frequently no one selling and institutions are shut. This often has a good effect on stocks at the smaller end of the market.

Of course, I am making it all sound too easy ... it's never going to work out every year. But the use of tight stop losses should ensure that when you meet a year without a Santa bump, your losses will be minimal.

Bad news

On the downside, one thing to watch out for is companies sneaking out bad news between Christmas and New Year. It's the same as political parties burying bad news on a day when a big story emerges elsewhere. With so many people away, the companies hope the stinker will go unnoticed. So it's worth keeping an eye on news that's related to your stocks. I get out quick if any kind of bad company news is released on one of my shares at this time.

Strategies

So where do I put my money to make the most of the benign conditions?

First (and I do this most years): I buy the FTSE 100 index in early/mid-December and I sell in early January to take advantage of the fact that the FTSE usually rises in this period.

I usually just make a simple 'long' FTSE 100 spread bet, with a stop loss in place just in case it's the one occasional year when the festive uplift doesn't happen.

I find December is also a good time to have a look at some of the smaller, tiddler stocks in the market and sometimes have a bit of a gamble on a few stocking-filler shares. But only a little gamble, mind. Let's not be idiots.

Time for Tea and Toast

Yes, it's the tea and toast chapter. Yippeee!

It could also be entitled 'Don't Panic, Corporal Jones'.

What do I mean by *tea and toast*? Well, I'm actually talking about periods of time when no trades are necessary. Instead of trading, just drink tea and eat toast.

You will often find that this downtime will save you a lot of money. Especially given that bread and teabags are still very cheap. If you don't like tea and toast, go out and take the dog for a walk. Or take up a new hobby.

Because sometimes markets are volatile – up 100 points one day and down 150 the next. When markets get volatile I sit back and tea-and-toast it. Or sometimes, if it gets really nasty, I hide behind the sofa. Had plenty of experience doing this during *Dr Who* when it was really good in the 70s. It's also a good place to hide if the wife's come home and I forgot to tidy up.

Every time the market has got very volatile, I rely on history – as long as I know I am holding good, strong companies, I can be sure they will in time bounce back.

Just remember: every time you exit or enter a trade it costs money (spread *plus* commission *plus* stamp duty). But on the bulletin boards you'll see messages like:

> "*I am 100% cash now.*"

So boast the writers – not mentioning it cost them a fortune to sell everything at bad prices. The next week, prices having gone up, they are suddenly:

> "*90% invested again.*"

Meaning they bought at bad prices too, and let's not even mention the stamp duty and commissions paid.

One thing I think worth doing when markets are going down a bit is to seriously considering exiting spread bet or CFD positions. That's because most people are leveraged on these, which means they might have a £20k market exposure, but only really have £2k in the markets.

These are the kind of people that get wiped out quickly because in effect they've bought their positions by using a credit card. And the spread firm will want its money back fast.

If, like me, you have a decent portfolio full of good companies in, say, an ISA, you can relax more. I'm not saying be smug and don't sell anything. But you can certainly keep hold of good companies for longer.

Generally speaking, it's always worth *not* being fully invested; it's worth having some cash on the sidelines in good times and bad. That's because then you can take advantage of a market slide by buying shares that have suddenly become bargains.

It's usually better to be buying when everyone else is selling and selling when everyone else is buying. (By this I am referring to the market as a whole tanking or soaring, not individual stocks – don't go down the Northern Rock route!)

I love buying on market dips. I bought some of my favourite shares at great prices, and in particular made some great buys in March and April 2009 when the banking crisis subsided (for the time being, perhaps).

Buybacks, AGMs and Perks

Share buybacks

Sometimes you'll see a company announce that it is going to buy back some of its shares. Companies can seek authorisation from its shareholders to do this. Generally, companies seek to buy back their shares because they feel the market is undervaluing their shares and the price is too low. By starting a buyback programme, the value of the shares are usually underpinned by the buybacks and the shares might gradually see a rise in value.

But **I'm not a great fan of buybacks**. If the market is undervaluing the company then there is probably a good reason. So don't rely on buybacks to improve the value of the share you are holding by that much.

I would even consider selling the shares concerned, because buybacks, in my experience, don't tend to lead to fireworks for the share price.

However, for those wanting a steady income from a steady share, I suppose a buyback programme would give you confidence that the share will have some support.

Shareholders' meetings/AGMs/presentations

If you're a shareholder of any company, you're entitled to go to the annual general meeting (AGM). These are usually pretty dull affairs, but if you've got a long-term holding in the company it may be worth considering.

Sometimes companies even invite shareholders to the company premises to have a peek. These are called investor/analyst open days. If you've got the time and energy, why not have a look and visit the company? I've visited a couple and enjoyed the visits.

Another way of finding out more about the company directly is by going to presentations. **www.proactiveinvestors.co.uk**, again, is good for this. What they do is get two to three company bosses together of an evening to tell you why their shares are worth buying. You also get the chance to put questions directly to the bosses of the companies involved.

I've been to one or two of these presentations and thought it was well worth the time and effort it took to go along. The website tells you which companies are presenting, so I usually research them before I go. It's quite fascinating to meet the people behind a company and it can be very useful. These presentations are free, and just like the AIM events, you get free drinks and nibbles.

As we saw earlier, often the companies involved are smaller oil and mining outfits, which can be quite hard to research. And so to be able to talk to the management is a definite bonus.

A friend of mine who regularly goes to these meetings often has an interesting way of deciding whether to buy the companies. She analyses the shoes of the chief exec. Apparently this works rather well. A nice pair of shiny brogues? Tick! A horrible old tatty pair? Black mark!

Well, look, it works for her!

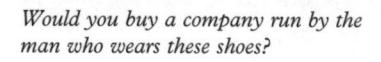

Would you buy a company run by the man who wears these shoes?

Share perks

You'll often see articles in newspapers and magazines written by lazy hacks regarding share perks. When I say 'lazy', this is because articles on perks are one of the easiest features for them to write – they can re-write an old perks feature in about ten minutes!

Perks are special privileges you can get if you own a certain number of a company's shares. For example, hotel chains might give you a 10% discount on their room rates.

You should buy shares to sell them at a profit: all perks do is make you hang onto a share longer than you should.

When the Excrement Wallops the Air Circulation Device

AKA when markets go bad …

One of the main reasons I wanted to write this new edition of *The Naked Trader* was to cover assorted changes in the last four years. The other was to talk a bit more about what happens when the markets turn savagely downwards.

There is nothing worse than seeing your profits made over quite a time suddenly start to disappear. In the four years since I wrote the last edition, there have been two market downturns and quite a lot of volatility. Most of 2008 was just horrible. Mid-2011 turned nasty too: after trading in a tight range the FTSE took just four days to crash hundreds of points.

There have been all kinds of events to make the market scared. The worst, of course, was the fall of Lehman Brothers and the banking crisis in the UK. Thousands queued outside Northern Rock branches in the first run on a British bank since the 19th century, and centuries-old titans such as RBS and Bank of Scotland (HBOS since the Halifax merger) had their value decimated.

Indeed we were pretty close to a major financial crash here, and then all bets, as they say, would have been off.

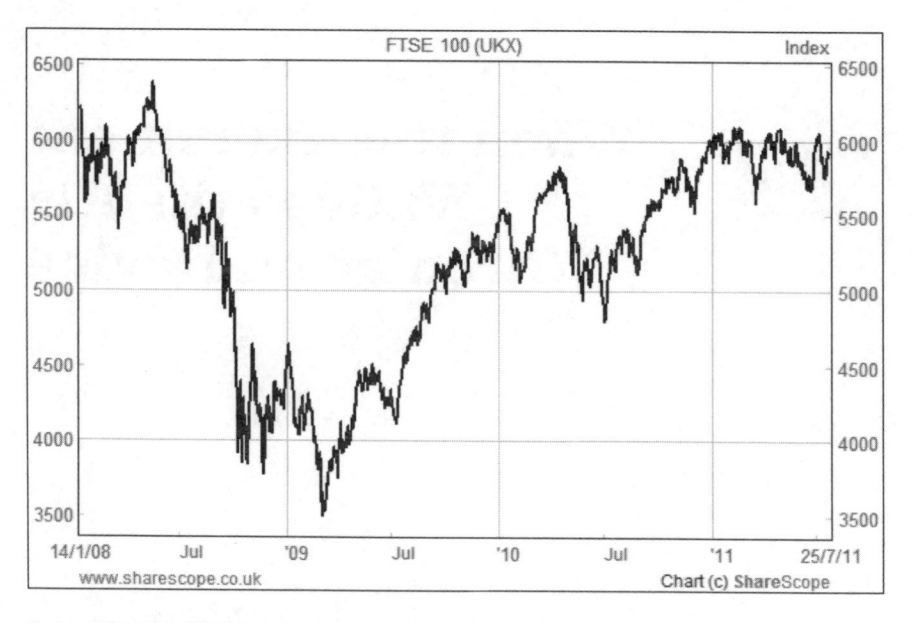

The FTSE 100 (2008 – 2011)

And then there's been turmoil across the Middle East. Bailouts across Europe. Debt swamping weaker countries and scaring even the stronger ones. The US had its credit rating cut in mid-2011, which worsened sentiment.

And to make matters worse?

At the same time, a very real problem – and it's a recent one – is that *Terminator*, and the rise of the machines, has actually started coming true in the markets.

Yes, Arnie is back. The robots really are taking over. Only, rather than being sophisticated humanoid murder machines, these robots are programmed by banks (and other financial companies) to buy and sell stocks as part of computerised trading strategies.

It turns out this can be rather more dangerous for the average citizen; it means a *lot* more volatility in the markets than there would otherwise be.

In May 2010, for example, there was what's been called the 'Flash Crash'. The Dow Jones crashed nearly 1,000 points in just a few minutes, leading to widespread panic. Remarkably, by the end of the day, it had bounced back up again. How? Why?

A large mutual fund had sold off a lot of futures contracts which caused an initial decline. However, the robo-systems of 'high frequency traders' – those looking for quick hits – then started selling them furiously too. After an incredible bout of buying and selling, their machines then decided to slow down or pull out of trading altogether. Liquidity in major shares dried up almost instantly. This then caused all the other robots (of banks, hedge funds, ordinary funds, perhaps central banks – all sorts of institutions) to start selling stocks.

Prices rapidly went further down. Lots of stop losses in the market were hit, resulting in countless other automated sells. Some shares even briefly went to zero!

The authorities are trying to stop this happening again by introducing circuit breakers to halt trading. In the UK, any stock down by more than 10% on the day gets halted and goes into auction for five minutes.

Now, in the big scheme of things, this kind of thing doesn't matter much to me – I'm a medium to longer-term trader. However, if you are new to the markets then you can easily lose a lot of money by being forced out near the bottom of these events. And all because of Arnie's cousins. Nothing legitimate.

So what do you do if things start to turn ugly?

There are various approaches you can take to all this volatility. One is to conclude: 'The stock market is a [naughty word. – Ed.] and I'm selling up and not coming back. I'm off into premium bonds and lottery tickets.'

Alternatively:

- 'I'll sell most of my stuff as I'm scared I'll lose the lot, and then buy back when things look better.'

- 'I'll try and short loads of stuff while keeping my long termers open.'

- 'I'll hide behind the sofa till it's safe to come out.'

- 'It doesn't matter, my shares will be higher in six months so I'm off out for a game of golf.'

- Or: 'If everyone is scared, I'm going to buy in at the height of the panic.'

None of these is the correct answer, because there ain't a correct answer. Maybe things will get worse in the Middle East. Perhaps more countries will default, and maybe we'll find ourselves in financial doo-doo again. Maybe we are worrying too much, maybe we aren't.

All I can tell you is what I do. And that is broadly *follow* the market as it changes rather than second-guess where it might turn. So, for instance, as markets turn down, I might start to gradually sell things and go short. As they lift up again, it's time to start buying. And I'll only go against the grain now and then if I think bargains are available and people have sold off unnecessarily, or if I think a rise looks unsustainable.

When to buy and when to sell (when all is going to hell)

My strategies when markets are falling

When markets are falling:

1. I tend to cut spread bets back a bit.

2. I go right through the ISA portfolio and skim a few profits off the top and dump anything that I have any question marks over. However, I usually hold onto my longer-term winners.

3. After that I make sure that there is some cash sitting in the ISA and plenty of legroom in the spread bet accounts.

4. I short the FTSE 100 and use an ETF to make money in my ISA from the market falling (more on that in a sec).

5. I keep an eye open for when to get stuck in somewhere near the bottom, if I can.

Industrial-strength portfolio protection

When things are bad market-wide, the FTSE 100 index as a whole (obviously) goes down. Perversely this gives you an opportunity to protect your portfolio rather than having to sell everything off: you can hold onto your stocks and short the index. And short it with a *vengeance*.

I use something which sounds rather scary but is actually quite easy once you get your head round it. It is the snappily entitled:

ETFX FTSE 100 super-short strategy (2x) FD

See, told you it was snappy (you can imagine what a barrel of giggles the person who came up with this awful name must be).

Now, I know what you're thinking. 'Screw this, it sounds complicated, I'll skip it.' See, I also hate finance books when they seem to get complicated. Try and bear with me for a sec. Off for a cup of tea? Coming back to this bit after *Match of the Day*? You bottler!

This really can make you money tax-free in your ISA if the FTSE 100 tanks. It's an ETF, which means exchange-traded fund, seemingly a scarily dull-sounding thing that will never be worth understanding – but which couldn't be simpler. ETFs are just funds that are purchasable in the same way that shares are – by being listed and traded on exchanges. Easy bloody peasy!

And this *ETFX FTSE 100 super ...* monster is ISA eligible. Its code is SUK2.

So you can tap SUK2 into your monitor and it should come up. If you want to use it, just tap SUK2 into your broker's dealing screen and you should be able to easily buy it in your ISA, just as you would with any share.

But what is it and how does it protect portfolios?

Here's the brilliant thing: it goes up twice as much as the FTSE 100 goes down!

So if the FTSE fell, say, 10% and went from 6000 to 5400, this little beauty could make you nearly 20%, as if the FTSE had actually risen to 7200!

Which is why it is called a 2X super short! (In reality, because of some slippage, it doesn't quite do 2X after a while, but it's close.)

You can buy and sell it just like you would a share. You don't have to worry about market makers or market manipulation or anything like that. It simply goes up as the FTSE goes down.

Fairly obviously, if the FTSE goes *up*, it goes down! And twice as much. **So use with caution.**

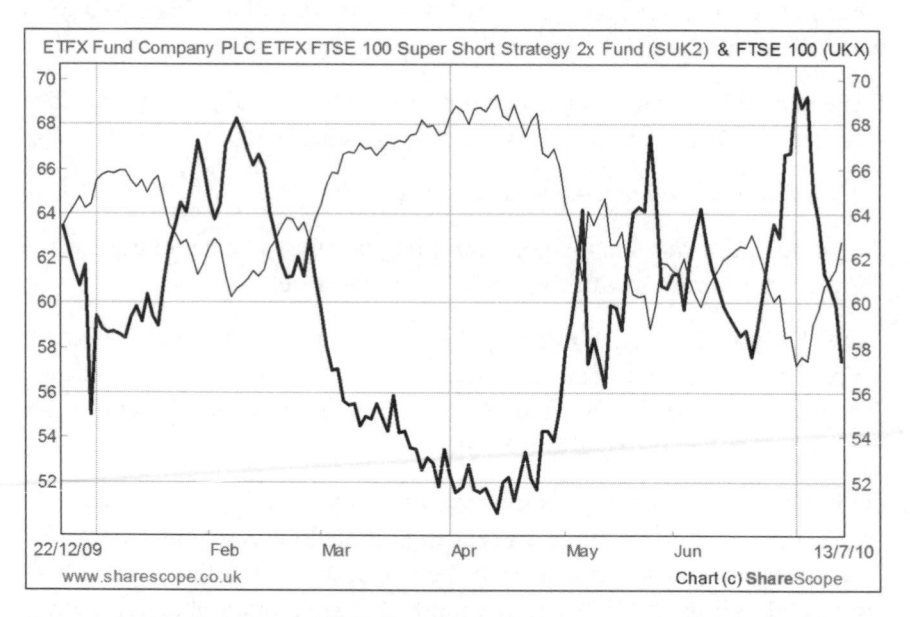

SUK2 in action (December 2009 – July 2010)

As I write, the price is 3844p to sell and 3855p to buy. So if you bought 100 'shares' in it, it would cost you £3,855.

If the FTSE then tanked by 10%, it would likely move the price up 20% to about 4600. Which would turn your £3,855 into something like £4,600. Or around £800 profit.

If you are a medium-term investor and think the market may go down for a bit but then spring back up, this super short is a great portfolio protector.

How about an example showing how I used it last, eh? Good idea!

Example – super short time

It's early 2011. The FTSE is at 6100. My portfolio has done very nicely. But the FTSE has tried a number of times to get through 6100 and I reckon, given the economic climate and bad news everywhere, it looks unlikely to go much further.

There is bad news coming out of the Mid East, a default looks likely in Europe, and there is an earthquake in Japan. I think my shares are likely to go down a little but I think the market reaction to the downside won't last long – it usually doesn't in these kind of situations.

So I don't want the hassle and cost of selling some of my strong companies. I would rather keep them but try to make some short-term money from the downside to counteract the likely small falls in the portfolio.

So I short the FTSE in a spread bet at 6102. More on that in a minute.

And what about the ISA portfolio?

Here's where SUK2 comes in! I buy 500 of SUK2 at 3800 or so. Costs me £19,000.

The FTSE falls and my stocks fall a bit – not too badly, though. The FTSE drops to 5600. Then tensions ease in the markets and it starts to go up. I sell the SUK2 at 4400ish, banking £3,500 profit. This nicely covers some of the losses made in the ISA on the shares.

The shares then start to go back up with the FTSE. I never had to sell them, so no cost to me. Eventually they recover. The SUK2 has done its job.

What about if I was wrong and the shares carried on going up and I had the SUK2?

Well, okay, that's fine! Let's say the FTSE carried on going up. I would have lost a few quid on the SUK2, but my shares would have probably gone up. I could have sold the SUK2 for a small loss, no damage done, especially as shares would be going up anyway.

If the FTSE had continued to go down I could have carried on holding – and perhaps increased – the SUK2.

Now tell me: what have we really been doing using the SUK2?

HEDGING! Yes, we have indeed been acting like a hedge fund, and making money on the downs as well as the ups! Clever old us!

Look, I hope I managed to explain it. If you are still unsure, stick SUK2 on your monitor and see how it moves against the FTSE.

The other strategy is easier to explain and that is simply shorting the FTSE in a spread bet account. Just log into your spread account, and sell the FTSE at whatever pounds per point you think you can afford or would help hedge your portfolio.

> In spread betting you don't need to own it in order to sell. There is no magical shorting button – 'sell' basically just means 'short' if you don't have a position open in a particular share.

The FTSE trades 24 hours a day with spread bets and the price can change a lot overnight, so if you're using a stop loss be prepared to get stopped out overnight ...

There's more on shorting in Chapter 24 and in my spread betting book. During a very quick fall for the FTSE in August 2011 I found a good way to make money was to gradually scale into shorts using different trades, adding more as it went down, then lowering stops on them into profit as it carried on falling.

Other things to think about when the market is sinking

- In general it is FTSE 100 stocks that get hit suddenly and quickly rather than the smaller stocks. They are also very volatile. So consider whether you should exit.

- In particular, commodity stocks tend to get hit a lot as investors bale out.

- Do a stress-check: can you afford to lose, say, 40% of what you have in the market if it crashes badly? Have you overdone it using leverage with spread bets or CFDs? It's a good time for a rethink and some checks and balances to ensure you are not in for more than you should be.

- It's also a good time to think to yourself about whether you need a few more 'defensive' shares in your portfolio. For instance, shares in supermarkets and utilities often go up in downturns, as people may abandon luxuries but they'll always need food and water. Earlier we met Mr Safe and Steady who foolishly buys only these and likes them all the time. But downturns are when they could start being really interesting.

Consider what sort of downturn you are in

Above all, you need to think carefully about why the market is tanking. Is it just a short-term overreaction thanks to a load of sell-happy robots? Or is it more serious?

The fallout from the Lehman Brothers collapse and the credit crunch is the most serious crisis of recent times. (There may well have been a worse one since this book came out, of course. In which case, let me go on record as saying: I saw it coming!*) There was a squeak of a chance the whole financial system was in trouble and so it really did seem sensible to keep a lot of cash on the sidelines to be on the safe side. Even if, when we were out of the woods, markets rallied.

In general, massively calamitous events don't happen very often. But perhaps one day we'll all get caught out.

Black swan events – a time to buy?

A 'black swan' event is not when your wife suggests renting that film Natalie Portman won an Oscar for. It's simply a neat, slightly buzz-wordy phrase for a highly significant event that comes right out of the blue.

There are usually one or two a year. For example, it could be the terrible earthquake that hit Japan in 2011. Or some kind of awful unexpected terrorist event.

---

* If there hasn't been a worse crisis since this book came out, of course, let me also go on record as saying: I knew there wouldn't be!

And this might surprise you: whilst a black swan event can often be a terrible time to be a human being, it's usually a great buying opportunity for shares. Sad but true. Often just a day or two after the event itself, you can pick up some very good bargains. I know it's not nice to think about, but it probably shouldn't be ignored.

Of course, if something apocalyptic happens – like a nuclear bomb being detonated in London – then all bets are off. But during nearly every unexpected bad event, the markets initially knee-jerk downwards, helped by crazy robots. Then when we've had time to think about things, everyone realises, 'Hey, it's not as bad as we thought it was,' and the market duly heads back up.

> I keep one spread betting account open with nothing in it except for the funds to buy cheap stock if there is a black swan event.

Look at any event. The terrorist attack in London. The earthquake in Japan. The uprisings in Egypt and Libya.

At each such event, the market gets scared and sells off, thinking the end of the world is nigh. Then a few days later it says, 'Oh, actually, it's not all that bad, things will work out.'

So don't be scared.

If you are a real scaredy cat then is trading really for you? I have a friend who thinks the world is going to end up like some brutal war-torn sci-fi movie. She has about 300 cans of Tesco's value baked beans stashed away. Oh, and just for variety, 100 cans of Tesco's value sausages and beans.

Personally I would rather kill myself staggering about in an alien-ruled nuclear winter than end up in a basement with cans of old beans.

Which leads me to two rough rules for trading against unhelpful grains.

- Buy when everyone is selling.
- Sell when everyone is buying.

In other words, buy when everyone else is crapping themselves that they will lose all their money. Sell when they are all feeling smug and that they've made a lot of money.

In either case, they are almost certainly wrong – fear or greed, not sensible investing, has got the upper hand with them – and you can make money from being a cool, calm, collected Mr Spock who is right.

> These rules refer to the market as a whole diving or soaring – not to individual shares. And they don't mean you can disregard research and buy any old thing. They're just good times to get in or out of worthwhile shares.

Simple? Well, it does work. But it's easy to write and harder to do. We are like pack animals, and want to conform and do whatever everyone else does.

That's why you don't walk down the street with no clothes on.

Okay, if you do, congrats, you must be very pleased with what's down there.

Downturn summary

- Consider cash and cutting positions but don't panic.
- Cut stakes in volatile stocks.
- Use shorting tools like SUK2 and spread betting.
- Consider buying after a black swan event.

Need a rest after that lot? Okay, off you go to put the kettle on or flick the switch on your fancy coffee machine. But there's lots still to come. Now we know the basics, how to find decent shares, and the kind of buying and selling strategies that will net us some juicy profits with them.

Next it's time to learn how to execute our buying and selling in the most effective ways. Vital stuff!

Part V

Charts, Timing, Targets and Stops

"The great rule is not to talk about money with people who have much more or much less than you."

– Katharine Whitehorn

Charts and How I Use Them

Don't mistake me. I strongly believe charts *are* very important to look at because they tell you at a glance a lot of important info about the history of a share price; where it's been, what it's been doing, which TV shows it likes, and who it's been knocking around with.

> But I also believe it's simply crazy to buy and sell shares on the basis of looking at a chart and nothing else.

There *are* some people who do this. They call themselves 'chartists' and I reckon most of them can hardly afford to get their round in. This isn't going to make me popular with chartists, but who cares if I'm not popular with everyone. Evict me and see if I'm bovvered.

Chartists say things like:

> *"The MACD divergence touched off by the Fibonacci Bollinger band at 202.4 shows an increasing likelihood of a golden cross over the 40-day moving average on the triangle double-bottom formation ... "*

Which is almost certainly just a load of cobblers. (Well it definitely is in this case, as I made it up, obviously. But the names are real.)

I gave a talk one day and the guy on before me, who was talking about charts, moaned like hell to me that he was having a rough time on the markets, saying he was fed up with being a chartist. He mentioned none of this in his speech.

You'll often see bulletin board punters talking chart theory because they think it makes them look good. Bit odd considering it's done under pseudonyms and no one knows who they really are, but people are funny aren't they?

Market commentators and tipsters tend to split into two camps:

1. Chartists (also known as technical analysts): they reckon they don't have to know anything about a company beyond its share price; they don't care what the company does, what sector it's in, whether it makes profits or not, or when the next dividend is due.

2. Fundamentalists: they feel you should be looking at the accounts, profits, etc.

What am I – a chartist or a fundamentalist?

Well, very much more a fundamentalist than a chartist – but one doesn't have to be, er, a fundamentalist about it: I always want to look at the whole story of a share, and that includes looking at charts. I like them for breakouts and for setting targets and stops.

But you've got to be careful about charts. They can easily be abused, and if you rely too much on interpreting them you can start to fall victim to wishful thinking or end up, like some heavy chartists, in a land of pure make-believe and extremely vulnerable to losses. But there are some basic ways of using them that will prove very useful. And this is what this chapter is about.

Charts and price ranges

You will very quickly come across charting jargon when you begin visiting bulletin boards – there are a lot of amateur chartists out there. I see no need, especially for new investors, to get bogged down in all the terminology.

I think it's far too easy to get tripped up by chartism – and many investors come a cropper when they rely on it. They read a few books about charting and then feel they're invincible! **Of course what inevitably happens is the chart turns on them, and bites them on the bum.**

So let's keep it simple. The main purpose I use charts for is checking out a share's *price range* in the recent past.

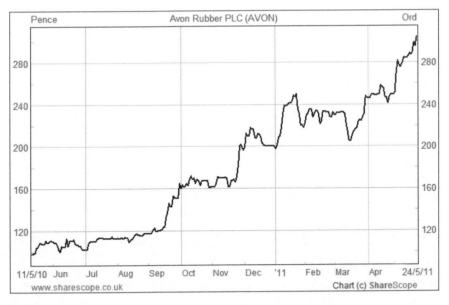

A year of Avon Rubber's share price (May 2010 – May 2011)

A chart like this – available or linked to by any trading site's quote page – shows what's happened to a share price in trading days gone by. And in doing that, it can reveal what's very important: the prices at which investors are likely to buy and sell in the future.

Here are the major ways in which charts might prove helpful for your trading.

Playing the range

As we discussed in a strategy in Chapter 11, charts are useful for flagging up shares that are trading in a tight range. A share price might move back and forth in the range 200–220p over a few months, and you could try to play that trend: buy at 200p and sell at 220p.

Breakouts

A breakout is when a share price is moving out of a previously established price range. As looked at in Chapter 9, it is an excellent indication of a potentially juicy share. And without a check of a chart, and seeing its price range in the past, you would never be able to spot them.

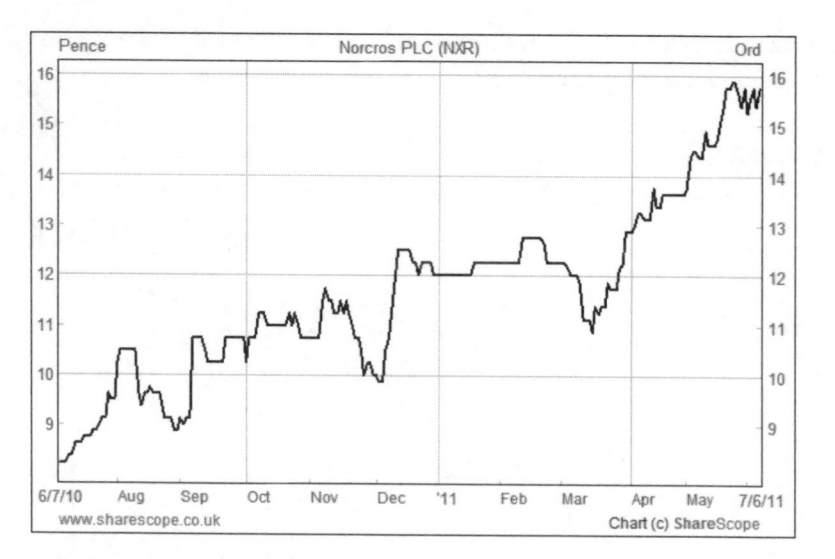

A 52-week upward breakout

The related ADVFN toplist gives you all the shares currently breaking out of previously established price ranges, and enables you to search for 52-week, 12-week and 4-week breakouts. My preference is for 52-week breakouts. A 52-week upward breakout often means a share is about to rise steadily higher.

Resistance and support

As well as breakouts, you need to know about resistance and support.

- *Support* is jargon for the level a share's price doesn't tend to go below.

- *Resistance* is the level the shares can't seem to rise above. (Resistance is futile, after all.)

As you can see in the next chart, Andor keeps dropping to 400p or so – but it bounces whenever it does so. That means that *support* is at 400ish.

And you can also see that when it climbs, it can't quite manage to get above around 480. So that is *resistance*.

There is resistance against it going above 480 and support against it going below 400.

What does this tell us?

That whenever it gets to 400 the market thinks it is too cheap and buys; and that when it gets to 480 it thinks it's too expensive and sells.

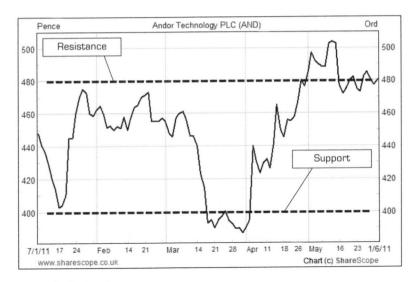

Support and resistance on Andor

How can this help us?

Well, it helps with setting the trigger level in a stop loss order. You could consider a stop at just below 400 because you know there is support. Though better to set it at 380 to steer clear of the support area.

And it could help you to decide when to buy. If it fell back to 400, this could be a good point to buy as you know it is supported and likely won't drop lower. But if it fell back much below 400 it could mean support is slipping and it's time to get out. Hence a 380 stop.

As said, it's also often considered a markedly good sign when a share breaks out over resistance. So if Andor broke out over 480 and started to trade towards and over 500 it could be that resistance is broken and a new rise is coming. 480, the previous high, could then become support. Time will tell.

Phew! Gettit? It's quite handy, really. This is probably what technical analysts would call back-of-a-fag-packet technical analysis. And they will hate me for it. But keeping it simple like this has worked wonders for me. This is how I look at a chart of any company I am interested in.

Think: where is support and where is resistance? Then you can more easily plan a buy or sell strategy.

Trend spotting with longer-term charts

I often look at charts over some *longer period*. I find this works better – any trend you find is then generally more reliable. I like to hop on a share whose price chart continues to go up like this:

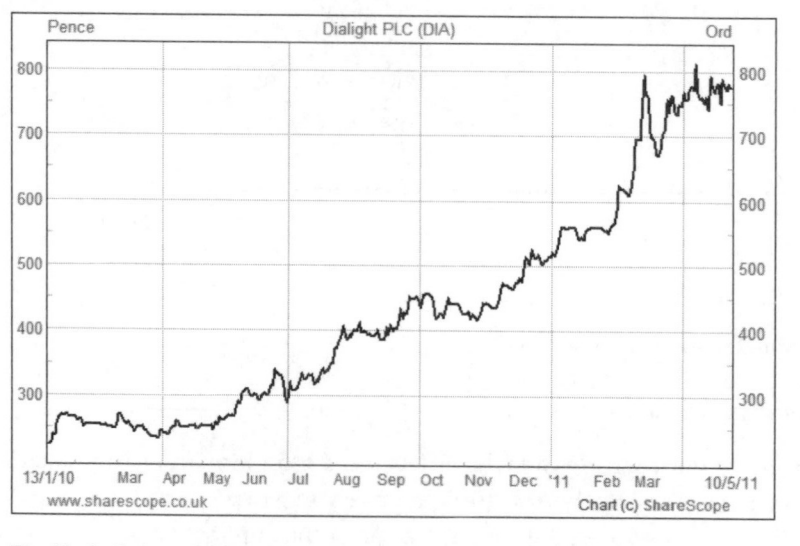

The kind of chart I like longer-term (17 months of Dialight)

I don't like to buy charts like this:

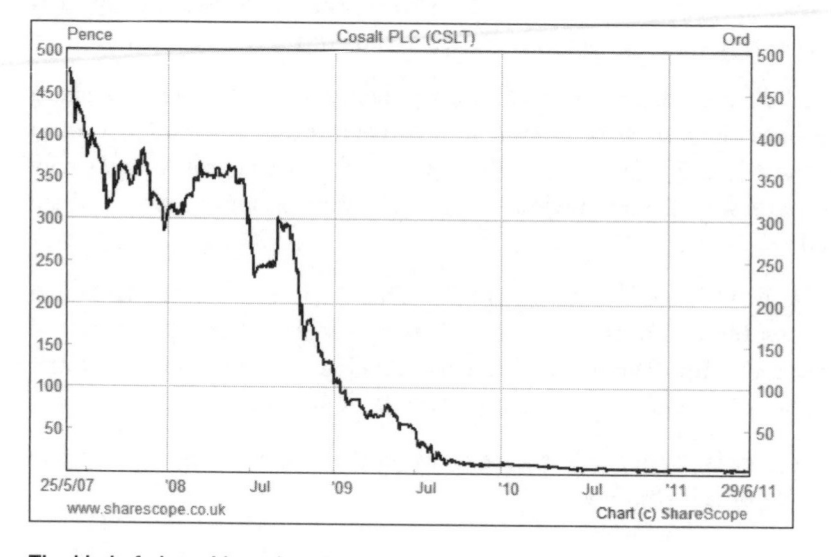

The kind of chart I hate longer-term (four years of Cosalt)

More charts I like

I am either looking for a chart that is simply gradually going higher – say, a beautiful one like this:

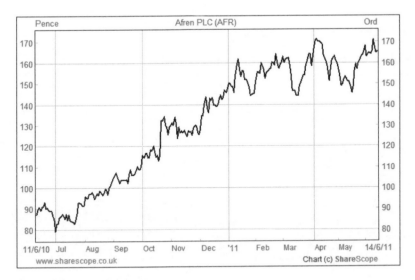

Afren (June 2010 – June 2011)

As you can see, this one just gradually keeps going profitwards in a nice rising uptrend.

Or I am looking for a share that is breaking out of a previous range like this (you can get these from 52-week breakouts):

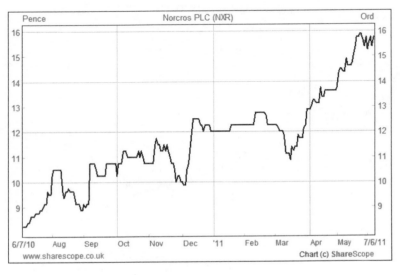

Norcros (July 2010 – June 2011)

In this chart Norcros breaks over 12p very nicely having stalled there before.

Both these kinds of charts, after my other research, I tend to view as green lights to buy.

I don't like these charts

I do *not* like charts like these, which show a falling price and very little meaningful support:

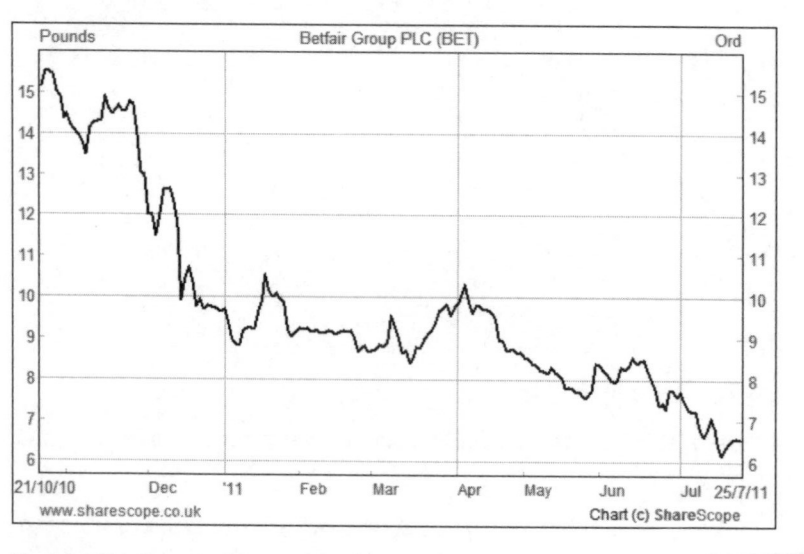

Betfair (October 2010 – July 2011)

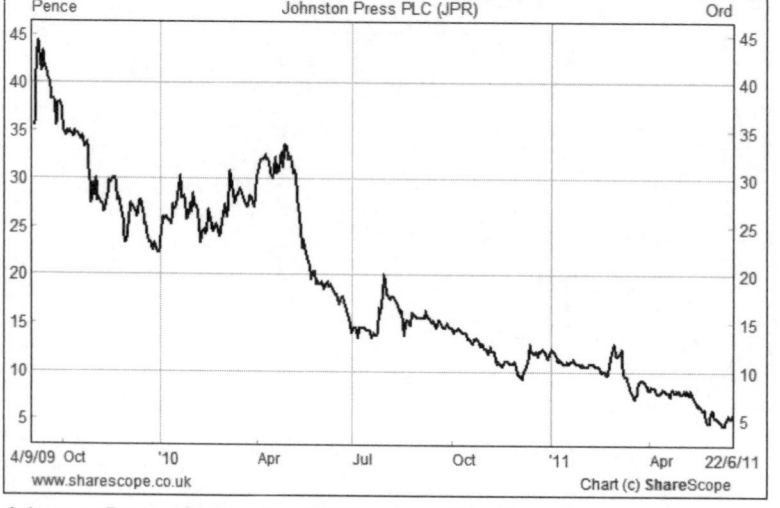

Johnston Press (September 2010 – June 2011)

Basically, they're disaster zones!

As I've said elsewhere in this book, a lot of traders prefer things the other way round: nothing looks more like a buy to them than a share with a chart that has just kept on plunging downwards (and vice versa for shorts). I'm afraid you must always remember that in such matters shares are no different to human beings: falling a great height is not a guarantee of being able get back up again and go higher. In fact, after a loud splat, usually quite the opposite is true.

Don't get suckered into thinking every share that goes down must come back up, or that every share on the up is destined for a fall. It's the oldest piece of foolishness masquerading as cunning.

Reader spot – gravity doesn't work both ways

"I 'invested' in Marconi because the price had dropped from £12 to £4 – surely, therefore, it was good value. I lost several thousand pounds on that bit of common sense."

Chart patterns

So now you have hopefully learned about support, resistance and breakouts. What about chart *patterns*? I'm not really so keen on these but let's have a quick look at them. The most famous chart pattern (let's call it Sir Chart Pattern) is called *head and shoulders*.

Head and shoulders

A head and shoulders pattern (and we're not talking dandruff-control shampoo here) is so called because that is kind of what it looks like: a head and shoulders! It's formed because the share hit a new high then fell off, tried to get back up again but couldn't and tried again. It really shows the share has run out of momentum for the time being and it might be time to take profits. So if you're ever going to consider looking at chart patterns, this is the one!

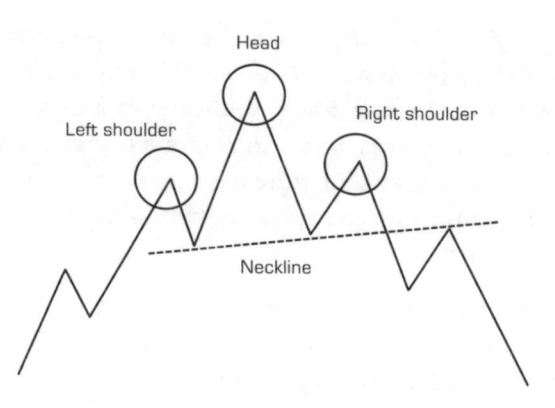

Head and shoulders

Double top

Another popular pattern where a share is expected to move lower is called a *double top* – as you can see it, well, looks like two tops:

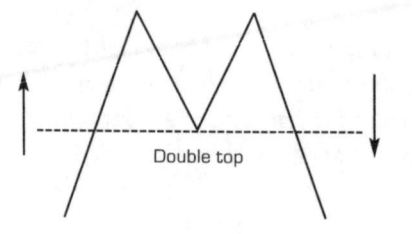

Double top

Once the share has tried twice to break up though a certain point it gets tired, needs a rest and a cup of tea and therefore goes down. So chartists argue (and boy do they argue!) it should be sold once the second peak is reached ... and so forming the double top.

Double bottom

And now the naughtiest sounding pattern – the *double bottom*.

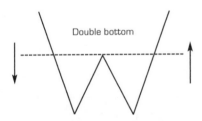

Double bottom

This is where the stock is expected to go *up*! It has gone down to the same price twice and bounced off that price. That, say chartists, is a bullish signal and the share should now rise a lot as it has found support.

Oh, talking of tea, another chart pattern supposedly bullish is the 'cup and handle' – i.e. the chart looks like, you guessed it … a cup and handle!

The share's gone up a lot, gradually fallen away, risen back up to form the cup shape, goes down a bit (to form the handle) and then is expected to rise sharply …

Round bottom

Then we have the err … (cough) round bottom. Lots of people like round bottoms (so I'm told). This is when a share falls away slowly, then bottoms out slowly before gently rising to form, err, the bottom.

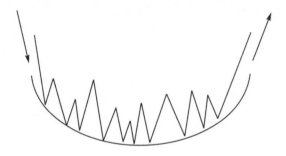

Round bottom

This is a bullish chart and the share should rise.

Triple top

And there's also the triple top. This is not good news. A share hits the sameish price three times. After it has hit the price for the third time it is expected to drop away sharply ...

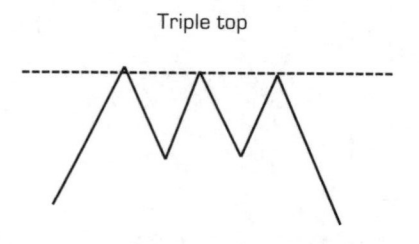

Triple top

Whether you believe in all this is up to you. The chart patterns sometimes work, sometimes don't, but they are worth a thought or two.

I would look on all these as things to just think about before you buy or sell; as an extra rather than using them solely. Sorry, chartists!

Further reading

An excellent guide for beginners, and to help you get more advanced in charts, is *The Investor's Guide to Charting* by Alistair Blair. This covers charting in depth, and if the subject interests you, the book covers most angles. And bottoms too.

# **Market Timing**

Timing is everything in life, and it's the same with shares.

It's pointless buying a good company if you're buying it during a general market slump, as the share will probably go down with the rest regardless of your careful research.

You have to time the best entry point you can with any share.

So I always ask myself: although I might have found a good company that I really like the look of, is today a good day to buy or not?

Just because the company is doing well doesn't necessarily mean the share price is going to go up. You could wake up one morning and see a great statement from a company. The share price is going up and you think: with results like that this share is going to rocket!

Not necessarily.

Suddenly, just after you've bought, the price starts to head south because many investors were in this one already and have now decided to take their profits and move on, leaving you holding the baby.

So how do you get your timing right?

Patience

There is always going to be some luck involved, but the key word here is patience. If you see that great company statement, add that share to your monitor and watch it like a hawk. Take a look at the share chart over the last three years and get a feel for its movements.

Watch how it moves up and down over the days and weeks.

And pounce when you feel the time is right! Never just buy it immediately.

Okay, the share might start going up and you end up missing the boat, but so what? There is always another day, another share. There is simply no substitute for experience in these matters, and as you learn to buy and sell shares you will gradually learn about timing.

> If you are very new to trading, the best advice I can give you is: if it is obvious that your timing has been wrong and the share starts to move against you – just get out.

There are many things to take into consideration regarding market timing. These considerations include:

- How much buying is going on in the share?

- What is the chart telling you?

- When is the next statement due?

- What is the general state of the markets? (Remember seasonal trends.)

- Is momentum with the share or not?

- What sort of share is it and how does it normally move?

First things first: you need to *plan* your trades – to get both your entry and exit points firmly in your head.

Plan your trades

As a trader or investor you *must* try to have some kind of plan. Too many people plunge into a share without having any idea why they bought it or how long they're going to hold it.

Make sure you plan every trade:

1. Write down every trade.

2. Think carefully about why you have bought the company.

3. Set a stop loss and profit target and stick to them.

4. Decide on your timescale.

5. Is it a short-term or a longer-term trade?

Keep a diary of all your trades and be honest. If you're losing money you can then look back and try to work out what you've been doing wrong.

Not having a plan is one of many fundamental errors made by traders. Entering a trade without knowing what you want and where you are going with it is the way to the poorhouse.

And in your plan one of the most important parts must be your timing.

Back now to timing

So what exactly are the signs I'm looking for to get in there and buy?

In no particular order I want to see:

- positive momentum
- plenty of trades
- positive chart
- it's in the run up to results
- Level 2 shows me it's a good time to buy (more on Level 2 later)
- it is not tanking badly.

Let's say I have a share I am interested in buying. I've done my research and it's just a question of when.

First, I am looking to buy when the price is *rising* on the day I am buying, not falling dramatically. I don't mean rising a lot. Just a small amount will do to show me that others are buying in.

Next I want to check volume by pressing the 'Trades' button on ADVFN. Is there some reasonable buying volume coming in and has there been for one or two days? To check this go back over the trades for the last four weeks. Are there more trades and bigger amounts showing in the last week or so than in the previous weeks? E.g. are there 200 trades instead of 100?

Then I'll check the chart (see Chapter 17). All good? A few final checks and then it's show time.

When is the next statement due? If it's tomorrow I might leave it and see what results are like. **I prefer to buy, if I can, around four to six weeks before results – this is often when shares start to motor if results are expected to be good.**

What sort of share is it and how does it normally move? If it's a small company, that makes buying easier as the price doesn't move that fast. If it's a medium to large one, sometimes I have to be pretty nimble to get a good price as the buying price could move 5p or 6p just like that.

And that's where my final check – looking at Level 2 – comes in. Basically Level 2 shows me what the market makers are doing and where the support is for a share. (More on Level 2 in Chapter 22.) Sometimes I'll put in a buy order and see what price I get on the 15-second countdown. If I think I'll get a better price in a few minutes by using Level 2 I'll wait a bit.

And that's that! *I'm in.*

Timing tip

Here's a reason why it's worth having at least two broker accounts.

Say you want to buy a share – let's say 4,000 shares. The share is moving up quickly and is in big demand. You put in an order but no 15-second countdown appears with a price.

You have to send the order through to the dealer or phone them. That'll take time and you'll miss the price.

Instead: put in orders for smaller amounts and see if a price is offered and the countdown appears. Let's say you're able to buy 2,000 of the shares immediately.

Now you can buy the full 4,000 shares. Put in an order for 2,000 with one broker and 2,000 with another at the same time. You ought to get the countdown clock with both firms and so get the price you want for the entire 4,000.

When it comes to selling shares, you should be able to play the same trick. I don't suppose the market makers would be that happy about it, but they're not going to know it's you – so who cares?

Volumes

Trades – buys and sells

Volume is simply the amount of trades made in a share.

Why is it important?

Because unusual volume activity with a share can indicate that something interesting is going on.

> To access trade volumes, press 'Trades' on ADVFN for the stock you are interested in. This gives you an up-to-the-minute list of buys and sells going through.

You should be able to see trades coming in on your share monitor pages too.

Best way to check volumes is, as said, to click through the last four weeks and see if there are more trades in bigger sizes in the last two to three days compared to previously.

I often get emails from confused investors who follow the volume of buying and selling in particular companies. They raise questions like:

"Why is the share dropping when there are so many more buys than sells?"

Apart from market maker shenanigans I've already discussed, such as tree shaking, this is because all the buys and sells you see listed on the trade pages are only *guesses* by a computer!

So when you see trades listed under 'buys' or 'sells', that 'buy' could easily have been a 'sell'! The trouble is, market makers can delay the publication of trades that are over the normal market size of a stock. So the trade you see at 14.20 could well have been made at 10.20.

Also when you see an 'AT' trade, that is effectively a buy *and* a sell. Someone has bought it but someone also sold it and the two parties have exchanged shares automatically.

> The lesson here is to treat volume trade data with great caution. To keep it simple, if the share is going up it's likely to have more buyers and if it's going down there are probably more sellers.

ADVFN 'Trades' page

Trade codes

You'll notice that there is a letter displayed next to every trade, which at least gives some sort of clue as to the sort of trade it is. Here are what the main ones mean.

T trades

This doesn't mean nice relaxed trades made over a cup of tea. 'T' by a trade, in market jargon, means 'single protected transaction'. The trade you see going through is someone who has bought or sold a lot of shares over a period of time and it all goes through as if it was one transaction.

That makes it hard to know whether the trade is a buy or a sell. But again, as a general rule, if the share is rising it's probably a buy, and if falling it's probably a sell.

X trades

When you see 'X' by a transaction, even if it's for a big amount of shares, you can kind of ignore it. This is just a parcel of shares being swapped between two parties. One wants the shares, the other doesn't. So there are no real conclusions to be drawn and the share price is rarely affected.

O trades

'O' means it's an ordinary trade; could be someone at home or an institution etc. This is normally broadcast immediately, unless it is over six times the EMS (exchange market size – the amount you can deal in per share). In which case it can be delayed.

L trades

'L' means a late reported trade.

M trades

'M' is a deal between two market makers. It usually means one of the market makers is short of stock.

AT trades

'AT' is an automated trade dealt through the order book. Generally means it's a trade made by a professional or regular market player and often via CFDs. More likely to move the market.

NO CODE

Probably went though a rival market to the LSE such as PLUS Markets.

Other markets

Now you might think that you would see all the trades coming through. You've got to be kidding – it's the stock market, so as usual expect the unexpected ...

There are other rivals to the LSE and they include PLUS Markets, CHI-X and Turquoise.

PLUS Markets deals in the small cap end of the market and a lot of small trades go via them. And the bigger shares you will find on CHIX and TQ.

CHIX and Turquoise even offer 'dark pools' where buy and sell orders are hidden.

On most sites you can't see these trades coming through. You *can* on ADVFN if you have their Level 2 service.

So if you have bought or sold a share and wonder why you do not see your trade published on ADVFN it's because it will have gone through PLUS Markets instead. To find the trades of yourself (and others) on PLUS go to **www.plusmarketsgroup.com**. Type the symbol of your share top right and you'll get the trades.

Setting Stop Losses and Profit Targets

Since I wrote the last edition, investors and traders have become more and more sophisticated. Stop losses – a tool for preventing heavy losses from occurring – are now more widely used than ever before. Here's everything you need to know about them and their brother, the profit target.

Stop losses

First, what the heck is a stop loss? (It is also known as a stop order.)

Diverting the wife from visiting an expensive boots 'n' bags shop? Yes, that is definitely a stop loss! But market stop losses ... well they are a figure you choose at which point you agree with yourself or a broker or your spread bet firm or your therapist to take a loss on a share before it goes down any further. You set them up in advance, when you make your trade in the first place, so that your account automatically sells out of a share when things get ugly and a certain price is hit (rather than being reliant on your own monitoring and changeable, oh so changeable, inclination).

This is about preserving your capital and ensuring you don't lose more money on a share than you need to. Often shares are going down for a reason and once they start going down they can really tank.

As I said earlier in the book, one of the main reasons that people lose money in shares is their inability to sell anything at a loss. So this is where your stop loss comes in.

Before diving into the detail of stop losses, let's first look at a simple share investment made by an investor, who we will call Bob.

By the way, I have nicked this example from my spread betting book (in case it looks familiar). I am honestly not being lazy, it's just a cracking example!

Bob and his shares that were going to the moon

The following chart shows the share price for a company – for the moment it's not important to know the name of the company.

Bob has been following this company and notes that while the shares had been stuck in a horizontal range for much of 2003–2005, the price then broke out of the range from around mid-2006 and started heading up.

Bob liked this type of situation and decided to pile in if the shares broke through the 600 level.

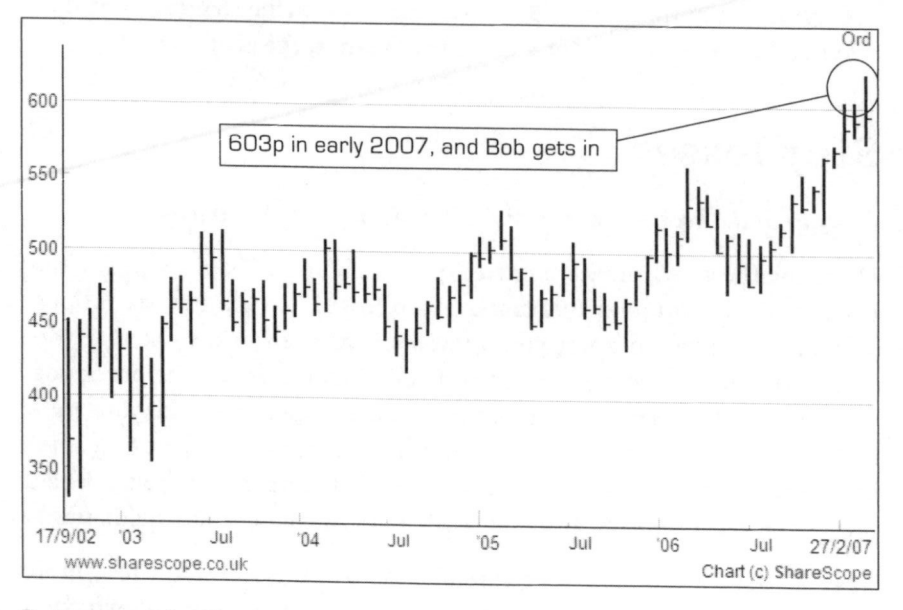

To the moon, baby!

As can be seen, the price duly rose through 600 and Bob ended up buying some shares at 603p at the beginning of 2007.

In the following couple of months the price moved around a bit but basically looked to be continuing the trend higher. Bob felt pretty smart. Next stop, 700, and then on to the moon.

And then …

Temporary correction, baby!

"Typical, typical, typical," thought Bob, "I always seem to buy at the high".

However, he wasn't overly concerned as he knew that prices never went up in a straight line. The chart showed clearly that the uptrend was still in place and this was just a temporary correction.

And then …

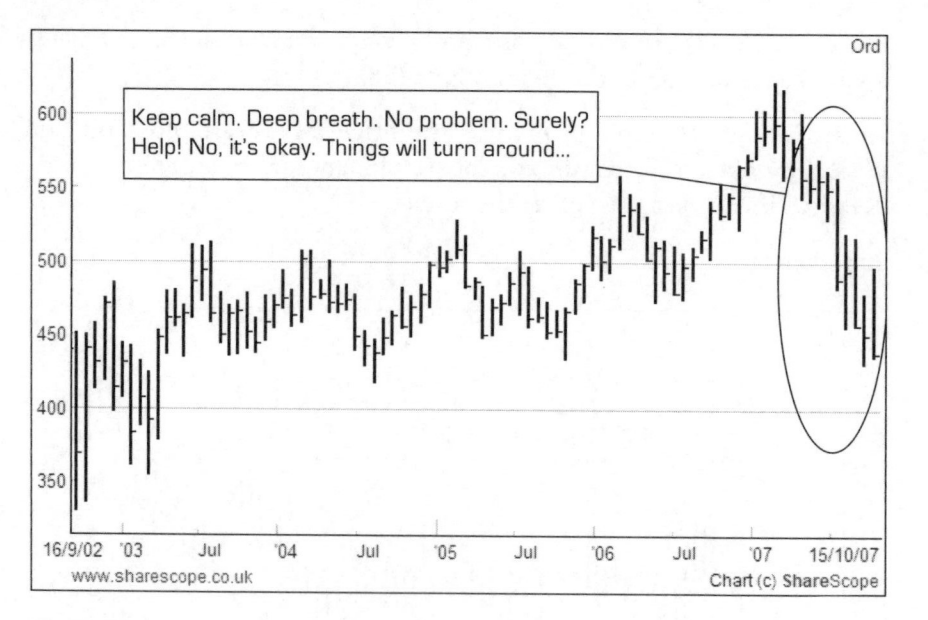

www.sharescope.co.uk

Chart (c) ShareScope

Er … baby?

"Hmmm," thought Bob, "that's not so good. In fact, bugger!"

However, Bob was damned if he was going to sell now and take a 30% loss.

He reasoned that the shares were sitting solidly on a support level of around 420 – indeed they had most recently shown signs of bouncing off from this level. If he sold now, he just knew the shares would rocket up and he'd end up feeling stupid and cheesed off.

No, reasoned Bob, these shares were still a good investment; it was just a case of holding one's nerve and sitting tight.

And then …

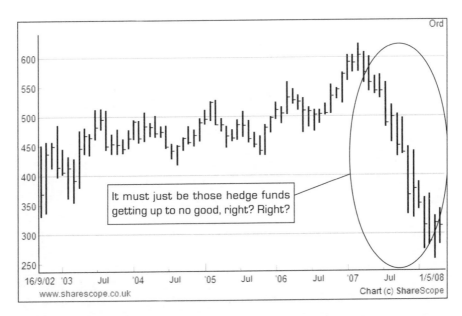

It must just be those hedge funds getting up to no good, right? Right?

Oh my

"Double bugger!" Bob was really annoyed now. "What the heck is going on here, this is ridiculous. There's no way these shares are worth just 300p now when they were worth over 600p just a few months ago."

Bob had read something about hedge funds shorting the shares which had driven the price down, and while he didn't understand the exact details of that he thought it was exactly the sort of irresponsible thing that hedge funds *would* do.

At least the shares seemed to have consolidated at the 300 level. And, anyway, there is absolutely *no way* that he was going to sell at a 50% loss when the shares were obviously worth 600 and had been just temporarily depressed by the actions of a bunch of shysters.

And then ...

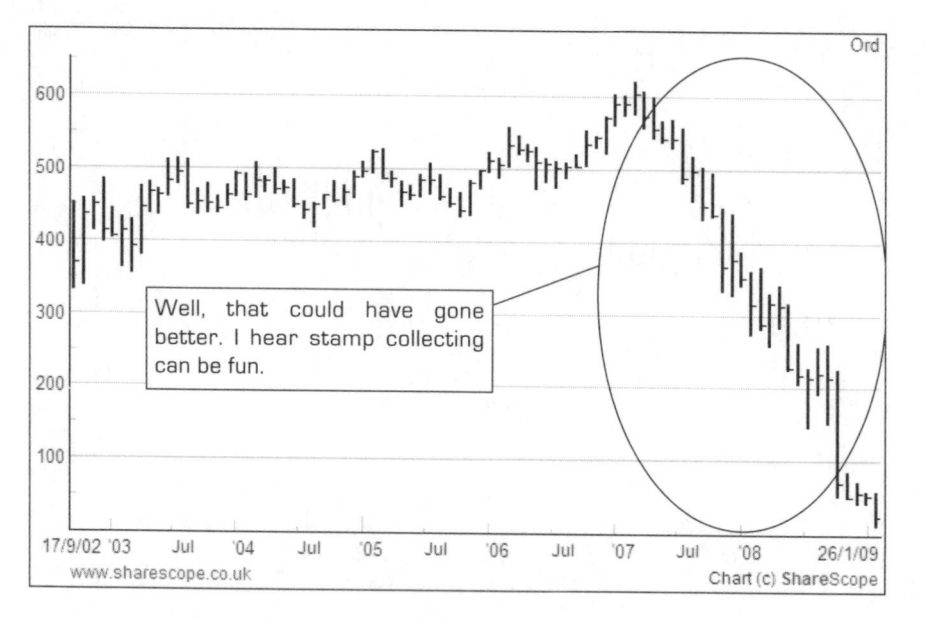

This isn't funny any more

"Triple bugger!" Two years after buying the shares, the price was 24p. A fall of 96% from 603p. Bob still owned his shares, but was 'fed up with this stupid share stuff'.

No wonder. This share is Royal Bank of Scotland!

Money or balls

The above is a good case study in how not to invest; there are many things that Bob did wrong.

One thing we can observe is how good Bob was at rationalising his bad decisions. All investors – especially bad ones – can be extremely creative in coming up with excuses for why they are not wrong.

Quick question: is the purpose of investing

1. to make money, or

2. to prove you have bigger balls than Gordon Ramsay?

If you answered (2), then put this book down right now!

You must realise that (1) and (2) are rarely compatible when it comes to investing. Humility is the order of the day: accept your mistakes and quickly move on.

How stop losses work

So, what should Bob have done instead?

The answer: use a stop loss.

Let's look again at the chart at the time that Bob bought his shares.

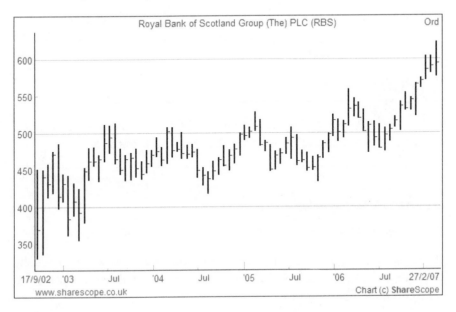

Before it all went wrong

After Bob had bought his shares, he should have placed another order with his broker that said something like: "if the price falls to 500 then sell all my shares". That is a stop order!

Now, the question of what exact level to set as the trigger point to sell the shares is a big topic (one that I look at later in this book). There are several levels that could be considered, for example:

- 550 – this was roughly the high set at the beginning of 2006

- 520 – this was the top level of the horizontal trading range from 2003– 2005

- 500 – a round number that might act as support for the shares

- 490 – a few points below the round number 500

- 440 – roughly the lower level of the horizontal trading range from 2003–2005.

And then there are any number of other possible levels; levels determined with reference to moving averages, trend lines, Bollinger Bands, etc.

A whole book could be written on where to set the trigger level for stop orders. The purpose of the trigger level is to set it at a level where you say, "Okay, this doesn't seem to be working I'd better get out just in case".

But the important point at the moment is that finessing the trigger level is of second-degree importance – the most important thing is to set a stop order in the first place!

A bad stop order (and it is difficult to know how to define a bad stop order exactly) is better than no stop order at all.

Mental stops don't work

So, a stop order is a precise order that you give to your broker.

To do it, most brokers have a 'stop loss' button near to where you usually press to buy or sell a share. You can put your stop in there. It's the same with the spread betting firms.

And you can enter them even after opening a trade without them, or adjust them as a price moves (more on that in a sec). They let you get in at a price of your own choosing (or as close as possible, if the market is dropping badly). And you don't have to be glued to the screen all day watching to see if the shares fall.

There are some traders who think that they don't need to place such an order. They believe they can monitor the performance of the shares themselves, and if the shares go down they will sell them. But this requires a level of discipline that is beyond most people. We saw in Bob's example how easy it is to rationalise our mistakes in the heat of the moment.

One of the useful features of a stop order is that it is an order that can be placed when we are thinking rationally; it can even be placed when the markets are closed. So we can and should determine ahead of time what is the critical level below which, should things fall, we will accept it is best to get out with our shirts still on our backs.

Stop losses limit losses

In the example above, if Bob had invested £1,000 in the shares at 603p, his holding would have been worth £40 two years later. A loss of £960.

Bad news.

Whereas, if he had placed a stop order with a trigger at 500p, his broker would have sold his shares when the price fell to 500. This would have incurred a loss of 17% (or £170). Nasty – but much better than losing 96%.

> Academic studies (hey, wake up at the back, this is important stuff!) show that the important thing in investing is not to beat the index by a few points when prices are rising, but rather to avoid the big losses when markets fall.

That's the key thing – avoid the big losses. And that's where stop losses are useful.

But at what point do you set them? When should you be quitting a share?

Good question.

I have changed my stance on this since the last edition. In the second edition I wrote that stops should be 10% away from the price you buy in at. After all, as discussed earlier, when a share has dropped 10% we really ought to start thinking about cutting our losses.

I have changed my mind since then and think that in some cases, especially with very volatile FTSE 100 and mining shares, stops should be further away. *Not because I don't believe in cutting losses at 10–15%.* I still do. It's just that sometimes the share price of such stocks will briefly jump down first thing in the morning – when the spreads become momentarily enormous – and that can simply knock out your stop loss.

So at 10% on some shares you can find yourself taking a needless loss, with the share almost immediately swinging back up again afterwards. We live in volatile times.

I therefore now start at 10% (away from the current price) and then tweak stops further away from there, depending on where punters have bought and sold in the past, and adding a little breathing room if it's a volatile FTSE 100er or mining share.

Best to have an example, eh?

Stop target examples

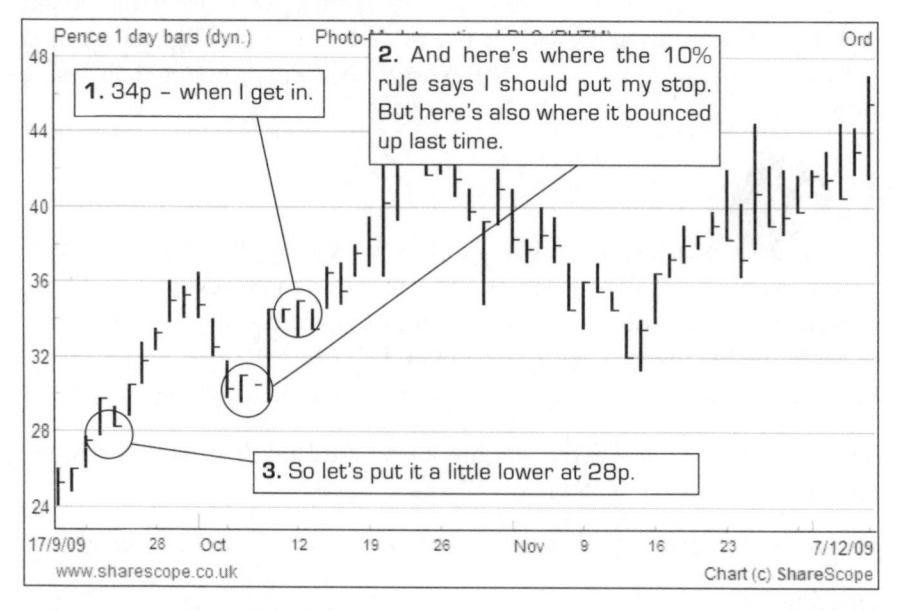

Photo-Me, October 2009, open at 34p, close at 30p

I bought Photo-Me at 34p in October 2009.

Now, what about the stop loss?

First, the 10% rule of thumb would place the stop at around 30.5 (34 - 10% or so).

Then I look at the chart and see the last time it bounced after going down was at 30! So I lower the stop a bit further, to go under that at 28. The reason is that history often repeats itself. It bounced before at 30 so it could easily do it again. I therefore don't want to go with the 30.5 in case I get stopped out at the 30p bounce (after which it could rise again).

The share then rises but falls back to close at 30. Pushing the stop under 30 means it did not get activated and it carried on rising. If I had set my stop *too tight,* I could have made a loss at the wrong time. That's something else to watch out for.

Let's look at another example.

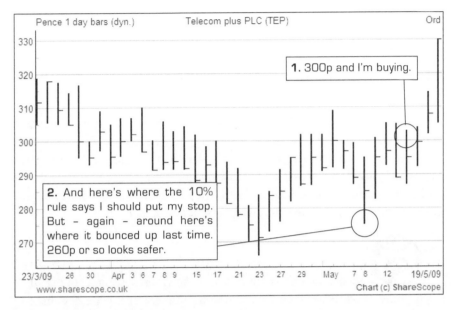

Telecom Plus, April 2009, 300p, 270p bounce

I bought Telecom Plus in April 2009 at 300.

10% of that is 30p, so I put my stop at 270. But look at the chart – it bounced right off 270 before. (Called 'support' in jargon, remember.) With a wide spread, I want to lower the stop a little just to be sure, and I go for 260.

See what I mean? Have a look back in time, check where the price bounced before, and set your stop a little below that price. In other words, set your stop just a bit lower from where everyone else might be setting their stops. Then you have less of a chance of being bounced out.

The challenge when setting a stop is to set a level that will be activated when the share makes a decisive move, but is not activated on a small, insignificant move (which is often quickly reversed).

Obviously this is just what I do, and you might want to design your own methods for setting a stop loss.

With shares priced over a tenner, you really have to be careful where you place a stop.

Stop losses and market makers

I have already mentioned tree shakes – beware of their effect on your stop losses!

Let's say a market maker has a huge buy order and needs some shares. All market makers are ruthless and will have a pretty good idea where investors have set their stop losses. In order to start a *tree shake* (a hideous but survivable experience we looked at in Chapter 7) and push the share down rapidly to scare you into selling them, they will look at the share, have a guess where the stop losses are, and *try to take you out*!

> So it's always worth considering when setting a stop, that you may need some slack should market makers be a little devious.

Tree shakes only last for around half a day and if your share has come down violently it will also come back quickly. You will soon get to grips with this through experience.

Trailing stop losses

Some investors use what they call *trailing stop losses*. That means as the share you've bought into rises, so does your stop loss, automatically.

Some brokers now offer to manage your trailing stop losses for you.

What does it mean?

Example: trailing stop loss

Say you bought a share at 200p, and you set a trailing stop loss of 20p. Then –

- If the share price **falls to 180p**, your holding is sold. (This is a normal stop loss.) But, there's more …

- If the share **rises to 260p**, your stop loss will track it upwards, and then be set (automatically) at 240p.

- If the share then **rises to 300p**, your stop loss is re-set at 280p.

Effectively, your broker will sell if the share goes 20p lower than its recent high.

In other words, **your trailing stop takes a profit for you, removing emotion out of any decision**. I think this is a marvellous idea, especially for newer investors or those who can't be at a screen all day watching prices.

You can set any trailing stop loss you like as a point difference or percentage.

In the end it's down to experience – and trial and error. But better to set some targets than having no plan at all.

Monitoring stop losses

You have got to decide whether to set your stop loss and simply monitor it yourself or set it with your broker or spread bet firm.

Fortunately most good stock brokers – and all spread betting firms – accept stop loss orders. In other words, they will monitor the stop loss themselves – you don't have to worry about it.

BUT! Beware. Your stop loss might not get you out in some circumstances. Remember your broker still has to sell the shares in the market. If you have a large holding it might not be possible to sell them. Or the price might be moving down so quickly that they can't be sold.

Some brokers allow you to set a 'range' where you want them sold. So say your stop loss was 100. You could set 95p for the bottom of the range. So if they tumbled fast your broker can still sell them down to 95p.

It is always worth checking what the policy of your broker is. Give them a call and ask.

> Trailing stop losses are a bit special and are not offered by everyone. If you think they'll be important to you, it is worth checking that a broker/spread betting firm offers them before opening an account with them. You can of course always implement them manually.

One other point to make is, if your share tanks overnight obviously your stop loss won't work if the shares open way down. Again, check your broker's policy on that.

Changing stops

You should check your stops from time to time if you aren't using trailing stops. If the share is going well, you could simply start raising your stop under the price yourself. Some brokers let you do this online; with others you may have to call them.

How do I use stops?

Well, I've used them in all these ways in the past. But now, after so many years in the markets and because I trade full time, I no longer set stop losses in my ISA portfolios. I would rather take the decision myself. Remember, for beginners, this isn't recommended. I didn't start out without stops! I do hold some stop losses in my spread bet account, though.

Now what about target prices?

Profit targets

Before opening a trade you should decide on a price level which you would be happy to sell at – this is called a profit target. I believe profit targets should be at least 20% higher than your buy price. **After all, why buy a share unless you think you can get at least 20% out of it?**

But I certainly do not automatically sell once a share gets to the target price. This is a point at which I look at the share again and decide whether it is still cheap. Is there further to go? If there is, I may well set a new target and stay with the shares or even buy more.

Because as I pointed out earlier, I am really looking for 50%-plus profits – some big winners.

I do the same thing as when I set my stops – look to around 20% (as opposed to 10% for losses), and then tweak it to where the share has peaked before.

So, for example, say I thought Hornby was a good buy at 110p in Spring 2011.

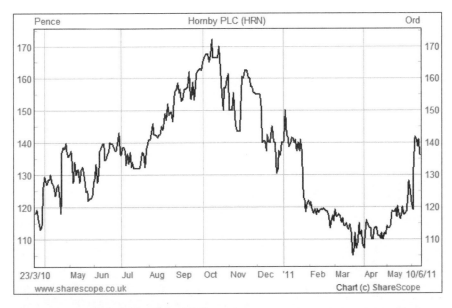

Hornby (January 2010 – May 2011)

I would initially want 20%, which is about 132p. However, if you look at the chart you can see 140 has been an area of consolidation in the past – so I would look around there for a target. Further down the line (Hornby makes toy trains, gettit?) you can see it has previously run out of steam (hee hee!) at 170. So again I would look to this area for my next target if the price raced through 140.

Summary

- Before you buy a share, set yourself a stop loss and a profit target.

- And remember what I said earlier – write them down!

- If you stick to a stop-loss system, your losses will generally be minimised.

> You'll see if you go to my website, **www.nakedtrader.co.uk**, that I have a list of my current positions. Every one has a stop loss and target. You need to ensure you have done this too.

Part VI
The Next Level

"The best way to keep money in perspective is to have some."

– Louis Rukeyser

SIPPs

The next level? You mean there's more?!

You bet. And hey, some of it's pretty flipping exciting. In this part we're going to look at some stuff that beginners don't need to worry about *too* much at first. But I think if you haven't fainted yet, you're well qualified to keep reading. If pensions don't do it for you, the chapter on spread betting should. It's a lot simpler than you think. Heck, it's an essential tool.

First, some sipping ...

SIPPs (self-invested personal pensions) mean you can take control of your own pension fund rather than letting the professionals look after it. I think they're brilliant. The question is:

Should you take the plunge and run the fund yourself?

The answer is: could you do any worse than the fund managers?

I watched the pension fund I had with the company I worked for, BSkyB, go up for a few years and then sink like a stone between 1999 and 2001, at which point I'd had enough. So when I left full-time work I immediately transferred all the money from two frozen company pensions into my SIPP and began trading.

I'm glad I did as I soon built it from £40k to £165k. Much of that rise was detailed in my *Sunday Times* column 'DIY Pension'. Now it sits at around £250,000. I reckon if I had left the pension money with the company scheme it would probably be floating around the £50k mark.

So I run my own pension fund, buying and selling shares. Of course, I'm confident when it comes to dealing in shares, but other people need to think carefully about whether to run their own fund.

For this section, I'm going to assume you feel reasonably confident about investing. Or you are going to be confident. So I'm going to discuss how to set up a SIPP and what to do with the money once you get hold of it.

One rule of thumb is: only go for a SIPP once you have about £25k or more to put in your pension – it's not worth it otherwise, taking costs into account. Also if you still have a final salary scheme, it might be worth keeping hold of it instead.

Setting up a SIPP

I wrote in the last edition that setting up a SIPP can be a pain in the bum. It used to take absolutely ages and it was a paperwork nightmare. Ah, but things have changed for this edition of the book! I've talked to loads of people who have set up SIPPs who tell me the transfer has become quite easy and smooth.

There are still lots of forms to complete. But some of it can now be done online. Assuming you mainly want to trade shares, you need two things:

1. an execution-only stock broker

2. a pension trustee.

The trustee basically looks after the money and keeps it secure for you – usually for a yearly fee of around £150–£300. You then trade the shares as normal and hopefully watch your fund rise.

It's probably best to choose the broker first – maybe the one you use for normal dealings – as they should have a list of trustees they recommend and work with. Trustees are much of a muchness, so just choose the cheapest.

You can transfer in as much of your salary as you want, and currently you then get 20% added, or 40% depending on your tax bracket. For instance, if you're a 40% taxpayer and put in £10,000, the government adds another £4,000. (This could obviously have changed by the time you read this, so you need to check.)

You just send the money to the trustee, it's put into your stock-broking account and away you go. Buy and sell shares using the money as you wish – and that includes AIM shares which aren't allowed in an ISA.

It's slightly easier if you want to start from scratch, without transferring in any money.

Transferring frozen schemes

You can transfer in frozen schemes. You have to chase up the company the schemes are lodged with as they need to send you forms (yawn!). You fill them out and return them – the company should then release the money to your trustee.

It can take time and you need to keep hassling them along. The other issue is that it can be difficult to transfer in a *final salary scheme*. Some trustees won't let you because final salary schemes are supposed to be the bee's knees, and it could be argued you don't need a SIPP because the FSSs are excellent payers. This is something you will have to look at closely. These days there are hardly any final salary schemes around; most have been closed.

Anyway, all the hassle is worth it in the end. It's a great feeling to be in charge of your own destiny.

You can carry on trading your SIPP till you're 75, at which point the government reckons you'll be too ga-ga to trade any more, and you have to buy an annuity. As I write this, the government is thinking of changing things so that you don't have to (with some conditions!). You'll need to check the latest online.

Trading in a SIPP

Trading in a SIPP is exactly the same as trading your shares normally. You buy and sell shares as per usual – however you can't get at the money till you're 55 (if you're over 55 you can take 25%). There is a limit on the amount you can build up, check or Google for the current max.

Once you have your SIPP, what sort of shares should you deal in?

You really ought to be sensible. You probably have many years to go before you want to cash it in. Don't go crazy – buy some decent, sensible shares with good yields. You're looking for a decent lift for the fund over time. You have time, and do not have to worry so much about the ebb and flow of the market, and can look longer-term.

Look for shares you'd be happy to hold for a while and follow the practices I've already outlined in this book.

Aim for growth of around 10–20% a year – the fund will soon grow nicely at this rate. Don't take too many risks, as you may be relying on this money in the future.

You could do some shorting in your SIPP by using SUK2 (see page 199) or covered warrants (see page 287).

For example, when the market headed near a high recently I bought a few FTSE put covered warrants. This meant if the market tanked short term I would make quite a lot. This would help to cover any losses in the longs.

Just recently, I have been using my SIPP to buy high-risk AIM stock, which has worked quite well for me. However, it is easy for me to do this because I have built up tons of money within my ISA which I can take at any time and I have decided to try and grow my pension money more quickly as I can afford to take the risk.

So all in all, why not give it a try? Just think: you can be your own fund manager!

And unlike the fund manager who handles billions, you can nimbly get in and out of shares. They can't do that so easily! Give it a bash and good luck!

Summary

- You can run your own pension fund.

- You can make contributions and transfer in frozen pensions.

- You need a stock broker and a pension trustee.

- It can take time to transfer in funds.

- Buy any shares you like, including AIM.

- You can short shares using covered warrants.

- Be cautious with your fund – you may need the money.

Level 2 and DMA

When it comes to timing a trade, I always use Level 2 for a final decision. In fact, I personally wouldn't ever trade without it.

Level 2

At last! Just what exactly is Level 2 and is it worth having?

Two very good questions which I will try and answer for you now.

But just before I do, I have to say that it's next to impossible for me to go over Level 2 properly here. It would take 1,000 pages to do it and even then I'm not sure I could. I just about manage it, but only live at my seminars. I can give you a little summary. No need to get frightened, it just takes a little time.

If you are just starting out I wouldn't worry about it until you find your feet. But if you're starting out you *could* get into this now – the reason being it will help you to understand more about how shares move and why.

You will find it an eye-opener and will quickly understand much more about how and why shares go up and down.

There's no way I could trade without it. Personally? I'd look at it now. I think even if you're very new to the markets it's worth considering finding out about Level 2. But expect it to take *ages* before it's of help to you.

So what is it exactly?

Level 2 used to only be available to professional traders in the City, but thanks to new technologies and price cuts by the stock exchange, it's now available cheaply to anyone that wants it. In short, it provides far more information about a share, including not only full details of the current bid and offer price but also prices that exist at other levels and the offers of individual market makers.

Without Level 2 you simply see the current best sell and buy price. But you have no idea what other bids and offers there might be in the market.

Let's say you were interested in buying or selling Avon Rubber. Without Level 2, here is what you would see:

Avon Rbr.(AVON)									Click for Financials		
Name	Symbol		Market		Type		ISIN		Description		
Avon Rbr.	LSE:AVON		London Stock Exchange		Equity		GB0000667013		ORD #1		
Change	%	Cur	Bid	Offer	High	Low	Open	Volume	Time	RN	NRN
↓ -9.75	-3.9%	240.0	234.5	239.0	245.0	230.75	245.0	88,466	11:36		
	Sector		Turnover (m)		Profit (m)		EPS - Basic	PE ratio	Mkt Cap (m)		
	AEROSPACE & DEFENCE		117.6		4.3		15.2	15.789	73.7		
Type	Size	Price	Tr.Time	Units							
O	10,000	240.0	11:06	GBX							

Simple (Level 1) price quote for Avon Rubber

You can see the sell (bid) price of Avon Rubber is 234.5p and the buy (offer) price is 239p. These are the *best* prices, meaning:

- 234.5p is the *highest* selling price in the market

- 239p is the *lowest* buying price.

This is all very well. *But those aren't the only selling and buying prices in the market at that time.*

Now here's a Level 2 quote for Avon Rubber. You can see it is completely different. You can now see the other orders in the market:

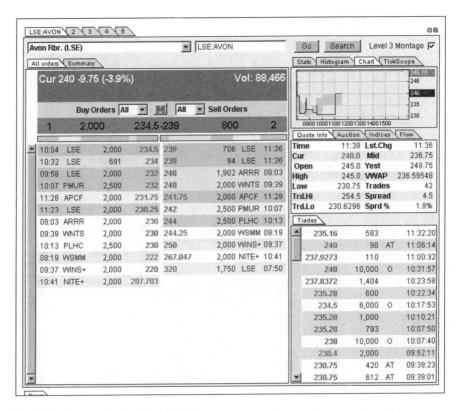

Level 2 price quote for Avon Rubber

What's the use of it?

Well, you can see the market makers begin to move their prices *before* it makes a difference to the Level 1 price. And what that means is, you can get in and buy or sell *before* the crowd knows there is going to be a price change. I find I can often get in ahead of a big price jump.

On this Level 2 screen you can see the market makers such as Winterfloods (WINS+) and WSMM and all the others. On Level 2 you can see them start to move their prices up or down. This means you can buy or sell *before* most people know the price is about to change. Which is rather handy!

When you see a lot of market makers moving up it is a good sign.

Moving onto the bigger stocks, here's a view of the Level 2 for Charter.

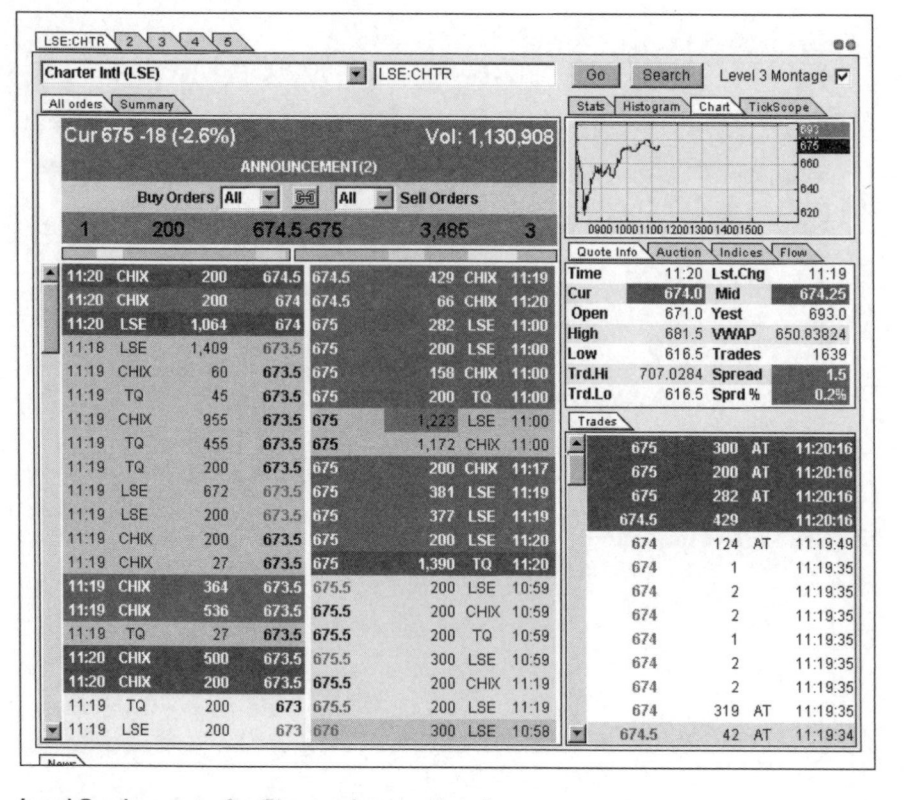

Level 2 price quote for Charter International

With bigger stocks, you still have market makers (you can see they are still there), but there can also be all and sundry putting in buy and sell orders. You can also see buy and sell orders from all the exchanges: LSE (London Stock Exchange), TQ (Turquoise) and CHIX (Chi-X).

The prices and amounts of shares you can see are all real buy and sell orders. The price of the share moves when someone has bought or sold the amount you see on the screen.

What may confuse you is that it says 'buy orders' on the left and 'sell orders' on the right. This is from the point of view of the people putting on the orders. For you, you are therefore 'buying' the right-hand side prices and 'selling' the left-hand side ones.

A quick way to remember this. You always have to:

- *buy* at the **higher** price, and

- *sell* at the **lower** price.

In other words, you always buy or sell at the more disadvantageous price!

You may look at this Level 2 screen and think: "Bloody hell, I'm never going to understand it."

But once you're used to it, it's much easier than you might think. What you're looking at here is not only where the market makers are, but with larger stocks you can see *all* the buy orders and *all* the sell orders. By seeing how big the buy orders and sell orders are, you can judge where support might be on a share price. And this information really is valuable.

The other valuable thing about it is that it teaches you how and why share prices are moving – you can see everything going on in the background that affects a price.

Level 2 will stop you from taking profits on a share too early and buying a share at the wrong time.

The best way to understand Level 2, though, is really to get it and play with it on your favourite stocks. And as I said, expect it to be a long process but one worth persevering with.

How do you get Level 2?

It's available (at the time of writing) at anything from free to £500 p/a. If you trade an awful lot, some brokers and spread bet firms will give it to you for nothing – a rule of thumb is roughly 30 trades or more per quarter to qualify.

ADVFN promise to offer it to *Naked Trader* readers at way cheaper than their normal price for the first year. Click on my website for news on that or email me at **robbiethetrader@aol.com** with 'Book Level 2 offer' in the subject line.

If you don't trade that much, don't worry – it's a lot cheaper than it was, and costs keep coming down all the time. Probably in five or six years or so it'll end up being free regardless.

I personally use the ADVFN Level 2 because I like the layout. Also, at the time of writing, it is the only Level 2 that includes all the trades made through PLUS Markets (the rival system to the LSE), so you can see all the trades out there. It also gives you access to what are called dark pools, or hidden trades made on exchanges like Chi-X.

I really wish I could do an in-depth book entirely on Level 2, but it's probably too difficult to bring over the complexities in an easy, non-terrifying way. It's just one of those things that really is much easier to explain in the flesh. At my seminars I go through everything I do with Level 2 right there and then, using live shares, and I think this works really well. If you really want to get on top of Level 2 quickly, it may be worth coming along to one of those. Check my website to see if I have one coming up.

Direct market access (DMA)

More and more brokers and spread betting firms will allow you direct market access.

What's it all about, Alfie?

It means you (yes, *you*!) can be a market maker, and you can put your own buy and sell orders directly into the market.

Let's say a share price quote is currently 500–502 (500 to sell and 502 to buy).

Now, normally, if you wanted to buy the shares you would have to pay 502 – as that is the buying price.

But DMA allows you to input an order direct onto the order book, which means you could input an order to buy at 500.25. You would then become the best (i.e. highest) selling price, and the share would officially then be quoted as: 500.25–502. If someone then wanted to sell some shares, your price would be the best and they would sell to you at 500.25.

Brilliant for you, because you are effectively buying them at the sell price.

Alternatively, if you wanted to short the shares you could put in a sell order at 501.75p and effectively sell at near the buy price.

Most direct market access is done via CFDs (explained in a mo). All the orders, including yours, will show up on your Level 2 screen.

As I said, you can get DMA at many places now.

As with Level 2, in the end DMA can only be properly explained live and again if you come to a seminar I would be happy to show you. I place orders live on the book at the seminars so you can see exactly how it works.

Spread Betting

Introduction

Here I should really just write: buy my book about spread betting! It's all in there! However, of course, if you are starting out you may not feel ready for it yet – so this big old chapter will provide a jam-packed overview of for you.

There *is* much more in *The Naked Trader's Guide to Spread Betting*, of course, with tons of trading examples, the biggest mistakes spread bettors make, visits to the two top spread bet firms, and plenty of spread betting ideas and strategies. But here's what you need to know for now.

> You can probably find my spread betting book in the bookshop near where you found this one, or else it's easy to order on the internet. This link will get you it for a discount:
>
> - **www.global-investor.com/nt**

First, let's find out why traders can't afford to be without a spread betting account.

When I say the words 'spread betting' to someone, their eyes glaze over.

Much easier to say the words: "Would you like another pint and some crisps?" Then the eyes light up.

However, I'm going to explain spread betting in a very simple way here. Don't be scared of spread betting – it is easy to understand.

I have used it more and more since I wrote the second edition and I've surprised myself by how much money I have made from these accounts: well over half a million quid between four of them. And those profits are all tax-free, too! My belief is that all investors and traders should use spread betting alongside their ISA to trade totally free from the clutches of the bowler-hatted Revenue men.

Okay, so explain what this strange-sounding activity actually is in a nutshell, please!

It's really simple. With spread betting, instead of buying or selling shares in the market, you are betting on the shares to go up or down with (what's essentially) a bookmaker. Which is why it's called spread *betting*!

The *spread* part simply comes from the fact that, as every trade is commission-free, firms make their money from the spread between the buy and sell price (that and the monumental losses that quite a lot of people build up through twatting around with leverage).

So, you're having a *bet* something is going to go up or down rather than making an investment in a company by buying its shares. You do not buy or sell any real shares at all in the process. It's like visiting a bookie at the races, rather than buying an actual share in a racing horse.

But why bother with it at all – why not just buy or sell shares in a normal account? What's the big deal about having a spread betting account?

Well, there are some amazing attractions.

Attractions of spread betting

Attraction #1: it's tax free

It's tax free because it's considered to be gambling. Governments reckon you are more likely to lose and don't fancy you being able to offset spread betting losses against tax!

Attraction #2: you can trade on credit – but be cautious!

Being able to trade on credit is quite amazing when you think about it. It's a bit like having a spread betting credit card.

For many trades, spread betting firms give you what's called *margin*. What this means in practice is many firms will let you buy shares on credit!

There is no sign up at the spread firms like in shops in dodgy areas to the effect of: 'Don't ask for credit or you'll get a punch in the mouth.' Indeed, the motto is more like:

> *'Please ask for credit and we will give you as much as we can.'*

Why are they so keen to give us credit? Well, spread firms make a profit out of every trade (winners and losers: the spread nets them something each time). Therefore it is in their interest for you to bet as much and as often as possible.

And boy, they give you a lot of credit. Give them £10,000 and in many cases you will be able to trade up to £100,000 of shares! In other words, you only have to put down 10% of the money to trade.

So you could buy ten grand's worth of a stock for just one grand. You're thinking: "Ah, now I can see why it's getting so popular … "

However, this must come with a warning. You shouldn't use all the credit available – the mantra *only bet with money you can afford to lose* must remain in place.

Attraction #3: bet on things to go down (short)

If you think the market is going to crash or you want some insurance against that happening, you can go *short*. (More on shorting a bit later in the book.)

Attraction #4: play the indices or commodities

With spread betting you can make money on whether the FTSE goes up or down, and ditto for the DOW. Or gold. Or oil, yen, sugar – loads of other things.

Attraction #5: You can bet on AIM shares tax-free

You can't put most AIM shares (the junior market) into an ISA. Without spread betting you would have to trade them outside an ISA, and if you made any big gains you would get taxed. So if you were lucky enough to make a lot of money on a couple of smaller AIM shares, the government would take a slice. You can avoid this with spread bets and bet on the smaller stocks tax-free!

Of course, as with anything that sounds too good to be true, there's always a downside isn't there?

So what are the downsides to spread betting then, Mr Naked?

Downsides of spread betting

Downside #1: wider spreads

Well, it's fair enough – the spread firms aren't a charity and part of the way they make money from you is by charging you a wider spread when you open your bet and when you take a profit or loss on it. So it costs. In other words, if the spread in the share market is 500 to sell and 501 to buy, expect the spread betting prices to be 498 to sell and 503 to buy. That's why they make a profit every time you bet!

Downside #2: longer-term trades get pricey

The longer you keep open a spread bet, the more it costs you. Every three months or so you have to close your bet and re-open it, which means you pay the spread again. And the further out you set the expiry date for your bet, the bigger the spread. More on that in a mo.

Downside #3: spread betting could make you over-trade

Spread bet sites are designed to be addictive. After all, the spread bet firms make more money the more you trade. It's very exciting to see the amount of money you are making or losing going up and down. And everything is made out to be as sweet and simple as chips. But this can make you trade too much, so beware!

Downside #4: losses are unlimited

If you don't set a guaranteed stop loss when opening your bet (which costs you even more on the spread) your losses aren't limited to your stake.

We'll discuss all of this shortly. But first I want to show you how easy it is to spread bet (either shares or indices). The best way to describe spread betting is to dive right in and look at some examples.

Example – a spread bet, long, and held to bet expiry

BSkyB shares are going up and you want some of the action. The shares are currently priced at 500–501 (500 to sell, 501 to buy) in the stock market.

However, your ISA is maxed out, and you only want a relatively short-term exposure (say three months), so you decide to take out a spread bet.

You log onto your spread betting firm's site (or give them a phone) and find the BSkyB spread betting price is 500–505 (i.e. 500 to sell, and 505 to buy).

Now it's very simple:

- If you think the shares are going *down*, you want to short them. Sell at 500p.

- If you think the shares are going *up*, you want to go long. Then Buy at 505p.

In this case, you think BSkyB shares are going up, so you buy at 505.

The next decision is how many pounds a point you want to stake. If you're very optimistic you'll bet a high amount, but if you're more cautious (and risk-averse) you'll bet a low amount. In this case, let's say you bet £10 a point.

The following table shows what your profit will be, depending on the BSkyB share price at expiry of your bet:

BSkyB price	Profit (£)
480	-250
485	-200
490	-150
495	-100
500	-50
505	0
510	+50
515	+100
520	+150
525	+200
530	+250
535	+300

For example, at bet expiry if the BSkyB share price is 530, you will make £250. (This is a cash profit that will be deposited in your spread betting account.) But if the BSkyB share price is 485 at bet expiry, you will lose £200.

The formula to work out your profit is simply:

```
stake amount x (final price - price bought at)
```

So, if the final price is 515, the calculation is:

```
£10 x (515 - 505) = £100 profit
```

If, instead of betting £10 per point, you had bet only £1 per point, then the profit numbers in the above table would be divided by 10. Or, if you had bet £100 per point, then the profit numbers in the above table would be multiplied by 10.

It's usually easiest just to think in terms of numbers of points made or lost. For example, if the BSkyB share price is 520 at bet expiry, then you've made 15 points (520 minus 505). Then simply multiply the points you have made by your original pounds per point.

Example – a spread bet, short, and held to bet expiry

In the previous example we looked at the case when you were *bullish* (optimistic) on BSkyB and so went *long* (i.e. you bought a spread bet).

In this example, we'll look at the case where you are *bearish* (pessimistic) on BSkyB and so will *short* it (i.e. you will sell a spread bet).

Don't get confused here: you don't have to own in order to sell. It's just the way they phrase a bet on something to go down.

To quickly recap prevailing prices:

- the **share price quote** is: 500–501

- the **spread betting quote** is: 500–505.

In the first example, you bought the spread bet at 505. This time you will sell at 500. Again, you will bet £10 per point.

The next table shows what your profit will be, depending on the BSkyB share price at the expiry of your bet.

As you can see, the profit profile of the trade is essentially the reverse of that in the first example. If the share price falls to 490 at bet expiry, then you make a profit of £100. But if the share is at 535 at bet expiry, you will lose £350.

BSkyB price	Profit (£)
480	+200
485	+150
490	+100
495	+50
500	0
505	-50
510	-100
515	-150
520	-200
525	-250
530	-300
535	-350

```
stake amount x (price sold at - final price)
```

So, if the final price is 495, the calculation is:

```
£10 x (500 - 495) = £100 profit
```

As before, just think in terms of points made or lost. And then multiply that by the pounds per point to get the cash profit.

Example – a spread bet, long, and closed before bet expiry

All spread bets have a date at which they expire. At expiry the bet is settled at the prevailing price in the underlying market. In the first example above, if the underlying market (BSkyB shares trading in the stock market) was priced at 520 at bet expiry, the spread bet is settled at 520. Expiry of a spread bet can be considered like the end of a horse race – when the result is known, and the winnings paid.

However, unlike a horse race, spread bets can be *closed out before expiry*.

Think about that for a moment – that's quite a useful facility.

Imagine placing a bet on a horse race and after two bends your horse is out in front. Wouldn't it be good if you could stop the race right there, and collect your winnings immediately? But you can't, you have to hold on to the end of the race, and possibly see your horse being overtaken by others.

But this isn't a problem with spread betting. You can effectively 'stop the race' whenever you like. This is what is meant by closing out before expiry.

This can happen because the spread betting firms are quoting prices all the time – even after the 'race' has started.

Let's look at the first example again.

You bought the spread bet at 505 for £10 per point. After a few days the spread bet price is 515–520. The price has moved up and you want to close your bet immediately and bank your profit, instead of waiting to expiry of the bet.

No problem. You close your bet by making an opposite bet. In other words:

1.   If you *bought* the bet originally (i.e. had a *long* position), you would close it by *selling* the bet.

2.   If you *sold* the bet originally (i.e. had a *short* position), you would close it by *buying* the bet.

In this case, you are long, and so you would close the bet by selling the bet (at the same pounds per point: £10). To recap, the spread bet price is 515–520, and so the selling price is 515.

The following table summarises the prices and action taken to open and then close out a bet before expiry:

Market action	Value
original spread bet price	500–505
spread bet bought at	505
stake (pounds per point)	£10
spread bet price a few days later	515–520
spread bet sold at (effectively closing the bet)	515
points made	10 (515 - 505)
profit	£100 (£10 x 10)

So, we can see that this facility is very powerful indeed. It allows the spread bettor to close bets when they're winning.

You can't do that at Goodwood!

Expiry dates

Most expiry dates for spread bets are set at three-monthly intervals – March, June, September and December. The expiry date itself is usually the third Tuesday of the month for shares, and the third Friday for indices.

Recently spread bet firms have tended to allow expiry well into the future – at IG Index, for example, you've been able to go nine months ahead.

I usually go for the furthest quarter possible. Otherwise you can go for a rolling daily. Here the spread is tight but you pay a small charge every day for keeping the bet open.

A rule of thumb is that a rolling bet usually works out at costing more after two to three weeks. But in the end there isn't that much in it so I wouldn't worry too much.

But one other thing to note: although you have chosen an expiry date you can *extend* that date if you want to. That's called ...

Rolling over

... rolling over. Normally, when your bet expires you will *have* to take your profit or loss – not a bad discipline. But you *can* keep a trade open by what's called a *rollover*.

A rollover means you close out the current trade, and open a new position in a spread bet with a further-out expiry date. Effectively, you roll over the position. You take your profit or loss and a whole new trade is set up. Unfortunately, you have to pay for this via a new spread, but most firms will give you a decent discount on that.

> Some people argue that you should just let all bets expire on their expiry date, clear your slate and start again. Some merit to that I think as it forces you to re-assess your current strategy.

Phew – that was a lot to get through. Still with me? Look, if you're not, don't worry, put your feet up and read it again. It will sink in, I promise. Took me a while to get my head round it too.

Dangers of over exposure

When you're spread betting, you get exposure to shares without putting up all the money you'd have to if betting on a normal share account. That's good and bad news.

For example, I could buy £10 a point of BSkyB – giving me, in effect, exposure to £5,000 of shares without having to put up the five grand. Most spread firms will allow you to trade that with only 10% upfront – so you'd only need to have £500 in your account.

This is called 'margin', 'leverage', 'gearing' and 'being an idiot'.

What happens if the shares sink 200 points and you suddenly owe £2,000?

Can you afford to pay?

And what happens if you open a lot of trades and they all go wrong, leaving you with a whopping great bill?

Always check your spread account. Think about a few worst-case scenarios and check carefully that you are not overdoing it, buying or shorting shares on tick. You must work out what your exposure is and whether you can afford that exposure.

Here is my handy cut-out-and-keep guide to spread bet exposure. Make sure you don't put on a bigger bet than you realise.

Cut-out-and-keep exposure check!

Spread bet size	Equivalent size in share market
£5 per point	500 shares
£10 per point	1,000 shares
£20 per point	2,000 shares
£50 per point	5,000 shares

Your bet	Share price (p)	Exposure
£10 per point	500	£5,000 (10 x 500)
£10 per point	1000	£10,000 (10 x 1000)
£20 per point	100	£2,000 (20 x 100)

> Exposure is where you have to be careful and make sure you are not playing with money you can't afford to lose.

(Cartoon from *The Naked Trader's Guide to Spread Betting*.)

Opening an account

In the days of yore, there were only two companies that took spread bets – IG Index and City Index – but now there are tons of spread bet companies with various offerings.

Many traders have two or three accounts and use different firms depending on a particular trade.

Some firms specialise in tiny bets, others have minimum stakes. Some have smaller spreads than others.

Beware of firms that offer very small spreads. Remember, they have to make a profit somewhere. You may find (and there are instances of this I know of) trouble 'closing out' a trade. The spread may mysteriously move against you when you try and take your profit or loss.

Most spread bet companies want you to win. That's because every time you put on a trade they should make money. They should simply put on whatever trade you make themselves in the market and they pocket the extra spread charged.

A winning client is more likely to carry on spread betting, and so make them a profit, whereas a client is more likely to call it a day after racking up losses.

But some companies take what can be described as an adversarial stance against you. You put on trades and they don't take out a similar trade in the market to ride the trade with you and just make money on the extra spread. In effect, they want you to lose! They want your trade to go wrong and so they cash in. In particular, they will do this against clients who mainly lose. If you're a winner, of course they will trade with you!

It's up to you to pick one or two firms – get to know them and see if you like the way you get treated. If you don't like them, there will always be plenty of others!

The two companies I personally now use most are Tradefair and IG Index.

I use Tradefair for bets on the bigger shares because its spreads tend to be very tight and the site easy to use.

And I use IG Index for bets on the smaller AIM shares as they tend to have the widest range of shares to bet on – they will pretty much quote everything on the market bar the really really tiny companies.

So if you are starting out I would recommend those two. I have visited both firms and I believe neither take an adversarial stance against you.

Both firms are happy to offer readers a little something, as well, which is always nice.

Check out **www.tradefair.com/promo/spreads/nakedtrader100** for a Tradefair account. They will offer you a nice credit of £100 right now. (If this link stops working check my website for any fresh offer.)

IG offer a pretty decent weekly educational programme at **www.igindex.co.uk/nakedtrader**.

Spreads and costs

There is no point in moaning about being charged extra spread whenever you do a deal with a spread betting firm. Remember, you do not have to pay commission when spread betting *and* you don't pay the dreaded stamp duty *and* you don't have to pay capital gains tax on any winnings.

How do the costs compare between normal trading and spread trading?

It's quite hard to work that one out. Different spread firms charge different spreads at different times. It also depends on how you like to trade.

Let's take the BSkyB example again, and work out a rough cost comparison between normal share dealing and spread trading.

In this example we will say the shares were 500–501 in the stock market and 500–505 in the spread market when the shares were bought.

Then we'll say the shares go up to 549–550 in the normal market and 548–553 in the spread market.

Normal share trade

- Buy 1,000 shares at 501p. Value = £5,010

- Buying costs: broker commission = £12.50; stamp duty = £25.05

- Sell 1,000 shares at 549p. Value = £5,490

- Selling costs: broker commission = £12.50

- Gross profit = £480. Costs = £50.05

- Net profit = £429.95

Spread trade

- Buy £10 a point at 505p. Sell at 548p. No costs.

- Profit = £430

The comparison trades are summarised in the following table:

	Shares	Spread bet
position opened	buy 1,000 shares at 501	buy at 505 for £10 per point
broker commission	£12.50	£0
stamp duty	£25.05	£0
position closed	sell 1,000 shares at 549	sell at 548 for £10 per point
broker commission	£12.50	£0
trade profit calculation	1,000 x (549 - 501) = £480	(548 - 505) x £10 = £430
Costs	£50.05	£0
net profit	£429.95	£430

So, not much in it there – and I reckon generally there is no difference.

It is probably cheaper to use spread betting if you are a larger trader (not particularly holding for the longish term) and you easily make more than £10,500 profit a year (the CGT allowance for 2011).

Say you'd already used up your capital gains tax allowance: top-rate taxpayers would have to pay 28% tax on our example profit of £430; a massive £120! In this case, it would be much better to spread bet than buy in the normal market. An ISA should be your first port of all, though.

I could come up with loads of different examples and each one would throw up a different cost comparison.

For example, Vodafone – the most actively traded share on the market – would probably be cheaper to spread bet as the spread will always be very tight. But a company with a 3–4% spread might be better off being traded elsewhere.

> The rule of thumb is: the tighter the spread given by the spread firm, the more cost-effective spread betting is.

Also, remember, if you are rolling over you are increasing your costs again.

Stop losses

I talk about normal stop losses elsewhere in the book. One of the greatest benefits of spread betting is that you can set a stop loss. They tend to get you out faster than a broker can.

This means discipline is imposed on you, and your trade will be closed out at your stated stop loss. It is much more difficult in the share market.

But there are a few points you should understand.

Let's say you've bought a BSkyB spread bet at 505p. You decide your stop loss should be about 50 points, so you set a stop at 455p. If the share goes below that, you'd rather take the loss now than rack up any more.

There are *two* different types of stop loss:

1. *Ordinary stop loss*

    The spread firm will try to get you out at the stop price, but if the share is moving fast you may end up being closed out at, say, 445p rather than 455p.

2. *Guaranteed stop loss*

    A guaranteed stop loss means what it says – you will be closed out at 455p. But a guaranteed stop loss will cost you a bit of extra spread, so your 505p buying price may be adjusted to something like 507p, costing you the equivalent of £20 on your £10 per point buy.

> I would say it's generally worth paying the extra spread and getting the guarantee if you are a very new trader. Once you are confident then perhaps it isn't worth paying the extra spread every time. I generally don't use guaranteed stops myself.

Take this example. You've bought BSkyB at 505p but a week later the company issues an early morning statement. The market doesn't like it and the shares open at 355p.

Under an ordinary stop loss you will be closed out at 355p – a full 100 points lower than your stop loss. That would cost you £1,000 more (at £10 per point) than if you'd used the guaranteed stop loss of 455p. Because the firm guaranteed you 455p, that's the price you'd get even though the shares opened at 355p.

Here's another view on guaranteed stop losses from one of my readers who is a profitable trader using spread bets:

> ❝ I think of the charge for the guaranteed stop losses as an insurance premium, debited via the greater quoted spread. It's an insurance policy with an agreed excess. You have to consider whether routinely paying the premium and occasionally falling foul of the excess whenever the stop loss is triggered – either by the real dive which you wanted protection against, or by the all-too-frequent momentary spikes in share price movement – is justifiable in relation to your own circumstances.
>
> It probably makes sense, especially in somebody's first year, and particularly where s/he is unable to constantly monitor the market. But the user needs to be aware that it is an expensive form of protection – thanks mainly to those unexpected and unwanted excess charges which kick in unnecessarily whenever a transient spike occurs or is engineered. They kick in far more often than the real situation of a share price collapse. What's more, the spread bet companies know that when the annoyed punter has been kicked out of a bet by one of these many false alarms, s/he will quite likely reopen the bet – paying the added spread again each time. ❞

One word of warning on stop losses in spread betting – as with those in your broker trading, set them at a decent point away from your trade. That's because, during the first few minutes of trading, spreads can be stupidly wide and you could get caught and stopped out on one rogue early trade.

I've had horror stories from several readers who got stopped out early in the morning by some rogue trade. And if your spread firm is especially nasty they might even close you out on purpose!

You must handle and control your stop losses in the best way you can and learn by experience. It could well be that the best plan is to use guaranteed stop losses on all your trades. At least then you know, and can control, your maximum possible loss.

Margin calls

This is a call you don't want to get! I'm glad to say I haven't had one since 1999!

A margin call means one or more of your positions are losing heavily and the spread firm wants to see the colour of your money. Don't worry, they are very discreet, so if you don't want your other half to know you've been losing they won't find out. (But keeping trading secret is never the best of ideas for long-term happiness.) They will normally ask you for the money needed to cover some of the losses you are racking up. The best solution is to use a debit card and hand the money over right away.

Is it a wake-up call?

If you get a margin call, you may also want to consider whether it is a wake-up call. Have your positions got away from you and should you close out, take the loss and go flat for a few days? Are you definitely playing with money you can afford to lose?

Be honest with yourself. Don't pretend the losses aren't too bad and you're 'gonna get them back'.

 When you get the margin call, treat it as a wake-up call!

If you owe a spread firm money, it is backed by the law – so they can send the boys round. Cough up!

The case of Nick Levene, who famously lost £50 million-plus spread betting, shows how big debts can mount up – quickly.

Spread firms have actually put some structures in place to try and stop this happening, and will call and email you very fast if you go over your limit. Even so, the above scenario could still happen.

Here are my thoughts on leverage.

Say you have £15,000 you can afford to lose and you want to spread bet. Put £5,000 into the spread account. This could give you access to £50,000 of shares. But only use a little of that leverage. In this situation, ensure you only give yourself access to £20,000 of shares. Once you have too much exposure, close out some positions or bank profits.

Spread betting strategies

My main uses of spread betting are (in no particular order):

- shorting FTSE 100 and FTSE 250 companies in a bear market

- buying companies when I'm out of cash in my ISA

- buying or selling the FTSE 100 index at certain times

- buying AIM stock to avoid capital gains tax.

I treat most trades as short-term (anything between a week and six months). But if they are going really well, I'll stick with them; I have held the odd spread bet for over a year.

> The major lesson I've learned with spread betting is: keep an open mind and change strategies as the market changes.

Just to make you aware of how volatile spread betting can be, a contact at a spread betting firm told me this story:

> *"A client opened an account and put £9k in. He turned it into £220k within a week. Sounds good. But two days later, he owed £40k!"*

So beware!

Playing the indices via spread betting

One of the advantages of spread betting is it does give you the chance to bet on the indices – although this is not something I do a lot of.

To spread bet the indices is similar to buying or selling a normal share. You're just betting on a number (in this case the index value) going up and down.

So, if the FTSE is, say, 6500, you can take out a quarterly or daily spread bet. You can buy at the offered price or sell at it. You can bet on it to go up or down. Or you can bet on the DOW, Nikkei or any other index.

As I've already said, I don't buy or sell the indices much, as to me it's just gambling. One use I do have for it is to have a short on the FTSE if the market has had a very good run and looks toppy.

For example, if you had a FTSE short open during 2008–2009 you could have made a lot of money!

Naked Trader's 10 golden rules for spread betting

1. Use it for shorter-term trading.

2. Beware of trading volatile indices.

3. Don't open too many positions.

4. Keep stakes to a level you can afford.

5. Be strict with your stop losses.

6. Make sure you know what you're doing!

7. Remember to trade the opposite way when closing.

8. A margin call could be a 'wake-up call'.

9. Consider a guaranteed stop loss on every trade.

10. Don't tell the wife how much you're losing.[*]

---

[*] That's a joke. If you're having to hide losses, STOP BETTING NOW. Gambling is even more dangerous in spread betting. Houses have been lost.

Shorting

One of the major uses of spread betting is shorting, where you are doing the opposite of buying a share. You make money if the stock goes *down*.

I would urge new investors to tread carefully before getting into shorting, but it's something that must be considered because it means you can make money during a period when the market is going down. And while I do urge caution, it is something you should learn about quite quickly.

There are various ways of shorting: CFDs, covered warrants and spread betting. But the easiest method is to spread bet. That would certainly be the method I would use first.

I usually have at least two short positions open.

Markets often turn down for quite a while and shorting could be the only way to make money. I tend to only take out short positions in quite large companies. The reason is mainly the spread. The spread firms usually quote much wider spreads in smaller companies, and for shorting purposes I find the spread is simply too much.

During crisis years I have held more shorts than longs (buys) because it made sense. I believe at some point in the future I will do the same again.

Hedging

Many investors use shorting as what's called a *hedge*. As we saw earlier, that's not something that separates you from the nosy neighbours; it's a way of protecting a long position.

For example, you may hold 5,000 shares in a company, but are worried for a short-term period (perhaps the company is about to announce results). You could sell the shares, and buy them back after the cloud has passed, but that could be very expensive (what with broker's commission and stamp duty). An alternative is to hold the shares, but take out a down spread bet in the company to an equivalent value of your holding. If bad things do happen, and the share price falls, the amount you lose on your share holding will be approximately offset by the gains in your spread bet trade.

Finding shorts

So how do you find shares that are going to go down and make you money?

Well, during the bear market of 2007–2009 it would have been easy: short anything and it would have made you some money! Ditto for early August 2011. And ditto for tech stocks in 2000 and 2001.

But outside of a bear market, you have to do the exact opposite of finding buys. You need to look for shares that are overvalued, on a downtrend; or, if the market is in a downturn, a share that should sink with it.

I am personally not much cop at trading indices, but I can see the point of setting up a FTSE short if you're generally holding loads of share buys and the SUK2 seems a bit intimidating. If something happens, like a terrorist event, and the FTSE 100 goes into free fall and your shares with it, at least you'll make some money.

However, I would advise you to hold off from shorting indices until you are confident in your trading.

Here are the kinds of things I look for in shares I'd like to be short of:

- **Profit warning**

  These tend to come in threes. If a share issues a profit warning there could be worse to come. This could be a good time to short. For example, furniture store Courts began issuing profit warnings long before it went bust – you could have shorted and made a killing.

- **General downtrend**

  A share that just keeps going down, maybe breaking through 52-week lows. It often means there is something amiss.

- **High P/E**

  If a company has a very high P/E or it's making, say, £5 million but has a market cap of £280 million, it may be all the promise (and more) shown by the company is already in the price and it could fall heavily on any negative news.

- **Watch for 'challenging'!**

  Check the latest reports on the share you're interested in shorting. If you see the words 'challenging', 'difficulties' or 'problems', then it could be worth a go!

- **Broken down through support**

  Remember earlier in the book I talked about support levels for shares? You don't remember? You skipped that bit? Bad reader! Go back and read it again. If a share has been coming back to a price a number of times and then falls through it, a lot of people sell up, pushing the price down even more, so it could be time to short. You can find shares going down through support by going to ADVFN's premium breakout lists but selecting breakout *downs* instead of ups. You should then get a nice list of shares that are breaking down and could be worth considering as a short.

- **Big debt**

  Check the net debt of the company – if it sits at much more than six times pre-tax profit, that could be a big burden.

My ideal short

My ideal short is on a share that is:

1. breaking down through support

2. in a sector that is not in favour

3. has issued a not-so-positive statement recently

4. is unlikely to be a bid target in the short-term.

Short example: Yell

One example of a short I made some good money on is Yell.

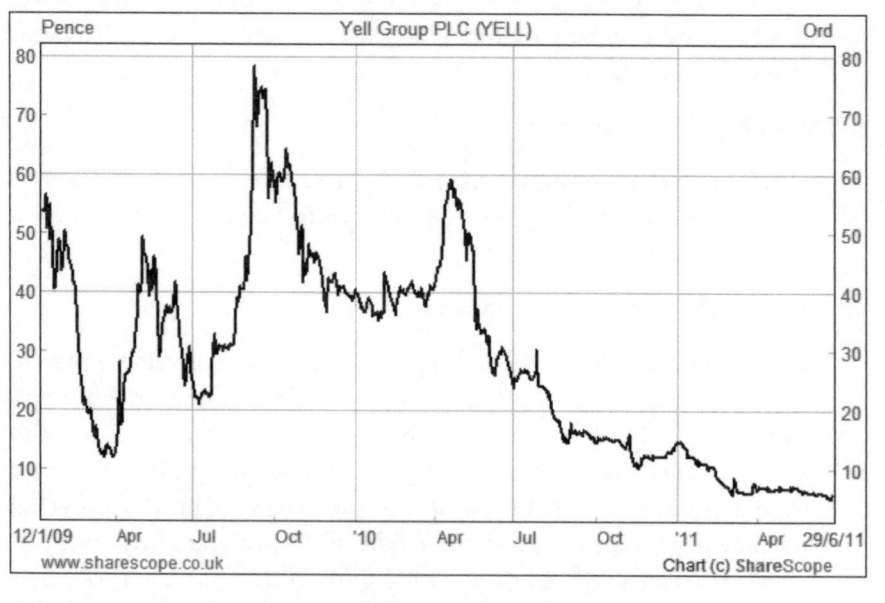

Yell (AKA Aaaaaaaaargh) (January 2009 – June 2011)

This one simply had a massive debt: something like £4 billion compared to profits of just £200 million! So I shorted at 50p or so – and it kept on falling ... all the way to under 10p. It was in an out-of-favour sector, too, which no doubt helped.

Some short DON'TS

- Don't go against the trend and short a share because it's already gone up a lot. It could go up an awful lot more!

- Don't short a share because some big market guru has. He's probably already in at a better price ... and he might be wrong!

- Don't short shares in a strong, generally rising market. Even if you're right, and it's a bad share, it could still go up with the market.

- Don't hold on to your shorts for too long [Robbie, please, have some self-respect! – Ed.] – consider them as much shorter-term trades than normal. If you see them starting to rise after you have obtained a good profit, it might be time to take your profits.

- If you're a bloke over 40: just don't wear short shorts in public. Well, someone had to tell you.

Remember: indices like the FTSE and Dow can move very fast – be very careful when shorting them that you don't get blown away by a big move.

What are the signs that the markets are going to go down?

You probably hear all the time about bull and bear markets:

- **Bull markets** are basically when shares go up most days, but with the odd sudden correction when shares fall for a short period (say a month).

- **Bear markets** are when shares are generally going down most days with the odd sudden upward thrust.

The good news is that bull markets last an awful lot longer than bear markets. Bulls go on for years and years, whereas bear ones usually only last a few years.

For example, a long bull run ended in mid-2000 (having had a blip in '98), and we then had a bear market for two years through to 2003. Many people thought the bull run had ended in May 2006, when share prices were savaged for a while, but it proved only a correction.

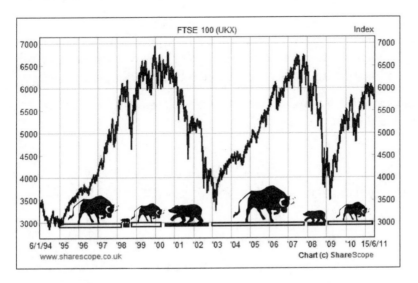

Bull, bear, bull, bear ...

There was another small correction in February 2007. Then it went up again for most of 2007.

Things really got bad in 2008 when the banking crisis caused a nasty fall for most of the year and for the first part of 2009.

After that things went back up, and got to around 6000.

Then, whilst I was writing this edition, the FTSE broke down through a previous tight range and started heading below 5500 on Euro and US debt worries, with shorters having a good time all the way.

What next? It's impossible to call. It could recover. But any move below 5000 would signal a bear market.

> The thing to remember is: don't believe everything you read in the papers or hear on TV from commentators. Just because they wear a natty suit (£129.99 M&S), doesn't mean they know what they're talking about.

Commentators/pundits use loads of jargon to make themselves sound good but they have no more idea than you or me really. So just because a commentator says the markets are about to crash doesn't mean he's right. The same is true if he says there is much further to go. Same goes for bulletin board gurus.

There is no point trying to forecast the markets. Best to trade the markets as they happen and don't expect to be able to sell your shares at the top and buy at the bottom – this is not something anyone can do.

Do you know what the biggest clues are that a bear market might be about to get underway?

Here they are ...

Incoming bear market signs

- Sunday newspaper headlines say things like: 'Markets soar as investors pile in', 'Our experts predict the FTSE will hit all-time highs'.

- You take a cab and the cabbie says: "Got some shares? Mine are doing really well."

- You visit the doctor or dentist and you see share prices instead of medical notes on his computer screen.

- A friend says: "I've got this really hot share tip, this company's got this amazing new product, everyone'll want it and you'll be in right at the bottom!"

- The bulletin boards are full of subject lines like "Fill ya boots with _____".

- Coffee shops are jammed with people paying £4 for a coffee.

- And the possible tipping point: Starbucks starts doing tastings and free coffee afternoons ...

> A bear market is a 6 to 18 month period when the kids get no pocket money, the wife gets no shopping and the husband gets no sex.

Other Instruments

CFDs

CFDs are becoming increasingly popular. It is easy to see why: no stamp duty, commissions are very low and the bid–offer spread is usually very narrow.

In fact, CFDs are probably now the instrument of choice for very active, short-term traders.

> I would advise new investors to avoid CFDs to begin with, as they are too easy to trade using credit and they could lead you to over-trade.

But once you are experienced there is no reason why you should not add them to your trading arsenal.

I don't tend to use them that much for the moment, because profits are subject to capital gains tax – unlike spread betting. However, I *do* use CFDs in my SIPP. And I have found that quite profitable.

If CFDs interest you, make sure you read up as much as you can about them and only go ahead when you're sure you know everything. Make sure you understand completely what you are doing first!

What are CFDs?

Instead of buying a share you are buying a contract for difference (hence CFD). In effect, like a spread bet, you are buying a contract with a bookmaker or broker, rather than buying the share directly.

So, if a share is 500 to sell and 501 to buy, you should be able to buy or sell a CFD at that price. The difference is:

- You can *sell* at 500, without having to own the share (i.e. you can short easily). So you can make money on it if it falls.

- You don't have to pay any stamp duty. But you *do* have to pay an interest charge each day instead; expect roughly 70p a day on a £5,000 long.

Because of the interest charge, CFDs should be treated as a shortish-term tool: say one day to three months.

Again, CFDs *are* liable to capital gains tax unlike spread betting.

My feeling is that it is worth looking at CFDs *after* you have used up your self-select ISA allowance. Remember, though, once you have used up your capital gains tax allowance you will have to pay tax on any CFD profit above this. (Bastards!)

You will find there are two types of CFDs:

1. *Straightforward* (no difference really to shares); expect to pay about £10 a deal.

2. *Direct market access* (DMA); expect to pay nearer £20 or a percentage.

With DMA CFDs you can put your order directly on the order book and therefore become, in effect, a market maker and try to buy at the sell price.

As this is generally a book for beginners, I'm going to leave it there. If you want to know how to place DMA orders, I can show you live at a seminar. Explaining it here would take too long.

I do believe CFDs are going to get more and more popular. The main thing if you open a CFD account is to take it slowly. Start with one or two small trades until you are certain you know what you are doing.

Remember: CFDs are not suitable for long-term investment. If you are thinking of buying a share with a one or two-year view, just buy it in the normal market as it will end up cheaper. **Six months max for CFDs, okay?**

Covered warrants

I gave a talk at a conference a while back and on after me was a speaker dealing with covered warrants. After he'd spoken for ten minutes, my wife nudged me and whispered:

"Look at that row over there, they're all fast asleep."

And indeed they were. In fact, some of them were dribbling a bit. Well I guess it had been a long day.

Covered warrants sound extremely boring, and they're also quite difficult to explain. Which is quite handy for me as this book is for beginners and they are a complex derivative, so I'm not going to cover them here.

If you want to learn about them, go to the bookshop on my website (**www.nakedtrader.co.uk**) and order the book *Covered Warrants* by Andrew McHattie. He is the expert on this subject and the book will tell you everything you need to know.

Warrants *are* useful and I do use them occasionally if I need to do any shorting for my pension fund. However, for the moment ... forget about them.

If you are a real beginner, I would suggest you leave covered warrants alone until you've had at least two years' experience of the markets.

Investment trusts

Investment trusts (ITs) are often overlooked by investors, but I've bought a few of these and made some decent profits.

Investment trusts are funds that buy shares in other companies. You invest in them just like normal shares – there's a buying and a selling price for each. Usually the investment trust has a theme, so it will buy shares of a particular kind and, in some cases, buy shares in other investment trusts.

In essence you are buying a fund. You buy or sell them just like a share.

For example, one investment trust I have profited from in the past is Resources Investment Trust (RIT), which buys shares in gold and mining companies. The argument being that if you buy RIT, you're getting exposure to this sector, diversified across a number of shares, and the benefits of a fund manager who knows the sector and does the legwork of research for you to select the best companies.

Okay, it doesn't always work out like that, but that's the theory.

I've also done well out of the Templeton Emerging Markets Trust. That gave me exposure to emerging markets. Alternatively, if you fancy getting exposure to the Japanese market you could buy a Japanese investment trust. Of if you fancy growth in India there's one that invests in Indian companies.

And so on.

One of my recent favourites has been the Montanaro IT – this one buys shares in small companies across Europe and has done very well. It would be difficult for you to buy smaller European companies; buying the Montanaro IT, they are bought for you. Easy.

There are many types of ITs specializing in smaller companies, pharmaceuticals, German markets, etc. The list is endless. ITs give you exposure to a sector you like the look of with a bit less risk than just buying one share in that sector.

Are they worth buying?

Well, why not? Personally, I don't buy that many or that often, and I treat buying them like any other share, though they do require a different research focus. Investment trusts rise and fall in line with their *net asset value* (NAV). This is a rough calculation of the value of the fund at a point in time. These get published monthly, weekly and even daily.

Certainly, having one or two ITs in a portfolio could be a solid move. But if you choose a risky one it will definitely be worth imposing a fairly tight stop loss.

Investment trust summary

- Research them as carefully as ordinary shares.

- Check the net asset value.

- Find out the top holdings and research them.

- Work out how risky/volatile the trust is.

- Make sure you want exposure to its particular market.

Part VII
Trading in Real Life

"Money won't buy happiness but it will pay the salaries of a large research staff to study the problem."

– Bill Vaughan

It Shouldn't Happen to a Share Trader ...

Top reasons traders lose

This chapter is about mistakes, cock-ups, blunders, gaffes, screw-ups, clangers ... you get the idea. It includes the top mistakes made by traders and investors, my biggest idiocies, and some horror stories from private investors.

If you've been losing money on the markets, I reckon you should find it all pretty enjoyable (or possibly painful)! But seriously, it's amazing what you can learn from making mistakes. I know I've learned a lot. And it really is true how many of us make exactly the same ones.

The secret is to learn from them.

It would have been next to impossible not to lose something or other during the years of 2007–2011. But at the very least losses could be kept low.

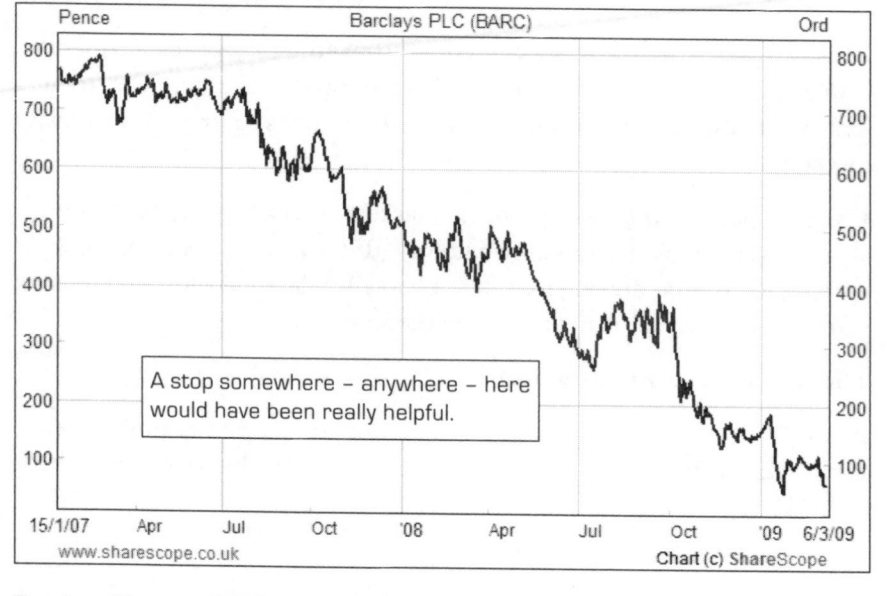

Hint: when you see Robert Peston (how irritating is he?) come up on the BBC news with a big red arrow behind him, get the hell out of the markets!

Top 20 mistakes

Like the strategies, just to give you that extra bit of value – a bit like Poundstretcher – I'm doubling the number of top mistakes covered in this book from ten to 20.

These come from mistakes that I have made in the past, and mistakes that other people have made and I have learned from.

The best thing you can actually do, in a way, is make a mistake. The lessons can be invaluable, and going forward you should be less accident-prone. There are no right and wrong answers to the markets but the following boobies can be easily avoided and will save you/make you money over time if you avoid them.

Mistake 1: not using stop losses

A stop somewhere – anywhere – here would have been really helpful.

Barclays (January 2007 – March 2009)

2007–2009 were pretty bad for stinkers! Especially if you owned, dare I say it, bank shares!

When the banking crisis hit, if you owned part of a bank, boy were you in trouble.

They all sank without exception. Even the big ones like Barclays (see the chart on the previous page) – which went all the way from 800p to 80p! A ten bugger, you might say.

(Sorry if you were in it.)

Then there was Lloyds. (Yikes!) And, dare I even mention this one ... Northern Rock?

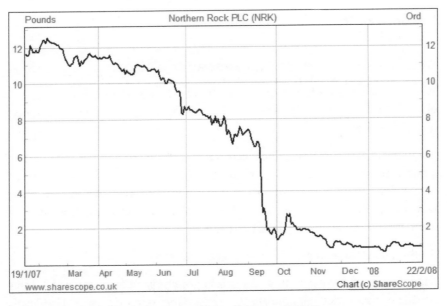

Northern Rock, crocked (January 2007 – February 2008)

Also caught up in the banking crisis were all kinds of other shares that tanked.

The lesson? When a sector is being hit like this for a very good reason that plainly will not go away or correct over night ... USE A STOP LOSS! If investors had used stops on their banking shares they would have taken small losses instead of huge ones.

The mantra 'Why didn't I get out of [insert crisis share here]?' rang out from everywhere. And investors found that no matter how far they fell, they just couldn't press that sell button.

Other shares then got hit by government spending cutbacks. Companies relying on government contracts like Connaught got badly hit – they went bust, catching many people out.

What's worse is that with a lot of these shares many people kept buying as they went down. They were trying to average down, but any reason for buying the shares had departed, which just meant they wasted more money. (See Mistake 12.)

In this kind of crisis: have the balls to get out and take your losses. Don't just sit there and see your money go down the drain.

It really is as simple as that. Once out, you can wait until the really bad crisis blows over and then perhaps consider getting back in.

Because then at least you have some capital left!

Mistake 2: setting stop losses too tight

We discussed this earlier in the book. So, yes, set a stop loss, but be careful on the stop level. It is silly to set too tight a stop as you will just get stopped out all the time!

If you're trading a volatile stock, setting a too tight stop all the time can be a particularly pointless move. It's understandable; you want to be out of something fast with a small loss by setting a tight stop. But the problem with doing this on volatile shares is that you are pretty much asking for each of your trades to be closed out too early.

So think carefully about where to place your stop.

Many traders get closed out as the market opens with wide spreads – don't be one of them. Set sensible stops a reasonable distance away. Use levels below resistance and support to make sure those stops do not get hit. The one that really annoyed me was in a share called Spirent. I bought at 107 and stupidly placed a stop at 102. This was really stupid. I was asking to get stopped out on a wider spread at 8am and of course I did!

I should have set it at 95p.

One good hint is to go through and check all your stops every night and ensure they are in the right place!

Mistake 3: not investing, or even trading ... just gambling

It's amazing how many people go gung-ho into the markets and just gamble!

I received an email from a 19-year-old who is obviously very intelligent and could end up being a good investor. But I despair when I read paragraphs like this (I've X'd out the company names):

> 66 I have read a lot of contradictory info on XX and XX across many of the message boards you will undoubtedly be familiar with. Being 5% to 10% down on both, reading this info begins to place doubt in my mind. I do however believe these are both potential ten-bagger shares. Could I have your views? 99

I take a look at the two shares he mentions. Oh boy. They both turn out to be tiny, illiquid penny shares that should not be touched with a barge pole the length of a pier.

For heaven's sake, one of them had a spread of 13% – you lose 13% just by buying it! Both were high risk, loss-making companies that could just as easily go bust as go up.

What my emailer – and so many other new investors who buy into these shares – don't realise, is that they are not investing, or even trading ... just gambling.

The words *ten bagger* is what really gets them going. Believe me, ten-times increases are highly unlikely to happen. Trouble is, it all seems so exciting to buy a share at 4p hoping it will become 40p. True, it does happen occasionally. But for every one that makes it, ten go bust.

You will simply lose money over time by buying rubbish and that's all there is to it.

People who make this mistake are invariably egged on by penny share pushers on the bulletin boards. Such pushers are only trying to get them buying something they haven't researched and know nothing about in the hope of getting a big, quick return themselves.

Mistake 4: buying companies with big debt

I covered this a little earlier in the book, but buying companies with big debt really is one of the biggest mistakes you can make.

The one thing no trader wants is to wake up one morning and get a lurching feeling in their stomach as they read:

"Shares suspended at request of company."

What's going on? Well, you hope it's good news. Maybe the company's about to be taken over and the share price is going to soar. But you kind of know something bad is probably up. And that possibly the share you're in … could be going bust.

Eeek!

How could you have made such a terrible mistake? It's a great share, it's been going up, directors were buying, it wasn't even really very risky! How are you going to tell your spouse you lost ten grand just like that?

Where did it all go wrong?

Did you check the debt?

If it went bust, it will, almost every time, be down to unsustainably large amounts of debt – and the banks have pulled the plug.

Remember my rule for debt (not including oil and mining): get the figure for the full-year pre-tax profit. Don't buy if the net debt is more than three times that. Remember to get both profit and debt from the latest results report from a company and not anywhere else. If you cannot find debt, look for net cash instead and use my traffic lights system!

A punter favourite that went bust was Aero Inventory – I remember going through this one at a seminar. Profits were rising as was everything else, but I immediately refused to touch it.

Why? Profit was £40m – but net debt? Nearly £500m! I thought anyone would be crazy to buy it. It went bust soon afterwards.

Same with poor old Woolworths. A tremendous debt. I do miss it, though – you could find all kinds of great crap in there.

Example – Homebuy ... definitely not a buy

Homebuy's results looked great in June 2006. Profits up 343% to £12m! The chairman said they were making 'excellent progress'. All the way through the report everything looked fantastic.

Why didn't I buy the shares after the great report?

When I read the Homebuy statement, at first glance I was very tempted to buy. The company had everything in it I like: a growing business, booming profits and turnover and an encouraging outlook. The shares looked like they had plenty of room for growth and I thought about buying some. But then, as usual, I used my traffic lights system to check the company's debt.

And my system picked out this sentence:

"Net bank indebtedness has increased from £28m to £78m."

Full-year profit for Homebuy? £12m. *With debt of £78m.* That's six and a half times profit. Way over my limit.

Once I established that, I had a look through the report using traffic lights again to find out what the banking facilities were (banking facilities are highlighted in blue by my traffic lights).

I was shocked. The banking facilities were just £75m. In other words:

They were already at the limit of what the banks were currently prepared to lend them!

At this point there was no way I was going to buy the shares. Although the company report was bullish in the extreme, the debt was way too high.

In the days following, the shares were tipped as a buy by many magazines, newspapers and tip sheets. And then, just a few days later, on 17 July, there was a further statement. Homebuy's chairman bought 25,000 shares at 231p, nearly £60,000 worth, and the deputy chairman bought 100,000 shares costing him a massive £231,000!

This provided the impetus for many other private investors to buy shares.

Amazingly, just a few days after these directors had bought shares, investors in Homebuy were greeted with this statement on the newswires:

> **"** Trading in the shares of Homebuy has been suspended at the company's request pending the outcome of discussions concerning further funding arrangements for the business. **"**

Homebuy went bust and shareholders never got anything back. *They lost all their money.* Judging from the bulletin boards, there were an awful lot of people who lost everything.

If they'd looked at the debt, they would never have bought.

Mistake 5: buying tipped shares

When you're new to buying shares, the biggest temptation is to buy shares you have seen tipped in the papers or a magazine or a tip sheet.

Be wary!

Firstly, if the tip is a very small company the market makers will see you coming a mile off, and the shares will be marked up before the market opens. If you buy, you will probably be buying at an inflated price. Market makers could well add 5% or more to the price of the share. And once they've got you in their clutches, what's the next thing they want you to do? Panic you into selling them – and that often works.

Using these wily tactics, the market makers will have sold you shares at a high price, and then buy them back off you at a much lower one. The only person who wins ... yes, you've guessed it, those dastardly market makers.

And with any tipped share, whatever its size, you'll see bogus uplift. This is where the bulletin boards come in handy. If a share is rising, che jck carefully it hasn't been tipped and you're not buying into a false rise.

Okay, so maybe you like the sound of the tipped share, but do your own research first before buying in. And if you still like it, maybe wait a week or two till the shares settle after the tip.

The worst tips to buy are the ones in the weekend press. So many more people read these but so too do the market makers.

Mistake 6: selling on ex-dividend day

You must know your ex-dividend dates! To warn you, ADVFN and other services have the code 'XD' by the share when you get a quote. If your share says XD and it has fallen, that could be the reason!

Why do investors sell on ex-date?

Because the share will have fallen from the off. Remember, shares normally drop on ex-dividend date by the amount of the dividend. So a 20p dividend share will drop 20p. What often happens on ex-day is you see a lot of small investors selling because they think the share they're in is going down fast!

But it's not really going down, because as the shareholder you are getting the equivalent of the drop in cash as a dividend. It's amazing the number of private investors who sell because they think their share is going down for a different reason. It may even be worth buying some more stock on the cheap when this silly blip happens.

So always, always check your ex-dates. If a share you own has dipped in price, it may just be because it's the ex-date.

Mistake 7: ignoring profit warnings/negatives

Profit warnings

It's crazy to buy into a company that has just produced a profit warning. And it's crazy to hold onto one of your shares that has just issued one.

It's more than likely it'll issue another one, and just because its share price has gone down doesn't mean it won't be going down some more!

Why take the risk? A profit warning means the company is in some kind of trouble or having problems. Why get, or remain, involved on the off chance of a quick bounce back?

A company issuing its first profit warning could even make a good shorting candidate.

Negatives

If you see the odd negative word creeping into the company's statements, don't hang in there, get out! Get the hell out! What's the point of being in a company with negatives coming out when you could be in a company with loads of positives?

Mistake 8: over-trading/smugness/greed

Sometimes traders have a good run and make some money.

Which is great. Except that after three or four winning trades they start to get a bit too smug and consider themselves masters of the universe. They feel they know everything and will never lose again.

And so, fuelled by an irresistible urge to carry on the good work, they go nuts and start to trade too much. The discipline goes (after all they are always right now) and soon the wins become losses.

I get told time and time again by spread betting firms, for example, of people who quickly make big money and then in just a few weeks not only lost the lot but began to go heavily into the margin and now owe them money!

"It's pure greed," said one. "They think they are king of the world when they start winning and blow it."

I guess it's the same as someone who wins a lot at the horses. He bets too much and ends up giving all the winnings back to the bookmaker.

Or someone who goes to a casino. A casino loves winners. Because they know the winners come back to win more. Then they lose and try and win back the money they lost and so lose even more.

So, if you've had some nice profits, don't be tempted to change your tactics. Stick to what you were doing and use your normal stakes.

And stop being so smug!

Mistake 9: buying boys-toys/one-product companies

If you're a woman reading this book, you'll know what I mean. Boys love toys! That is: gadgets, technology, *Star Trek*-type wizardry, computer games, new computer software, iPod imitators, in fact anything at all which has an *i* in front of it, things that go whirr … kzzpt, ping! – you know what I'm talking about.

And because boys love those toys, when boys look for shares they get drawn to companies that make the toys. There is a rationale behind it in their minds. The company that makes the gadget is going to go up in value 20 times because everyone is going to buy the toy they are developing!

This was the reason why so many of this type of investor lost money in the year 2000. They'd all bought into tech companies. And look what happened! Most of them went belly up. Or, at least, they lost huge percentages of their original values.

But lessons haven't been learned and investors still buy into tech companies with one or two products that may end up being a toy that's used in every household. Unfortunately, nine times out of ten a new technology struggles, time moves on and it becomes obsolete. I'm afraid there are dozens of these types of companies – and I can promise that boys will continue to buy them in the hope of that elusive big share win. Not everyone can be Apple.

Mistake 10: catching a falling knife

Don't try to catch a falling knife – it's an old stock market cliché, but it is so true. Don't be tempted to try and buy a share that keeps falling. This is the stock market. It is not like going to the sales and picking up a bargain.

One of the few traders I personally know loved buying fallers – he'd never buy anything I bought, because "it's gone up".

I wasn't so different when starting out. I thought I was pretty smart when I first began trading and I thought trying to buy into shares that had just plunged down a lot was a great idea.

Why?

Well, it's obvious! Surely because they've suddenly dropped a lot they must be a bargain, and they're going to go up! Buying shares that have come down a lot appeals to us traders – we start to think about how much money we'll make if the shares go back to their levels of just the previous day.

I remember the first falling knife I tried to catch: a textiles company called Hartstone. This was in the days before you could get prices on the internet. I used to watch the biggest percentage fallers page on Sky Text. I saw Hartstone shares had fallen from 450p to 280p on a profit warning. And they were starting to go back up …

Easy money? You bet.

Excitedly, I bought some shares at 280p. And what a flipping genius I turned out to be. Within two weeks the shares were at 320p and I had dreams of them going back towards 450p. Needless to say, I'd done zero research. Suddenly my dreams were shattered, another profit warning was announced and the shares slumped again – to 175p. I ended up getting out at 120p and with a lesson part-learned.

Only part-learned because I still tried to catch a falling knife another three or four times after that.

It doesn't only apply to me; buying shares that are falling is irresistible. Every single day of the trading year, you can look at ADVFN's list of the top percentage fallers of the day. You will find a share that's down by 20% – and inevitably you can watch as punters pile in to catch that knife.

Of course, during the noughties downturn there were any number of examples. The stop loss will always get you out. Use one!

Mistake 11: buying lots of penny shares

Beware of buying shares with a market cap of less than £15 million.

It might sound tempting to buy a company with, say, a market cap of £4 million. That's because you want to delude yourself that the company could really find its feet and suddenly quadruple its market cap, and you'll be in the money.

The fact is it is highly unlikely, and it's much more probable that you are buying a stinker. On top of that, they are usually very illiquid.

Some of the smallest AIM shares are the worst. They can fall very rapidly and often it can be hard to sell them if everyone else is trying to sell at the same time.

Shares in companies valued at less than £15m also have quite wide spreads, which make them even harder to make money on.

So unless you really think you have spotted a super company at the start of its life, steer clear.

I have met so many people that have bought them and had their fingers burned. The one that comes to mind most is called Provexis.

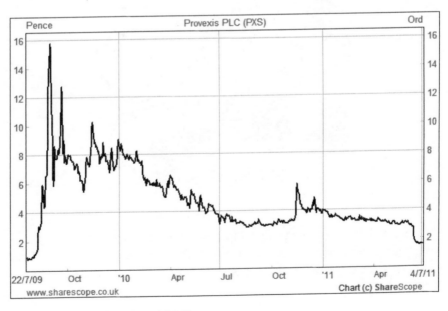

Provexis (July 2009 – July 2011)

I remember during one seminar everyone telling me they had bought in at around 15p. Apparently it had developed a new sweetener that was going to be bought by Coke or something. One chap excitedly told me in the bar afterwards that he'd bought millions of these shares and that it would turn him into a multimillionaire. It went to 3p.

I just really, really hope he got out in time.

Mistake 12: averaging down

Averaging down usually means. "I'm buying more of the crap share that I originally bought at a much higher price. It's fallen quite a bit, but if I get some at a lower price maybe I'll end up breaking even when the shares bounce back ... "

For example: you bought share X at 500p, it is now 400p and you buy the same number of X again at 400p. Your effective buying price is now 450p.

This means that at any price over 450p you're making money, whereas previously your break even was 500p. Good news, no?

No. This is a terrible strategy as your share is going down for a reason and if it goes down some more you will make even bigger losses. (And you've now almost doubled up your position size so your losses are going to be twice the size they would have been originally.)

Of course what you should have done is cut your losses on share X at 440p, got the hell out and moved on. This does not mean averaging down will never work, but more likely than not it won't.

It's far better to *average up*. That is, buy more of a share you've already bought and which is healthily rising.

So take my hint: don't average down in the hope you may break even!

Reader spot – holding on with your cold dead fingers

"I bought Tanfield at 366p and sold at 35p. The price dropped sharply over a two-week period, but I ignored all news and held on and on. Lesson: pay greater attention, respond to market news, drastic price movements and do something when a stop loss is hit. I learnt to let a share go, but not the cheapest way."

Mistake 13: trying to trade indices/day trading

Don't get involved with trading indices too early on in your investing life. Indices are things like the FTSE 100, the Dow, etc.

Index trading is very difficult. Indices move very fast and a winning position can turn into a big losing one in just an hour or two.

Say you decide the FTSE is going to go down or up and bet on that happening with a spread bet. The index can move fast and unless you can keep a very close eye on it, you can get in trouble. It is quite compelling. You see the FTSE 100 has fallen 70 points in the day and it's lunchtime. 'Well,' you muse to yourself, 'it can't fall much further. It'll probably go up from here!' So you take out a daily up bet. But it goes down some more and you get closed out at a loss.

Take it from me – this type of trading is hard.

Avoid it if you are new to the markets; this also applies to betting on all indices like the Dow and the NASDAQ.

Naked Trader says: index trading is like blind knife-throwing – not for beginners.

Mistake 14: hanging onto losers/snatching profits

I covered this a lot near the beginning of the book but it remains the biggest problem for newer traders. That is, hanging onto losing shares hoping they will go back up.

You have to learn to ditch the losers early. And the best way is by setting that stop loss discussed earlier. Quickly dump anything that is beginning to lose you a lot of money. If you have anything in your portfolio down by over 10% take a good look at it, and unless you really have a reason why it might come back it's usually best to bail.

Snatching at profits is the other big no-no. You need to be looking to make 20% plus on your trades even if it takes a while. If you are certain you have a good one, give it space to breathe and rise, and don't snatch at a very small profit – because if you do you will never make money overall!

Don't just take a profit because a share you bought has gone up 2p.

> You'll find this cutting losers/running winners theme running throughout all this book. I am hammering it home to you ... but it's on purpose.

It's one of the most important things to remember!

Do I have to carry on nagging you?

Mistake 15: buying against the trend or trying to spot a turn

This can end in disaster. You think, 'This company's share price has gone up quite a bit. It must be time for it to go down. I'll go short.' But it keeps going up, you keep your short open and you end up a sore loser. This can happen time and time again. Better to let the trend of your share dictate what you do than trying to guess when the trend has changed.

Try to follow trends and not go against them. Smart arses generally end up as just arses.

Remember: your few quid will be flattened by the rush of much bigger money. Trends stay in place longer than you think and they often go against all rational logic. Markets can be irrational far longer than you can stay solvent.

Mistake 16: buying small drugs companies

Many people get very excited about smaller drugs companies. They reckon all they need is for one such company to discover a drug that cures cancer (of course, let us hope this does happen) or another major illness. Then, having invested in their shares, they will wake up millionaires.

I just don't buy these companies. In all my trading years I have seen so many more failures than successes.

The biggest punter favourite that got hit really hard in 2011 was Renovo.

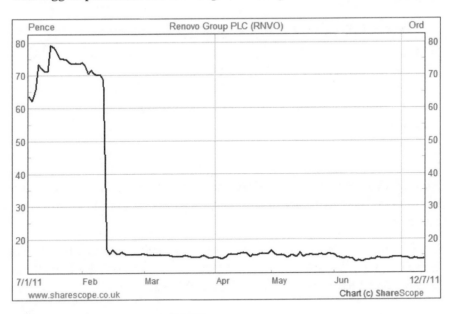

Renovo (January 2011 – July 2011)

Traders bought steadily into this one, up to nearly a pound. One morning they woke to the news that Renovo's flagship scar treatment hadn't met its goals in a major trial.

The shares sunk 70% the next day.

Cue plenty of wailing and gnashing of teeth. However, those investing should have realised what a major gamble this actually was. It's the same with lots of other smaller drugs companies. The share prices tend to get too high because of excited investors hoping for the big one. And then they collapse.

Mistake 17: buying just small oil and mining shares

It's amazing the amount of new traders who go into the market and solely buy small oil and mining exploration stocks and very little else. This really is crazy. Portfolios must be balanced.

I have met so many traders who lost fortunes backing a whole host of small oilers. Or actually, even worse, backing just one! Some really do put massive amounts into just one small oiler in the hope of making it big. But it is just too much of a risk.

Reader spot – a reader's lament

"I went crazy and bought just Desire Petroleum. And lots of it. Too much. Unfortunately I bought at 150 and now it sits at 40. What a lesson to learn. Wish I had bought other shares too, now. Having all my money in one has turned a single loss into a portfolio-wide disaster."

At least if you back a few, one might do well, but even then concentrating in one area – and an exceptionally volatile one at that – is still putting it all on one horse.

If your oil and mining shares are merely a sensibly controlled part of a complete portfolio, and a couple go bust on you, it won't be too bad. If they're all you have, you're in for a world of hurt.

Mistake 18: not running profits

Actually, running profits is one of the hardest things to do in trading. But it's amazing how much money you can make from keeping hold of a really good winner. We've discussed the 20–30% you should be aiming at. How do you know when to hold your nerve in reverses, or whether to hold on past this?

It's important you work it out. For example, I bought Petrofac in the mid-300s and held onto it while it kept on rising!

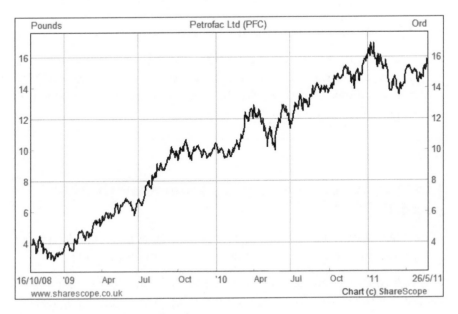

Petrofac (October 2008 – May 2011)

If I had taken the profit along the way I might have come out and never gone back in. This can happen so easily and has happened to me.

The best course of action if you're unsure whether to take a profit or not is this: pretend you never saw the share before. Would you buy it from new? Yes? Hold onto it then. This has helped me hold onto Petrofac even when it has gone down by 70 points on a bad market day.

If you have a winner, try not to let the market push you out of it, as long as no question marks appear.

Mistake 19: buying a system

Over the years I have never come across even one person who has bought a trading system that on its own has made them serious money.

Always ask the person selling you the system why they have not yet retired to the Caribbean with it.

The worst systems, I believe, are the ones which claim to be able to make you loads of money trading Forex/currencies. Nearly everyone loses trading Forex so it isn't possible. Don't fall for it.

Systems appeal to our laziness – something else is going to do the work for us, yippee! You lazy git. Do some work!

> ### Reader spot – systematically bad
>
> "I spent £3,000 buying the XXXXXX system. I was told it would be guaranteed profits. I was asked if I wanted to renew it after a year – I said I would love to, the only trouble was that I had lost £24,000 on it so far."

Mistake 20: buying directly from bulletin board pundits

Oh brother! I can't tell you how many emails I have had from devastated novice traders who have fallen for bulletin board writers.

I have seen it happen time and time and time again. There really is no excuse at all after you read this book for going onto a bulletin board and buying a share just because someone you never met tells you to fill your boots!

> ### Reader spot – on life support
>
> "My worst share was a biomedical company that is now barely alive. It fell from 300p to 15p. Gleaned from a BB, without due diligence on my part and too much deference to the poster's opinion."

Remember the bulletin board ramper is especially interested in getting you to buy small shares; the smaller the better. Sometimes the same person uses different nicknames to fake a buzz amongst BB posters.

Watch out for those who set themselves up as BB gurus. Don't fall for it and buy stuff just because they recommend it.

If you fall for the BB hype, there is only one person to blame: yourself!

And now, my big mistakes ...

... and the lessons learned!

Don't imagine I always get everything right. I certainly don't! I'm not like those dodgy tipsters who claim every little thing they do is magic. But over the years I've managed to put a stop to most of my original bad habits.

Coffee Republic

My worst trade ever was in Coffee Republic. First off, I bought the shares without doing any proper research. I bought them ... because there was a branch near where I lived and I liked their coffee. What kind of reason was that?

I bought loads at 28p. The share price started falling from the moment I bought it. I bought some more – averaging down. Coffee's got a great mark-up I argued to myself. The company will do better. I got emotionally involved with my local branch. I started buying more coffee in the hope it might drive up the share price ...

I started interfering:

"Why don't you put the muffins up there where people can see them?"

I asked the manager. After all, if everyone bought a muffin with their coffee the share price would start to rise.

I bought more at 8p. Then it became a terrible spiral. I was drinking so much coffee I was having sleepless nights for more than one reason. The company issued one bad report after another and eventually I sold at 3p, losing £8,000.

What a relief once I sold. And sod Coffee Republic.

I go to Starbucks now.

What were the mistakes I'd made. Want the list? Okay, I had:

1. got emotionally involved

2. hadn't set a stop loss

3. averaged down

4. threw good money after bad

5. ignored all the warnings.

Take heed and don't do as I did.

Senior

A slightly different mistake I made was selling a share too early, prompted by fear of losing profits.

I bought Senior shares at 25p. They did really well and doubled up to 50p. Hmm, I thought, yes that'll do – I think I'm going to take profits.

But I didn't do what I usually do and try and re-evaluate it. I never asked myself: if I was coming to this share for the first time, would I buy in at this point? I just lazily sold it. Guess what happened next?

It kept going up … and up … to more than 150p.

Why didn't I buy in again as it did so?

I let emotion get in the way. I decided the share was rubbish really, and hoped it would go down. What stupid trading from me.

And I thought I was the master of holding onto winners. No, sir.

Shares don't go up in a straight line and if you have a good one which falls slightly one day, if it still looks cheap, keep holding!

Want another mistake?

(Of course you do, you're lapping this up, I know. 'Robbie – what a plonker! Call yourself a shares expert, you pillock?')

Hardy Oil

Hardy Oil does not bring back happy memories. I simply bought too much of what was a risky oil stock. So when it plummeted overnight on some bad news, I lost more than a grand!

I'd bought in the late 400s and only got out at 350. 'Harmless punts', where research has been skimped on, or a lot of shares bought for no greater reason than gut feeling, are not victimless crimes!

And now it's time to move onto the mistakes made by some of the traders who read my website!

Traders' Tales

I got loads of emails after the last edition from those of you who thought Traders' Tales was a very important chapter. So here are some all-new stories that people have sent me which I think are excellently instructive. Especially as many have also shared the terrible lessons they have learned from making their mistakes.

Some of the stories are just awful. From people who have lost the lot, to people who lost a little but learned a lot, to those who started winning and then lost!

So, have a good read and stop and think carefully if at any point any of these stories start to apply to you.

(Identities have been disguised and some emails edited for length.)

The importance of protection

Charles's tale:

> ❝ I have a very sorry tale to tell. I lost around £250K and have precisely £89 in my bank account as of today. Mistakes? I've made more than a few.
>
> I used money I couldn't afford to lose. I was too quick to buy into shares. And I chased them when they started collapsing, out of

desperation. It actually didn't take too long to completely wipe me out.

Lessons I learned which I hope your readers will benefit from:

1. ALWAYS PROTECT YOUR CAPITAL. WITHOUT CAPITAL YOU ARE IMPOTENT. That means exposing your capital to measured risk *only* when the conditions are in your favour, i.e. the health of the general market and the fundamentals of the company you're investing both look good.

2. Investing is not a race but a learning process. Be measured in your decisions. Be patient, be very patient and only expose your capital to risk when the opportunity presents itself. October 2008, for instance, was without doubt the greatest buying opportunity in the last 20 years.

3. Never chase stocks. *Never chase stocks.* You will lose your money as sure as night follows day.

4. There will always be opportunities in the market.

5. Remain objective, calm, assured and remember that success is the result of HOW YOU respond to the markets. Psychology and emotion play such an important part when investing and trading. I became destructive, revengeful and bitter. Subconsciously I had decided to lose my money and take revenge against myself for making continuous errors. When in revenge mode exit the market and go for a run. Indeed go on holiday and forget the markets for a couple of weeks.

6. Being out of the market is taking a position, i.e. cash, similar to being long or indeed short.

I have no way back from here. I have lost my capital. I hope others don't.

I'm not sure what else to say except good luck to those who have decided to expose their capital to risk. It takes guts and courage to be a trader and shows a spirit of independence and a desire to take control of your future rather than remain a wage slave. **99**

NT comments: A real lesson here: be careful with capital. Really and honestly play *only with money you can afford to lose a lot of.*

Number five in Charles's list might be the most important lesson: avoid doing anything in revenge mode. Nothing worse than losing money in the market then trying to get revenge. It typically leads to worse losses.

Great story. I would like to thank this reader for being so brave and honest in admitting his tale in the first place.

I lost more than £100k thanks to bulletin boards

Andrew's tale:

66 The whole stock market thing really interested me and initially it was fun. I had (and still have) a reasonably well paid job. I did all of my own research and was moderately successful, investing small amounts and importantly had never heard of financial bulletin boards. Once I stumbled across these boards the rot started to set in. I believed the hype, the ramps, and started buying stocks which an experienced investor would not touch with a barge pole.

Obviously this increased my exposure and I ended up with over 20 AIM positions, which proved impossible to monitor. As each position amounted to no more than £500–£1,000, a 25% loss wasn't especially significant in isolation. But in total, losses were beginning to mount.

Naturally, I kept this information to myself and only discussed the winners. And through bulletin boards came the next step in futility, an introduction to leveraged markets. I recall reading a comment on a thread along the lines of, 'No investor should even think about leveraged products until they have invested successfully, buying and selling real shares.' With hindsight that was the best bit of advice I ever ignored!

I soon ramped up my bank, over-traded and I suppose it wasn't long before I suffered my first five-figure loss (it wouldn't be my last).

I turned to the indices and FX, spotting the potential to make a lot of money very quickly (or conversely lose a lot of money very quickly). Quite clearly I wasn't equipped to cope with such volatile markets, either from a knowledge or emotional perspective, but that didn't stop me trying.

Things weren't great in my personal life, and soon I didn't care if I won or lost (yeah, right) and ran up a number of credit cards to keep in the game – not to mention a personal loan.

It's difficult to describe the effect this had on my life, but take a spectrum somewhere between pissed-off and suicidal and you'll get the general idea. From having a generous disposable income to struggling to pay the mortgage was quite a feat in such a short time. Ultimately though, I did keep paying the bills and to my credit (I think) my house (and equity therein) was never really at risk.

So what lessons did I learn through this awful process? Some of the answers are already there of course: avoid leveraged products, BB hype, over-trading, emotional trading, gambling (because that is what it became), lack of knowledge/experience, reckless money management and on it goes. I imagine I have made every mistake in the book and the point of this email is to warn others.

I lost in excess of £100k. I was eventually declared a free man, and have spent the time since then addressing my debt (I could have bankrupted myself, but I feel honour-bound to repay the money I borrowed) and have reduced the figure considerably (I'm more than halfway there).

As far as trading is concerned I have gone back to basics, doing my own research, adopting a risk-averse strategy and putting into practice all those hard-won lessons. There is no quick and easy way to make a lot of money (unless you get lucky) and I truly despair at many of the posts I read on BB threads. Since I returned to trading seriously last year, my trading bank (albeit by circumstance relatively small) has increased threefold, but with a few blips on the way (old habits die hard).

Finally, I tell my story to remind myself to stay on the straight and narrow; I escaped from the abyss through the support of others, a belief in my own ability and a burning desire to succeed. That desire becomes ever stronger as I improve, but I won't let it lead me down the wrong path again. **99**

NT comments: I guess this excellent story speaks for itself, but the general lesson is: beware of bulletin boards and the influence that people you don't know could have on your trading. Don't believe everything you read at these places, especially when it comes to small penny shares. And the other thing, of course, is: don't trade if things in your life are going badly and you feel like you want to self-destruct.

Three early mistakes, then I made money!

William's tale:

❝ I started trading/investing whilst I was a student and had £500 spare. So what shares would a typical student buy who doesn't have a clue about trading/investing?

That's right, I bought a tiddler, Tadpole Technology, which I got for around 25p a share, thinking that I was going to turn my £500 into £50,000 in a year.

It went bust.

But I learnt my lesson … I thought. I then left trading until I had £1,000 spare. Obviously, having learnt my lesson, I wasn't going to buy a company offering 'jam tomorrow'. I was instead looking for a company that had huge potential … and fixed on oil company Desire Petroleum. So I bought DES at around 60p and watched it like a hawk.

I finally sold it for 28p (yes, near the bottom!).

That loss actually got me thinking for a very long time. Why was I making these mistakes? What was trading/investing really about? I really learnt some valuable lessons. When attempting a new venture such as trading, don't think you're more intelligent than people who do it for a living. Respect the market and approach it with caution.

So I started reading and paper trading for a while. Eventually, I learned how to avoid companies that are high risk, and I have made money.

Things I have learned along the way (not saying they're original, but hopefully my experience of getting on top of them will help others):

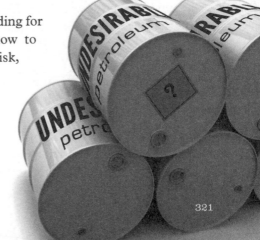

1. Let your winners run

How true the above statement is. Had I let my winners run I would be sitting on some bigger profits. One of the hardest things to do is to see a large profit on your screen and not be tempted to sell. You start justifying it to yourself by saying that the fundamentals aren't as strong as before, or where will the growth come from? Or markets are going bearish now.

This is where a detailed diary is handy. It should record not just why you chose that share but where will growth come from? Forecasts etc. also to be included and updated for each share you hold, especially when significant news (both good and bad) is out. Your diary should reflect all this so that when the market tanks and/or your share is down 5–10% you look at your diary which was written when you were making logical decisions and you can then decide on what to do.

2. Cut your losses

Outside of initial reckless stock-picking, most of my losses have been due to bad timing, lack of access to share price/news, and panicking. My remedy to this is to have an iPhone with decent software loaded on it, such as Shareprice, which I can check during the day. I'd also recommend signing up to an RNS alert that can bring critical news to your attention by text message (e.g. RNSzone or RNSAlarm). It only costs £5–£10 but could save you loads.

3. Minimise the number of high-risk shares in your portfolio

I know that 'high risk' could be subjective depending on each individual's appetite for risk. For example, I don't consider all AIM shares to be high-risk. But I tend to have only one to two high-risk shares in my portfolio, each with a real emphasis on the probability of high reward. I also don't understand mining shares at all and therefore do not touch them. If you minimise the number of high-risk shares your portfolio will be stronger.

4. Be sure of momentum (check volume!)

I saw a recurring theme in my trading which was that at times I was in boring shares that didn't do much for a while and then would bounce – but my patience was meanwhile *really* tested. I could have got out before they picked up. This goes down to timing. I think it is better to miss a few points and be sure of the trading volume, and that your share is truly going to be moving.

5. You won't get all your trades

I keep a diary of all the trades I am researching. I can't remember the amount of times I have missed a trade as I didn't see it move or didn't have an alarm. I compare the trades I make with the ones I have researched and find I have usually missed a number of trades due to not realising shares have risen or not having sufficient trading capital. **"**

NT comments: It's good to read a story about someone making money. Point three is the standout for me. If you have too many high risk shares you are heading for a fall! Good points to learn from here.

Lost the Desire

Paul's tale:

" About six months ago I decided I wanted to buy shares and try to make a part of my savings grow a little. I decided I could 'spare' £20k to see if I could earn some extra holiday money.

I didn't know anything at all about dealing, but blithely went ahead and started buying shares without doing any research. Luck stopped me losing everything – BP were at that time in trouble, so the shares were cheap, thank goodness, and I made a little as they went up.

But at the same time I made another of the mistakes in your list and grabbed quick profits like a 'real day trader'. Sigh.

Then – another mistake – I bought and sold different shares, making very tiny gains, all without research and going on sentiment on the bulletin boards. I was lucky. Just.

Then I became unlucky. I bought Desire Petroleum and I lost money. Not a lot to most people's thinking, but to me 25% of my original stake gone was a gut wrencher.

At the same time all my itty bitty profits seemed to have dissolved in fees and stamp duties and I was scratching my head trying to figure what I had done wrong. I should have been thinking: what had I done *right*? It would have been easier because it was a far shorter list!

I had done nothing right. All my shares were in AIM now, all of them had been bought without research, I sold too often and snatched tiny profits, and had nothing in an ISA (but then had no qualifying shares to use in one anyway) …

Desire Petroleum made me waver. But funnily enough, it also made me think and start looking for answers.

A free bulletin board mentioned your book, and then I read it and realised I had done it ALL wrong. I was damn lucky: December 2010 was a good month on my AIM shares and I was able to dump DES, crying inside at the HUGE loss but rejoicing that my balance sheet after six months showed I still had (just about) my original £20k stake left.

I could write off the last six months as a learning experience. 'Pretend' it was not real money, I was paper trading – yeah right. **"**

NT comments: Well, at least he ended up even. It could have been a lot worse. Interesting that this reader has actually learned by making mistakes. It looks like he will go onto better things. A risky oil stock like Desire: that is a memorable way to learn a lesson!

I nearly lost everything

Mike's tale:

" I had been buying shares/tracker funds for years and thought I could walk on water. I had made more per year through the late 90s than I could have earned as a wage. I had a good share portfolio and was doing very well indeed.

But I wanted more, so much more, driven by the fact that I wished to retire at 50.

So I got into CFDs without knowing what on earth they really were. I bought 1,500 contracts in one share at around 380. It went up, so I bought 5,000 more on the profit (still holding the initial 1,500). At around 430, I bought 5,000 more. Soon it was up to 501 and I was making a killing! So I bought 5,000 more at 510.

I was now holding 16,500 contracts. The share went all the way up to 586. I was so happy – on paper I had made a huge profit. I was invincible and a super trader! So very confident.

Meanwhile, I made a loss of £2,000 in another CFD position but learnt nothing from it. What was £2k when I was so far up on this one share?

I was paying around £300–£350 month in interest on my big successful trade, but the paper profits meant this was nothing … I never bothered looking at the global meltdown around me. And then the price started to fall.

I was too ignorant to act swiftly.

But it kept falling and falling. By the time I realised what was going on, I was way over my head but managed to close out the first two trades. I was left with an average purchase price of £5.05. The share fell down to around £1.08 that day. I was in trouble.

In this period, the broker moved the margin to 30% from 10% and placed a huge call and gave me until the end of the day for the funds. I borrowed on credit cards. I could not afford to lose; I had already sold every share I had to shore these contracts up. I borrowed from family, too. I actually had a wedding looming and my job was looking shaky. The next task was to borrow against the house.

I never told my family why I asked for funds, though they helped me all the same. Meanwhile I married my beautiful wife (a wedding which I paid for with a bank loan) who knew I was in trouble but was not in a position to help. I was so close to a complete nervous breakdown. Friends and family were growing concerned.

Soon we had a baby on the way, and a car that was on its last legs. Miraculously I managed to get a better-paid job a little closer to home, which helped with the funds. It was just enough to keep me going.

My health had suffered greatly, though, and when I hurt my back I was off work for weeks. It would have been easy to hit the bottle but I had a good upbringing whereby you face what you have done and sort it out.

The share has only just (January 2011) gone above the price at which I originally bought in. Now I am in profit and going on your course (and reading the book). I have set my stop losses and will now make a few quid on the buy price (ignore the thousands of pounds in interest I have paid). I have become quite hardy, although I am not sure why I did not have a complete nervous breakdown.

The moral of this story for me is: don't play with more than you can afford to lose, don't be a 'cocky sod' (that's over-confident in Northern speak), and ensure you understand what the hell you are doing and the risks involved. If you don't get it, then don't do it.

Before your readers start to slash their wrists, I have managed to re-build my portfolio and managed to make a good amount (for me) to the point where I've been able to make myself mortgage-free. Good things can happen, eventually. **"**

NT comments: Quite a dramatic story, and a serious warning, I think: never, ever, *ever* play with more money than you can completely, comfortably, safely afford to lose. And do not buy derivatives if you don't understand them. And always use at least some kind of stop loss!

You ought to never get in such a position. I hope this story might just save one of you out there that might be about to go down the same route. While you might note the story had a kind of happy ending, he knows he was really lucky. The share in question could have gone bust.

He is right, do not be cocky or smug.

I may have made a lot of money but I could easily give a lot of it back. My way round this is to only add the ISA money in every year. But to be honest, yes, I have on occasions felt cocky myself. And that is just when the market will come and kick you where it hurts.

Always treat it unemotionally, as a business.

Day-trading disaster

Alex's tale:

❝ I took two weeks off work to try out day trading. It's impossible: as soon as the momentum kicks in your order doesn't get filled so you get in late. You never know which stocks will trend steadily and the reversal is always sharp, meaning you get out with a tiny profit, if a profit at all. It's horrible. There could be any sort of news announcement completely reversing any share price action. And people that say they make money day trading! What a stressful, pointless waste of time.

I can't wait to get back to proper investing. It's noteworthy that the guys with the real money are the Jim Slaters, Warren Buffetts and fund managers like Jim Mellon of the world. They're not interested in making 20 pips a day! They must think day traders are clowns. ❞

NT comments: He's right. Day trading is vicious and not to be recommended for private traders if they intend to avoid having early heart attacks. The richest men in the world are not day traders. But quite a few are investors.

I took the loss

Dean's tale:

❝ I bought your *Naked Trader* book at the weekend. In all honesty, after reading it, I am not sure if I have the discipline to be a successful investor. But I did take your point on ditching loss-making shares, and I do feel that I can now can make more informed decisions about share selection.

I bought Hampson Industries earlier this year (a tipped share) and paid around 64.5 pence a share.

I have been stressing over it as I watched it languish since the moment I bought it, and finally on Wednesday I decided enough was enough.

I traded out yesterday at a loss of around 13% (though I had previously watched it drop to about 25%). I checked the news today to find the price had plummeted following a management interim statement this morning. I had absolutely no idea that this news was coming.

Yes I lost some money, and was a bit down yesterday, but it could have been far worse. I reckon had I not read your book I may still have been sitting on that share – so thanks! 〞

NT comments: Phew! Glad that you had the courage to take the loss. If only other traders managed to do the same thing! And I think that anyone can become a successful trader, as long as they're willing to ditch bad habits and put the effort in. You've already made a pretty good step. Remember: cut 10%+ losses with utter ruthlessness. Always.

Started off winning

Eric's tale:

〝 I started out in trading with a £2,000 bank. I saw the FTSE was plummeting and decided to short it. It kept going down so I sat at the screen and every time each trade went into profit, I opened another position, doing the same.

I doubled my bank in the day. But I was totally reckless, placing orders like a madman – but didn't appreciate it at all.

I had no idea how lucky I had been and assumed that things would keep going in my favour. Needless to say, I did not move my stop losses and lost the lot when the FTSE picked up again, including the original £2,000.

Insane or what!

In January 2009 I then got into RBS at 100p. I didn't set a stop loss and sold at 22p. 〞

NT comments: Oh dear. He really should have learned his lesson the first time, having gambled his winnings away. There's a chance it's the gambler in him that kept him from setting stops even after this.

Traders cannot be gamblers and remain in the markets long. If you find you can't shake gambling habits, it may be worth reconsidering trading altogether. I've said that anyone can become a trader, but actually there is an exception. Compulsive gamblers.

At it since 1965 and still make mistakes

Tim's tale:

    66 My worst ever trading idea – the worst EVER – began with the thought, 'Wow – Northern Rock Shares are down at four quid – gotta be worth a punt!'

A week or so later, having bought in, I was busy assuring myself: 'Northern Rock may have fallen to £2.50 but I won't worry. I know I'm down a bit but if I buy more, that makes perfect sense!' So I bought more.

And then, not long after this, I concluded: 'They are down at £1.50 now, it's got nowhere to go – but up! It makes even more sense to buy it. Doesn't it?' And so I bought even more.

northern crock

And then Northern Rock was nationalised.

I've been at it since 1965, and I still make stupid mistakes. Is everyone else like me? **99**

NT comments: Well you certainly weren't the only person to get caught out with Northern Rock shares. It seems nearly everyone bought some on the way down.

It goes to show: it doesn't matter how long you've been trading, it's still always easy to screw it up if you depart from the cardinal principle of cutting losses.

Took bad advice

Harry's tale:

❝ I took advice from an AIM broker called (erm, actually I'll leave the name out – I don't fancy being sued!). In total I 'invested' around £12k from 2004 onwards. With the exception of a couple of small profitable trades some time ago, my portfolio has plunged into a number of heavy loss-making positions. My holdings are currently worth about £4,300 – so I've lost two thirds of my money.

Two of the shares that they bought for me have gone bust. **❞**

NT comments: I hear this quite a lot. People give their money to experts to invest, thinking that nothing bad will happen. And sadly that's not always the case.

I have heard lots of tales of people losing money to 'brokers' handling it. Organisations calling themselves 'CFD advisory services' seem to be a recent source of such problems. They will gladly relieve you of your fortune in exchange for a very brief peace of mind.

Personally I think it's always better to try and handle your own money in the markets. And be wary of putting it into anything that looks high risk or offers the lure of big returns.

Lost after following magazine tip

Iain's tale:

❝ I lost £9k taking the advice of an investment magazine journalist. This was a covered warrant trade shorting the FTSE 250 that initially went nowhere, but started to slide. Over three or four weeks in the mag there were increasingly desperate-sounding articles emphasising that it was a matter of time until the next down leg. I believed it and watched the money drain away.

Eventually I pulled the plug. It was painful.

What did I learn? Never trade without a clear exit strategy. Never trade a geared instrument without a stop loss. Don't believe that the experts always get it right. This has absolutely hammered my confidence and I have not touched a warrant or spread bet for two months. **❞**

NT comments: Well you have to remember that journalists (I was one!) aren't on great money. You are probably taking advice from people who have to fill up empty space and who – with some exceptions, of course – are also obviously not good enough to trade themselves, or they wouldn't be working for the magazine.

Just because you see some idea advised, do not follow it unless you understand the risk.

And remember tips – however good – are invariably rendered useless (at least for a period of time) by canny market makers.

Rapid-fire drop

Stephen's tale:

> 66 I bought into Hardy Oil & Gas on the day they announced a dry well. Their shares had dropped 40% and I thought I could make a quick 10% in and out. The background to this was that I had got shaken out of Gulf Keystone Petroleum that morning in a rapid-fire 30% drop, before watching the share price rise to 15% above what I had sold at minutes earlier. I felt cheated, got mad and was determined to make up lost profit as quickly as possible.
>
> Well, Hardy Oil & Gas didn't go anywhere but down.
>
> After reading your book, I finally sold out at a 40% loss. Lessons learned: do thorough research, don't bottom pick, don't get mad! 99

NT comments: Well, if it's any consolation, I lost some money on Hardy too! The good news here is that it looks like you really did learn a lesson and you won't try and make a quick turn on a falling share for a long time.

It really seems like the most natural thing in the world to buy into something that has gone down. It must come back up! Not true ...

Bulletin Boards

It can be a lonely business buying and selling shares. But that's where the internet bulletin boards (BBs) come in.

The four most active and biggest bulletin boards are:

- ADVFN – **www.advfn.com** (click 'Free BB' or 'PBB' if you're a subscriber)

- Proactive Investors – **www.proactiveinvestors.co.uk** (click 'Forums')

- MoneyAM – **www.moneyam.com** (click 'Investors' Rooms')

- Interactive investor – **www.iii.co.uk** (click 'Community').

All BB contributors have to chose a nickname, so you have no idea who they are. If you want to contribute, you just register on the site, pick your nickname and you are away.

On ADVFN and MoneyAM, each topic is called a 'thread', and they appear in order of last updated. There are the main bulletin boards which are free, and both also have premium BBs which you pay a small amount to access. The premium boards attract a more serious investor and tend to be better.

BBs are like a big pub where blokes (generally) talk about shares in the same way they talk about football in the pub.

The main rule regarding the BBs is: treat them as light entertainment!

I used to be a contributor to the bulletin boards. But as my profile grew you can pretty much guess what happened. Every time I posted, some idiot would come on with something nasty about me.

I didn't mind at first – I figured I had put myself in the public eye so I could expect to be criticised. But I just got tired of it in the end. There are only so many online custard pies a person can take. I know it was just one or two people, but it was exhausting and distressing in the end. I guess they are the equivalent of spooky stalkers.

One guy got so obsessive he wrote about me all the time. Not just creepy but scary. I think he was a lonely pensioner with nothing else to do.

Bear in mind that many BB contributors are trying to push a share they've just bought. So treat everything you read with some scepticism. Especially comments on very small companies.

- A **bad sign** is if there are dozens of posters all enthusiastically discussing every tiny movement of a share. Even worse, if there are posters claiming it'll be a ten bagger and the like, or posters saying they've bought some and are going to buy more etc. And worst of all is when there is loads of inside bitching and backbiting between posters!

- The **best sign** is a reasoned, quiet but informed BB. It means the share concerned is actually more likely to be a winner.

Some bulletin boards are good, some not so good, and others a complete waste of time. There is a good filter function on the ADVFN BB. If you find a particular poster a waste of time, you can filter that poster so their posts just disappear from your screen and never appear in future. Handy!

My view on using them?

Well, I think the BB on the company you've just decided to buy is worth a quick look in case there is some additional info you missed. You never know.

Sometimes you might find some handy research done for you. For example, if it's a retailer some posters may have visited stores and reported back their findings. Quite often with oil stocks you can find very informed posters who know their way around oil exploration, digging for oil and the like.

Sometimes, really good BB posters will make life easy for you and will cut and paste in company statements and reports, dividend dates, etc.

However, don't take everything you read as accurate! Remember you are just using the BB to place another piece of the jigsaw.

Rampers and other species

'Rampers' is a term applied to those on BBs who continually talk up a share they are holding in the hope others will buy in and so raise the price of the share in question. They then hope to quickly sell on the strength generated and make a profit.

They will say or write anything to make you buy. They will often claim to have inside information or say there's a 'bid coming' or there's an amazing 'chart breakout'. They pick on the smallest shares in the market and make clever remarks about them intended to suck you into buying.

The lesson here: don't believe everything you read, especially if comments are made about an illiquid company with a small market cap.

There are different sorts of posters to bulletin boards:

1. **The complete idiots** who just like using naughty words or having fights with others.

2. **The really good posters** who are well-informed and come up with decent and well worked-out predictions.

3. **The wind-up merchants** who don't even trade and just like winding people up. Watch out for posters who can't post during the day. This is a big clue that they don't really trade much but want to appear authoritative.

4. **The in-and-out types.** They will breathlessly post their trades, one minute saying what a great share it is, then ten minutes later saying they sold because it wasn't moving. Best ignored.

5. **The gurus.** Often with their own blogs; they try to set themselves up as the wise ones. They will post trades but will quietly fail to mention the losers. Beware.

6. **Complete fantasists.** They really think they are the dog's proverbials even if they just have losers. Avoid.

7. **Approval seekers**. Will latch onto one poster and agree with everything they say for a bit, seeking their approval. It usually ends in tears.

Given time, you will work out which is which!

Do watch for those who claim to have inside information. Remember they are breaking the law if that's true.

And don't think you can hide behind a nickname. You can still get done for libel and if you deliberately post misinformation you can get hauled into court.

This has happened on a few occasions.

Summary

- BBs should be used mainly for entertainment purposes.

- Don't get conned into buying worthless shares.

- Treat everything you read as suspicious.

- It is worth reading a board before you buy a share.

The Market Can See You Coming

If it seems too good to be true – it is

I remember tuning into the revived Harry Enfield show a few years ago and seeing the sketch where the older bloke tries to chat up the young Polish coffee shop worker. The wife and I used to crease up because when we owned a café that is exactly what happened to our Eastern European employees – much to our amusement and that of the said workers. One customer even said to a young lady, "Would you like to come for a ride in my car?"

I digress! After that sketch, there was one about a trendy boutique owner in a rich area who bought crap and sold it at ridiculous prices to people with too much money because, as he gladly says: "I saw you coming."

It's similar with the stock market. From the moment you start trading, expect a barrage of emails, junk mail and phone calls.

Why's that?

Because a lot people will think – will *hope* – they've seen you coming.

As an inexperienced trader or investor, a lot of people want to make money out of you. There are loads of scams out there in the marketplace. These catch out new (and more experienced investors) time and time again.

The one thing that you can be sure of in the markets is: *if it seems too good to be true – it sodding well is!*

I get emails all the time from people asking whether so and so system works, or whether a £3,000 seminar will help them to make millions. No, is the answer, in both cases! But it's scary that it should even occur as a question. Because the markets seem bafflingly complex to outsiders (they're not), beginners are all too willing to credit the most ludicrous, expensive advice or products in attempting getting on top of them. Don't!

Seriously, some of these scam merchants should be locked up. There are *a lot* of scams out there. There are: phone calls from people offering to buy your shares from you at an amazing price; people who want to charge you for tips; bulletin board experts trying to get you to buy illiquid stock; companies with systems claiming they will make you loads of money. And a lot more. Ruddy sharks the lot of them.

Every time a scam is offered to you it will always seem like a great deal. But trust me: all they want is your money.

> Do not give out your real email address when you register for anything. Set up what I call a dump mail. For example, when I sign up for anything and have to register I use the mail address junkmaildump@etc, etc. It's a real address, but not one I ever use. It means the mailbox I *do* use doesn't get bunged up with spam.

Also, think carefully before you give out your real phone number to anyone connected to the finance world. Otherwise you will get inundated with phone calls. Check with whoever wants your phone number that it does not get sold on.

It sounds horrible, but think of everyone out there in the wonderful world of shares as your implacable enemy, unless over time you are convinced otherwise. The friendlier they appear, the more likely it is you will get led up the garden path (before being relieved of your wallet and pushed into the garden pond).

Of course, it is very tempting to believe a trading system works and you just have to follow it to make money, or someone will tip you the right shares. But ignore all offers and concentrate on learning about the markets slowly and cautiously – do not get side-tracked by the easy way out. It's invariably a trap door to somewhere nasty.

Here are some particular scams to watch out for.

Scams

Phone calls/boiler rooms

Phone calls from 'boiler rooms' often come from America. A plausible sounding bloke opens up with a question like: "You handle your own portfolio, how's it going?" When you mumble something like "It's going okay," he'll start his sales pitch. He has an incredible stock that is going to treble in a few weeks and he's offering *you* the chance to get in!

It could be one of a couple of scams.

This bloke will probably claim to be from a broker who can let you have this wonder stock cheaper than the current market price. What this *really* means is he, or even a reputable-sounding broker, has bought a shed-load of stock in a crap company and wants to offload some to you at a worse price, thereby making a guaranteed profit.

Or it could be worse; you could send your money off and not even get that pile of rubbish in return!

Alternatively, the call could come from a UK company offering tips or shares at a knockdown price. Again the share is likely to be a small penny share and they are trying to make money out of you in the same way as above.

Ignore all these and just hang up. You are unlikely to get rich quick and are more likely to become considerably poor.

Before hanging up, ask them where they got your phone number and try to get off the list – otherwise, in my experience, you'll be inundated with phone calls.

Here's a reader who just this week emailed me this very useful piece of info:

❝ Never buy a stock from a cold call or email. If it's that good, why are they ringing you and not eagerly purchasing it themselves? I have been called three times this month alone with boiler room scams. Just tell them you are not interested. If you really want to have a look at the stock (you think it's a real deal) then check out the details of the company, and the firm pushing it to you. Here are a few tips for doing so:

1. Use **whois.domaintools.com** – this will tell you when their websites were created (normally, if it's a scam or fly-by-night, this will be recently).

2. Check the IP address of any email you've received by using **whatismyipaddress.com/trace-email**. If it's not in the country they say they are emailing from, you're usually dealing with a scam.

This should be sufficient to find the scammers.

And always remember: it is a lot better to say 'I wish I had put some money into that, it's doubled', than 'I wish I hadn't bothered with that one, I have lost all my cash.' There will always be other profitable shares. There will not always be other cash you can use to trade! **❞**

Newspaper/magazine get-rich ads

I'm sure you've seen these. They usually say something like:

"Learn stock market secrets … "

or:

"Make £400 a day from home … "

What happens is you get enticed to a free seminar. The guru will talk about things like spread betting and technical analysis and then spend the rest of the time trying to flog his work manuals, books, and another paid-for seminar or expensive software. Sometimes the sell can be very hard indeed. (*Lock the doors, gentlemen, I have a proposition for these good people!*)

The plain fact (again) is: if it seems too good to be true, it invariably is.

It is highly unlikely you'll make half a grand a day or other ridiculous figures that get bandied about. The guru will make money out of *you* by selling you his books, videos and courses. Again, all you have to do is ask yourself: if the guru is such a phenomenal genius why doesn't he sit at home with his systems, rack up the millions and just be happy?

I'm not saying all such systems and all software are no good. I just don't think these are a great way to learn how to make a start in the stock market.

Seminars

My seminars are brilliant (of course), but watch out for the ones that demand a lot of money, £3,000 and the like. They usually suck you in by offering a free seminar, which is where a heavy sell is used to get you to stump up for the expensive seminar, where they will reveal 'the true secrets' of the market. I'm pretty dubious about these and haven't heard from anyone who has genuinely benefited or thought they were worth the money.

What they usually do is spend hours teaching you market gobbledegook. One good trick: ask to see their trading accounts!

> There's no substitute for learning to do your own research and gradually learning the ins and outs of trading.

Scams summary

- Don't buy shares offered over the phone.

- Be sceptical about 'get rich' ads.

- Software may be an expensive waste of money.

- Don't take the 'easy' way – take time to learn about the markets.

Tipsters – the bad

I'm afraid to say the market is littered with an assortment of what I can only describe as 'dodgy geezers' wanting to take your money in return for their hot tips. Some will even offer free tips, but of course they will exploit your email address or inundate you with offers of paid-for tips.

There are loads of share tipsters around, as you will very quickly find out. They usually charge a fee for access to tips, or they come in the form of a monthly newsletter. Like entertainers, they all have some kind of shtick to pull you in. Some claim to be maverick City insiders. Others 'read the charts and the signals'.

Every single tipster will quote what seems like amazing performance figures:

> *"Our tips are up 40% this year!"*

> *"Amazing profit every year!"*

> *"Three penny shares that are about to rocket … !"*

What they don't brag about is the ones they picked that halved in value or even went bust. So you won't see headlines like:

> *"We tipped a share and – whoops – it went bust."*

There'll usually be a list of shares with percentage profits made against each one. Amazingly, you'll see hardly any losing shares. Obviously following these geniuses is a license to print money!

Sadly, their claims are unlikely to be realistic. Some tipsters are very clever and use various manipulations of statistics to show performance that often just isn't true. Something else you won't find in their claims: all their tips that have gone south or gone bust. You'll only see the winners highlighted. My cat could have picked some of those by sticking her paw at random on the share prices in the *FT*!

Nearly all of the dodgy tipping organisations tip very small penny shares. You won't find them tipping many bigger companies. That's because in percentage terms they only have to hit on one or two big winners (out of the dozens of companies they tip).

Here are just some of the ways they create amazing performance figures.

Tipster tricks

They often use 'mid' prices. Never the real buy and sell prices. With the small company shares they tip, this means they are already up on the percentage game.

Let's take an example. A tipster tips a share that is 9p to sell and 10p to buy. So the tipster says his tip is at 9.5p – the mid price. No one can actually buy at this price, but never mind! The tip is published in a tip sheet at the weekend. On Monday, before the market opens, the market makers have seen the tip and raise the price to 10p to sell and 11p to buy (the mid price is now 10.5p). Subscribers buy in at 11p, but the tipster can now claim to have profits of an amazing 10%! (The difference between his mid-price tip at 9.5p, and the new mid price of 10.5p.)

What has actually happened is that those who bought the tip are already nursing *losses* of nearly 10%. They've bought in at the real buy price of 11p, but the selling price is only 10p!

What's worse is that the market makers know the mug punters have bought at 11p and during the next few days will drop the price, and those who bought will suffer even worse losses.

The tipster doesn't care: that now goes down as a 10% profit. On the table of winners it will show: tip 9.5p, high 10.5p, +10%!

But none of the subscribers could possibly have bought or sold at these prices.

Of course, most of the tipsters tip anything from 50 to 200 companies a year. There's no way subscribers could afford to buy that many of them.

So even when a tipster manages to tip a big winner, chances are the subscriber won't have bought it. It's Sod's Law, but they will probably buy the one that's gone bust!

None of it matters because, while people are cancelling subscriptions, there are always new mugs ready to start up subscriptions.

In particular, tipping publications love direct debit payments. That's because us Brits are so lazy we rarely cancel them, so they carry on taking money off you long after you've tired of losing money!

Tipsters – the good

Okay, of course, as with everything, there *are* some good tipsters out there. There are probably five or six names that are worth paying attention to. If you can find someone tipping who trades as well, that would be an advantage. Alternatively, someone who specialises in certain shares, for example those listed on the FTSE 350.

But if you don't feel like finding your own shares, how can you find the good tipping services?

It'll be difficult, and is another reason why you shouldn't be so lazy! The clue is to ask around. Try the bulletin boards, put up a message: 'Is so-and-so's tipping service any good? Have you made money by following the tips?'

Bulletin board writers are notoriously difficult to please, so if you do read a number of plaudits for a tipping service, then maybe, just maybe, it's worth a look. (Make sure all of the accounts aren't freshly registered and suspiciously united in praise, though.)

If you do subscribe to a tipster service, don't just buy the tipped shares automatically. Do your own research. Look on the tips as a possible basis for further research (always check the debt!). Monitor the service carefully and write down the real prices you could have bought or sold at and judge performance yourself.

If you subscribe to tip sheets, you must only use them to help you generate ideas.

Tips and market makers

And, whatever you do, don't buy a tip right away. **The market makers will have marked up the tips and if you buy right away the price will be far too high.** Wait for a few days for the share to settle down.

The other sort of tips you get are the free ones in investment magazines and newspapers. Again, beware of the market maker mark-up – these shares should not be bought (or sold) right away. Be especially careful of buying tips in the Sunday papers, as on a quiet Monday morning these will already be higher and you will be paying far too much.

In addition, remember these tips are being written by journalists. Many are probably only on £25k a year. If they were any good at picking shares they'd be trading full-time themselves! They are also under pressure to regularly come up with tips and ideas, so they are not necessarily going to be much good.

There are writers out there who are different, and do it for the love of investing (and even waive their fees). Take a closer look at them.

Tipsters summary

- Be sceptical of the performance figures quoted.

- Tips are marked up before you can buy.

- Do you really need a guru?

Systems

Everywhere you look in the stock market, someone somewhere will be trying to sell you a system. Not just the devious scammers we looked at earlier. Even vaguely legitimate outfits. They're not quite as seedy as the scammers, but will be just as bad for your wallet.

These people promise you the world:

"Spend just five minutes a day and make big profits."

"Our system picks all the trades for you."

"Trade from home and make a living from the markets – with no experience."

But just think about it.

Don't you think that if the people that came up with the systems had devised an easy way to make millions they'd keep it to themselves and end up in Barbados sunbathing? Don't be fooled by promises of big profits for no effort. And take anything they say, like their 'record of profits', with a giant pinch of salt.

The only dependable 'system' is to learn about trading slowly but surely through hard work and decent research. You get nothing for nothing. Ignore the ads and bin the junk mail.

Of course it is tempting: the system sellers are clever and they are playing on our inherent laziness (well I'm lazy, and I don't mind admitting it).

It sounds lovely: a computer will do all the work for you. Pure science fiction, I'm afraid.

Part VIII
The End (Almost)

"The ultimate risk is not taking a risk."

– Sir James Goldsmith

The Naked Trader Rules

I'm not really one for rules. I've always hated authority, so rules and me don't often get along. But I thought to finish up I'd set out a few of my investing rules, especially for the new investor.

You're not going to lose everything you have if you don't follow them. But after you finish reading this book and it's tossed on top of a lot of other dusty financial tomes ... and you come back to it one day ... these rules are a pretty good summary of what I've been banging on about.

They are in no particular order. In other words, number 1 has no more importance than number 30. Because they're all equally important!

Just for fun, five of them are WRONG. If you have read the book you should spot them!

The rules

1.   Only play with money you can really afford to lose. Be honest with yourself.

2.   Get the whole story about a company before you buy. Learn everything about it.

3.   Don't rush into anything or chase a share price. There's always another share coming along in a minute.

4.   Buy penny shares – after all, they can easily become ten baggers.

5.   Be wary of buying into systems promising you thousands of pounds for no work. If it's too good to be true, it probably is.

6.   Don't buy a share because someone on a bulletin board says it's going to double.

7.   Buy tips you see in the newspapers – journalists know what they're talking about.

8.   Cut your losses fast if you've bought a share and it's tanking.

9.   Don't take profits too quickly. If you've got a good share and it's slowly heading up, stick with it. Run your winners.

10. Don't be panicked out of a good share if it goes down for a day. The market makers may be trying to get your shares cheaply.

11. Beware of buying a share just because a director bought some. They can get it wrong. Some shares have gone bust two weeks after a director buy.

12. If you are buying more than £3,000 of a small share, check its exchange market size. If it is below £1,000 of shares, you may have trouble when it comes to selling them.

13. Never catch a falling knife. That means: don't buy a share because it's gone down a lot. Better to buy shares that are going up. That falling share may be a bargain – but end up even cheaper first. Or it may be a stinker that doesn't stop stinking.

14. In a general market downturn, think about using a FTSE short or SUK2.

15. Don't buy a share after a profit warning (like London buses, they often come in threes, so the first may not be the last).

16. Check the spread between the buying and selling prices. If it's more than 5%, the share could be far too risky.

17. Beware of buying before 9am – the spreads can be at their widest. Don't be suckered into buying a share at a silly price early on.

18. Don't buy and sell indices like the FTSE 100 or the Dow, especially if you are a new investor. It's just gambling.

19. Be careful with mining and oil exploration stocks. One bad report can see these shares tumble. They are impossible to value properly. You don't have to entirely avoid them, but caution should be your watchword.

20. Don't buy companies that are making a loss. You're gambling they'll make a profit one day. It may never happen.

21. Think about buying after a Black Swan event.

22. Use all the credit/leverage you can get hold of when spread betting.

23. Use stop losses. Set them around 10% away from your buying price and don't hesitate to act on them.

24. Try to have a plan with every share. Think about what your exit price will be.

25. Shares are for buying and selling. Do run profits but also take them sometimes.

26. Don't get involved with things you don't understand. So don't buy CFDs or covered warrants if you don't fully understand them.

27. Beware of trading too much on margin. Using money that isn't yours may feel clever, right up until the point where you start losing money that isn't yours. Think about what your losses could be and whether you can afford to cover them.

28. If you're losing heavily it may be best to cut all your positions and come back to the market another time.

29. Don't over-trade. Keep to about 8–10 open positions. Any more and you are going to have trouble keeping on top of them.

30. Beware of overconfidence. If you're on a winning run don't start increasing the size of your positions.

31. Don't only go long; do think about shorting stocks. This is not for beginners, though.

32. Be careful about relying on one method of stock picking. Cover all the angles.

33. Watch for tipping points. Don't lose control of your investments. Stay calm.

34. It's fun to gamble, pick a stock at random sometimes.

35. Always check your ex-dividend dates. Your share will fall on this date for the amount of the dividend, so don't panic.

36. Open more than one broking account. Then you can compare their services and systems.

37. Don't rely solely on charts, but certainly use them – along with other tools – to help your trading decisions.

38. Read the financial press – some of it is rubbish but you must keep in touch with what's going on.

39. Always 'average down' and buy more shares in one you're already losing badly on as you may end up breaking even.

40. Remember the good advice of Corporal Jones in *Dad's Army*: "Don't panic!"

Find out which rules were wrong at the bottom of the page*. Well done if you spotted all five!

---

* Wrong rules: 4, 7, 22, 34, 39.

 # Finally ...

I'm almost off – this book is nearly over.

In fact I'm about to shout for joy, given I don't find writing that easy and it's all been a right pain in the neck [I noticed! – Ed.]. I just hope, dear reader, that at least something in this book will help you along the way.

But before I do go, I thought I'd reiterate some of the main points in the book.

Simple questions to ask yourself before making a trade

Here are a few questions you should know the answers to before making a trade. If you really don't know the answer to all these questions before you trade, don't bloody well trade, okay?

1. Why do you think the **share is going to go up**? If you can't think of a reason, why are you buying it?

2. What is your **timescale**? Are you in for a quick buck, are you looking at two months, six months or two years? What sort of trade is it?

3. Why are you buying **right now**? If the share is going down, are you buying at the right time?

4. **How much money** are you going to put in and why?

5. Do you know how much you are hoping to make (**profit target**), and how much you are willing to lose (**stop loss**)?

Tipping point

Well, the tipping point is now. So you can tip me if you like for all the valuable information you've got from this book. It's worth a lot more than £12.99, so I suggest a tip of about a tenner will do. Please put your tip in an envelope and send it to me. Much appreciated. Thank you guv'nor!

Oh all right, I guess that ruse won't work. So what is a tipping point in reality, and how does it affect trading?

A *tipping point* in gambling, investing or trading circles is the point where you 'lose it'. Instead of making money you have a mental crisis – you go bananas and start throwing money away and losing heavily.

A tipping point is basically a small thing that tips you over from being a sensible investor or trader into a complete and utter nutter.

It could be something simple like: you started out doing really well but one stock lets you down, even though you *know* it's really a good one. So you throw more money at it. You get annoyed and take out some spread bets for it too. Suddenly the share lurches down more and you're losing capital hand over fist. But you buy more of the stock, as you're sure it's a good purchase.

Soon you're out of capital, so you get credit and invest all that into the stock too.

And then – the market tumbles.

You are showing huge losses. But you're now utterly beholden to the share and leveraged up to the gills to keep with its fall.

All of a sudden, from a reasonably good investor, you've become a crazed gambler. And all because one stock tripped you up.

The tipping point can be anything. In fact, usually – from a longer-term perspective – it's actually just a small issue. Maybe you had a good run, showing a profit of say £20k in your spread betting account. A couple of bad market days later you're back down to only break-even. You're determined to show a profit so take out more bets than you should, and now you're in a loss. You've tipped over.

You have to learn to stop before the tipping point catches you out.

What's the solution if you recognise you've reached a tipping point?

Cut your stakes dramatically. Or get out completely. Get rid of whatever it was that began to tip you over.

How do I recognise a tipping point?

You start to feel out of control of everything and lose command of your investments. You begin to over trade – anything to start winning again. Symptoms may even include feelings of excitement; though perhaps more common are irritation and bad moods that are seemingly only alleviated (briefly) by a trade.

So one day, when something tips you over, remember what you read here and do something about it before your brain and bank account take a hammering.

And if all the above isn't a good tip, I don't know what else is.

Final thought

A final (really final) thought.

An accountant came to one of my seminars. After I covered some basic analysis of various companies, he piped up:

> *"But don't you look at acid test ratios? And what about the PEG value versus historic P/E?"*

And various other things. As an honest(ish) person I replied:

> *"No, in fact I don't really know anything about them. But do you think all these measures are relevant?"*

He then went on to describe how he analyses accounts in the minutest detail. He carried on for ten minutes, leaving me and the audience a bit bemused. We didn't understand much of what he was on about, but I certainly wouldn't dismiss it as I don't mind learning something new.

And I did wonder: am I too basic? Should I be looking at a whole host of financial data? Should I try to understand everything in the accounts?

I had a chat with him in the bar later. He said:

"Actually, I think I maybe overanalyse. The fact is I can't bring myself to buy many shares because there's always one figure I don't like. I've hardly been able to trade because I get scared after all the analysis."

He realised there and then that overdoing the analysis had actually cost him a lot of money.

So, my parting shot to you is: *don't overdo it.* You don't have to analyse everything to the *n*th degree. My simple methods outlined in this book should work. And you will, in time, work out your own parameters. Simple can be best. Ask the best chefs. It's the same with shares.

And with that simple message I shall take my leave. Hope you enjoyed the book.

I wish you the best of luck and hope you make a fortune. Just make sure you do it over time and don't try and make your millions in a week. So long, and pick some good ones!

Make me proud of you!

And don't forget you can catch me every Wednesday at my website **www.nakedtrader.co.uk** – see you there ...

APPENDICES
This is Not Goodbye, but it is Au Revoir

"The thing that most affects the stock market is everything."

– James Palysted Wood

Useful Information Sources

Worthwhile websites

There are tons of financial websites out there, and most of them, today, are actually very good. That's partly because the useless sites that got set up in the dot-com boom have disappeared. But it's also because the people that set today's sites up enjoy finance and shares and that tends to come across.

Most good websites provide a decent amount of free information, then you pay a bit extra for premium information such as always-on access to real-time share prices. For example, once you've had some experience you may want to access Level 2 services, which will cost something like £40–£50 a month.

The sites tend to offer premium material all priced around the same level, but you may want to shop around. The best thing is to experiment. You'll probably end up using two or three sites.

For brand-new starters you probably only need the free stuff to begin with. As you get more experienced, you may need to start paying for decent access to real-time information.

ADVFN

www.advfn.com

This is the number-one site. I've mentioned it a lot in this book, and I use it all the time. Live prices and great research tools. Just use the free stuff to begin with.

I've negotiated a deal with ADVFN so you can get access to their premium lists and bulletin board for £41 a year instead of £60. Those are the great lists where you can find eye-catching shares. You also get access to my Naked Trader discussion forum, where you can chat to some very decent traders. Email me for details at **robbiethetrader@aol.com** with 'Bronze' in the subject line.

Naked Trader

www.nakedtrader.co.uk

Er, my website. Bloody good if you ask me.

Proactive Investors

www.proactiveinvestors.co.uk

This site has got bigger and bigger and keeps on improving. It features news and well-researched articles on companies. The site also hosts presentation evenings where you can meet the bosses of companies. And it's free! What's interesting is that it researches the companies no one else does – especially smaller ones – and comes up with some gems.

Hemscott

www.hemscott.com

Worth a look. Plenty of good research material here and a bulletin board worth dipping into from time to time.

Motley Fool

www.fool.co.uk

Despite its title, quite a serious site. Think pipe and slippers. Some interesting articles; worth a good gander.

MoneyAM

www.moneyam.com

A similar site to ADVFN. It also contains real-time prices, but its bulletin boards don't have as many contributors. Handy as an alternative to ADVFN and I use it as a back-up should ADVFN go down.

Citywire

www.citywire.co.uk

Breaking City news. I don't use it much, but I know a lot of investors do.

Books

Read. Read. And read some more. I know this book is superb, but you should be reading others too.

There are many trading and investing books out there and I've read a whole load of them. I've never regretted buying a single one because, generally, there's always a gem or two inside to think about. Such books typically don't cost more than £20, and invariably help traders make much more than that in return, so it's a good investment.

So here are a few I very strongly recommend. They are in no particular order. They are all excellent reads for stock market beginners and old hands alike.

- *The Disciplined Trader* by Mark Douglas

  An excellent look at good trading practices, including a look at why what's in your mind can affect your trading. There are also some tips on how to become a profitable trader.

- *Your Money and Your Brain* by Jason Zweig

  This is a great one. It is all about psychology and how your brain affects every move you make in the stock market. Feel the need to conquer fear and greed? This is the book for you!

- *The Naked Trader's Guide to Spread Betting* by Robbie Burns

  Just who does this guy think he is?

  Yes, this is my new book on spread betting. If you decide you want to take spread betting further then I hope this book will help you! It's not a rehash of stuff in here – it's brand new material that explores spread betting in depth.

- *High-Probability Trading* by Marcel Link

  This book tries to teach the mindset of a successful trader – what you should think about before you reach for the buy button. No complex material, just good common sense.

- *Financial Times Guide to Selecting Shares That Perform* by Richard Koch and Leo Gough

  This book uncovers ten ways to beat the market, and there are some very good ideas here. A good broad discussion of methods you can use to try and outperform the indices. I learned a number of excellent tips and I agree with pretty much everything the authors say.

- *Come into My Trading Room* by Alexander Elder

  This one is the book I've read and re-read the most. Entering Elder's trading room is a very interesting experience. His years of profitable trading show through the pages and many of his warnings regarding some of the pitfalls of trading are excellent. I think this one is an especially good read if you have never traded before. There is also plenty of market psychology discussed, one of my favourite topics. And talking of psychology …

- *Investment Madness* by John R. Nofsinger

  Subtitled: 'How psychology affects your investing and what to do about it'. This is one of the must reads! It is highly amusing but also very sharp. You may recognise your own character traits in the book – and once you recognise them, you can learn how to stop bad sides to your character ruining your trades. Topics include the problems of overconfidence, social aspects of investing, the 'double or nothing' mentality, seeking pride and avoiding regret.

- *The Investor's Guide to Charting* by Alistair Blair

  For those of you who decide charting is the way to work out which shares to sell and buy, this is the easiest read. Blair explains the art of a chart and what it's all about. Find out what all the chart jargon means, like 'double tops', and whether charting is suitable for you. What's really good is the discussion of how much of chart theory and practice should be taken with a pinch of salt.

- *The Investor's Toolbox* by Peter Temple

  Everything you need to know about spread betting, CFDs, covered warrants, options – all the funnies – to help boost your returns. The book goes through all the tools you need for successful investing. If there's any question on basic derivatives you need to know the answer to, it'll be here.

- *The Harriman Book of Investing Rules*

  Collected wisdom from the world's top 150 investors. Tons of unmissable rules from the greatest traders ever. Read and learn! It's one of those books you can keep in the bathroom because you can pick it up anytime and have a great read. A brilliant book of wisdom to keep dipping into.

- *The Investor's Guide To Understanding Accounts* by Robert Leach

  This may sound like a really boring one, but Leach has turned what could be a very unexciting subject into an interesting one. Ever wondered how to look at a set of accounts and know whether it's all good or there is trouble ahead? Are they cooking the books? There's also an excellent ten-point summary which will point you in the right direction.

> You can order any of these through my website, **www.nakedtrader.co.uk**. Delivery is usually very fast and often next day. Click on 'Books'.

I keep my website updated with reviews of the latest books as they are published, so do check in for those.

TOP 10 MOVIES FOR SHARE TRADERS

1. The Money Pit
2. City Slickers
3. Carry On Regardless
4. Carry On Screaming
5. Titanic
6. Rogue Trader
7. Trading Places
8. Look Back in Anger
9. Casino
10. Buy & Cell

Quiz – What Sort of Investor Are You?

Here's a fun quiz to test your skills as a potential investor. Answer all the questions honestly. Do not cheat and look up the answers.

Pick only one answer for each question. Note down the question number and which letter you picked. If you did badly on the quiz in previous editions I hope you do better now!

Questions

1. *You decide stop losses are a great idea. Where do you set them?*

a. Close to the current price so you can't lose much.

b. About 5% away.

c. In the pub.

d. 10% away then fiddle it using charts.

e. Around where the share last found support.

2. *A big newspaper tips a share over the weekend. You like it. Do you:*

a. Buy it later in the week.

b. Get in quickly first thing Monday.

c. Short it Monday afternoon.

d. Ignore the whole thing.

e. Research it, put it on a potential buying shortlist.

3. *You want to trade tax-free. Do you:*

a. Get a DMA account.

b. Open a self-select ISA.

c. Move to Switzerland.

d. Spread bet.

e. Go in for CFDs.

4. *You're new to trading. Do you:*

a. Buy loads of oil and mining shares.

b. Get penny shares, they double easily.

c. Buy a number of different shares – spread the risk.

d. Day trade the FTSE 100.

e. Get into Forex.

5. *When researching a share it's best to look at it from the point of view of:*

a. Gordon Ramsay.

b. Bernie Madoff.

c. Mr Spock.

d. Lady Ga Ga.

e. Lord Sugar.

6. *A share you are in has doubled. Do you:*

a. Bank the profit fast.

b. Bank and elope with the girl at Starbucks.

c. Re-evaluate it and maybe buy more.

d. Bank half, leave the rest to run.

e. Top-slice a bit to get something new.

7. *You have £5,000 and get offered a CFD account with leverage of £50,000. Do you:*

a. Say no thanks and stick with an ISA.

b. Say yes please and buy, buy, buy!

c. Open the account but avoid using the leverage.

d. Say no, but research what on earth CFDs are.

e. Use part of the leverage so you can short.

8. *A friend tells you about an amazing share that will 'ten bag'. Do you:*

a. Tell him he has had one pint too many.

b. Buy lots of it the next day.

c. Research it properly then make a decision.

d. Buy it, then tell all your mates in order to get the price up.

e. Get him pissed so he gives you more hot tips.

9. *What's the best time to buy a share?*

a. 10am.

b. 8am.

c. 5pm.

d. 2pm.

e. At the weekend.

10. All your shares are crashing. Do you:

a. Hide behind the sofa.

b. Hold your nerve.

c. Check why the market is falling and take a view accordingly.

d. Sell everything as fast as possible.

e. Think about buying some great bargains.

11. `You've read The Naked Trader *3rd edition. Do you think the writer is:*

a. Probably a genius.

b. The best thing since the iPad 2/3/4/5/6/7 (delete as appropriate depending on when this is read).

c. Too good-looking to write books on money.

d. A total tosser.

e. A complete bluffer.

Now look at the answers and add up the numbers.

Scores

1. a-5 b-4 c-5 d-1 e-1

2. a-2 b-5 c-2 d-1 e-1

3. a-5 b-1 c-4 d-2 e-5

4. a-5 b-5 c-1 d-4 e-5

5. a-2 b-5 c-2 d-5 e-1

6. a-3 b-4 c-1 d-1 e-2

7. a-1 b-5 c-2 d-1 e-3

8. a-1 b-5 c-1 d-5 e-5

9. a-1 b-4 c-5 d-1 e-5

10. a-4 b-1 c-1 d-5 e-1

11. a-2 b-2 c-1 d-100 e-100

(Anyone answering d or e to question 11 is disqualified from the quiz.)

Add up all your scores for your final total.

Analysis

- **18 or below:** Master investor!

You have every chance of success in the stock market. Your approach to shares looks to be solid and I have every confidence that you will soon be in profit.

- **19–25:** Good potential

You have the makings of a good investor, but you must be careful not to blow it by taking too many risks. Take it easy.

- **26–35:** A lot of work to do

You are too liable to take major risks and you're likely to make losses unless you temper your gambling instincts.

- **36–50:** Oh dear!

Did you really read the book? You need to get right back to basics before you lose all your money!

The Naked Trader

Seminars

If you enjoyed the book, and want to bring it to life, why not come to one of my seminars? You get to meet me (you lucky thing!) and we spend the whole day together looking at live markets. There's plenty of drinks in the bar afterwards, too! I hold the seminars roughly five times a year, always close to London.

The seminars are for beginners and intermediates and you need to know nothing about markets before coming – although it would be handy if you read the book! The seminars are held in a pleasant, relaxing and informal setting. A three-course lunch, coffees, snacks and, of course, loads of chunky KitKats and fruit gums are included in the price. For the current price please check my website **www.nakedtrader.co.uk**.

Best time to book is early because that's when I give out massive early-booking discounts!

The idea behind the seminar is *simplicity*. I don't use jargon or fancy words – everything is in *plain English*! The idea is for you to come away from the event a wiser and better investor with lots of new ideas.

The subjects covered in the seminar include:

- how to find value shares
- Level 2: how to use it to grab great timed buys and sells
- how to beat the market makers
- how to spot tree shakes and use them in your favour
- how to get a market edge when timing trades
- how to tell when not to buy a share
- spread betting – how to do it and why it's a good thing
- how to short shares
- the best ways to buy and sell shares
- how to become a confident investor
- charts: how I use them
- profit target and stop loss setting
- how to plan share trades: exits, entries and timescales
- how to research shares simply and effectively
- how to spot an undervalued share
- what to do when shares crash suddenly
- avoiding stock market sharks and tipsters
- how to handle market volatility
- direct market access.

Phew!

I give tons of live examples all day of how to research shares quickly, easily and effectively. We'll watch how shares move, live on screen. And we'll look at *why* shares move and how you can use the two effective tools I employ to produce a powerful buy or sell signal.

Not forgetting plenty of questions and answers – all the things that bug you about the market but you were too afraid to ask about!

So if you feel you are interested in a seminar, email me for details at **robbiethetrader@aol.com**. Please put 'Seminar interested' in the subject line. I will then send you full details and you can decide if you fancy coming.

The seminars are usually held at a hotel close to Heathrow airport in London, so if you live up north, in Ireland or further abroad you can easily fly in. Maybe I'll see you soon!

Offers

See my website for the latest tasty offers.

My two favourite spread bet firms offer stuff:

- Tradefair offers £100 credit and a book of trading rules: **www.tradefair.com/promo/spreads/nakedtrader100**

- IG offers an excellent education package: **www.igindex.co.uk/nakedtrader**

ADVFN offers cheaper bronze, silver and Level 2 services – email me for details.

My website

You can catch up with my trading adventures at my website, **www.nakedtrader.co.uk** (currently updated once a week).

My email address is **robbiethetrader@aol.com**. I'm happy to answer emails but one thing I can't do is offer any advice as to whether you should buy, sell or hold anything!

Also, I do get a *lot* of emails so please be kind and stick to 150 words or fewer – no life stories! And do check the FAQs on my website, as the answer you could be seeking might already be there.

The best and the worst moments of life at NakedTrader.co.uk

If you want to know a little more about me and what I get up to, here's a little compilation of some of the best (and worst) moments from my online diary over the last couple of years. Hey, it's fine if you skip it – I understand. Maybe it's a bit like looking at someone else's holiday snaps …

ON SCHOOL PROJECTS

We dread it when a note comes through from Christopher's school entitled 'Special Day'. This will always mean: you parents are going to have to do some work. It's the same with a project. Said project of course always ends up being done by the poor parents. As if we haven't got enough to do already. (Though I am a dab hand with a prit-stick.)

And here it was: "Your children should come to school on Friday dressed as their favourite book character. The winner gets a prize!"

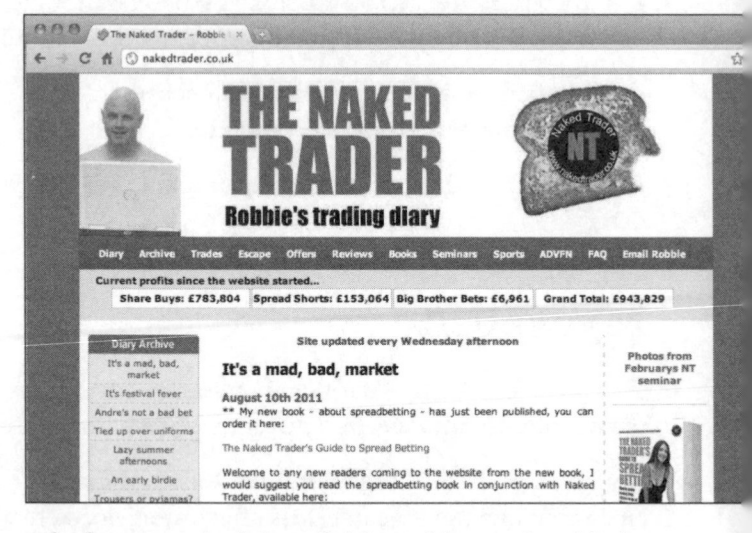

Arrrggghhh! This means the poor parents have to come up with the idea and the costume in a matter of a few days. And though it's nothing to do with the kids, you can't dress them up as Jack Reacher or there would be complaints.

You can imagine the competitive parents, can't you?

You know there will be one or two mothers who will work round the clock to be the winner. Their children will arrive in superb, intricately made costumes. And they will be brilliant choices, great characters no one else thought of.

The mum is saying: "I'm the number one mum. Don't even consider competing with me."

Personally, I'm with the parent who thinks: "Sod this, where's that old Spider-Man mask?"

We were kind of mid-range in the end, with a Cat in the Hat outfit. Though Christopher wasn't allowed to wear the whiskers we made. Health and safety, of course.

Speaking of schools, I met a sports teacher the other day. He has developed a great way of winning rugby games against other schools. He slips in one or two girls into the team!

"The boys on the opposing teams aren't sure whether they are allowed to bring the girls down. By the time they've realised they can, the girls have already scored a few times ... works a treat!"

Now that's my kinda teacher!

ON MISTAKES AT THE GYM

Sometimes we just wander around and don't notice what's going on around us, wrapped up in our own little world. Which is exactly what happened in the gym this morning.

I was getting changed after a swim, as were a few others, including the irritating 'whistler'. (The guy who always whistles. Not a tune even. Just, well, a stupid whistle. It takes a lot of strength for me not to say: "Yes, I know it's weird we're all in our undies and not talking to each other but the whistling does nothing to help. No need to be nervous!")

However, even the whistler stopped his tuneless din at what happened next. In walked a woman. She headed straight to a locker, and then promptly started to get changed in front of us all.

All being chivalrous, we turned away and pretended a lady changing in the men's was something quite usual.

After a while she looked round. Stating the blindingly obvious she said: "This is the men's, isn't it!"

"That's right," I said, deciding to break the weird silence that greeted her remark. "But I guess nothing here you've not seen before ... "

"That's true!" she said. (Which was a touch disappointing.)

She brazened the whole thing out rather nicely and disappeared, saying, "Thank you my men, and apologies … "

Well, after a decent silence, we all had a good laugh! And thinking about it, I'm pretty sure she was looking at the whistler when she made her "That's true" comment. Ah, could be why he whistles.

ON THE PITFALLS OF BEING A PARENT

When you are a parent there is just nothing like a playdate. Your child/children head off for a party or to play at someone else's place and you actually get some time off!

Not that Christopher isn't lovely, it's just that sometimes it's nice to clock off parenting duties for a brief bit.

Christopher was due for a party last Sunday between 2 and 6, and was duly collected.

So – wow! Sunday papers in bed! Haven't been able to do that for years! Hey! An oasis of an afternoon. Papers, tea and toast in bed and maybe some mummy and daddy time!

Ten past five, we had literally just finished playing mummy and daddy when … the doorbell went!

Uh oh. He was back early. "The party must have finished at 5 instead of 6," said Mrs NT.

I grabbed my dressing gown and rushed to answer the door.

I opened it to let Christopher in, but who should be dropping him off but Alpha Male Banker, a father of one of the other children.

He's big in the City. He is very alpha. I know he thinks I'm some waster. I dunno, fancy not having to get up at 5am and work till 8pm! Some people, eh? And all my wandering around in T-shirts and jeans. Where the hell are my pinstripes?

He gave me a pitying look – and then a withering one. His contempt was worse than normal. Then I realised why.

I was wearing Mrs NT's Cath Kidston dressing gown: a rich pink, covered liberally with purple and green spots. The very definition of girly.

"Was everything okay?" I asked.

(That's parental code for: did my child do anything awful to any of the other kids?)

"Fine," he said. "Goodbye." (I thought he was going to tell me I was the weakest link for a moment.)

One more withering stare, and he marched off. Probably put him in the mood to fire someone on Monday.

Christopher took no notice, but then again he was already guzzling something e-number-ridden from his party bag.

Mrs NT crept out of the bedroom.

"Suits you," she said.

"That was embarrassing," I muttered, and to relieve the stress I ate something yummy from the party bag.

It turns out the sugar content of Haribos steadies the nerves about as efficiently as a double scotch.

WILLY WOBBLES

I feel deflated. Christopher was out in the park with Mrs NT and his four-year-old friend. I was at home having a lovely bath.

Lots of bubbles and reading the *Sun* and *Hello!* maga ... I mean, er, the *Financial Times* and the *Investors Chronicle* ... Nice bit of peace and quiet. In a good mood.

Sadly for me, outside it had begun to rain hard, and they all arrived back early from the park. Before I knew it, the boys – told to wash their hands for tea – had run heedless into the bathroom.

Everyone froze where they were in shock.

Then Christopher's friend looked at me sadly.

"My daddy's willy is bigger than yours," he said.

Well that was the end of my good mood!

When I told his daddy this later, a look of, how can I put this, smugness came over his face. Indeed, there was pride mixed in there too.

"Of course, it's what you do with it that counts," I said, rolling out the old cliché not very convincingly.

Right, I'm off to look at my spam folder – bound to be something in there that can help!

ON TWITTER

I'm fed up with hearing about bloody Twitter.

Twitter this, Twitter that – nice and easy for journalists to make up loads of stories without having to do any work whatsoever.

Yes, you guessed it: we've now had the first woman to cover the birth of her child on Twitter.

What next? Tell you what, the next time I have a crap I'll do a live Twitter feed for you.

(2.30. Place the Sun carefully on floor of toilet. 2.31. Remove trousers and sit on seat ...)

Thanks for reading ...

I do hope you enjoyed the book. It was really tough to write. During the writing process I chomped my way through 500 pieces of toast, 44 chunky KitKats, 32 Yorkie bars (peanut and raisin), 698 cups of tea, 76 bags of cheese and onion crisps, beat my head in frustration against the wall six times. Said: "Why did I agree to write this bloody book?" 1,654 times. Stubbed my toe on the office desk eight times. Shouted "Arrrggggghhhhhh!" 18 times. And just before I sent it to the publisher I screamed: "Yeeeesssssss!" Then they sent it back highlighting all the mistakes and I went "NOOOOOOOOO!!!!!"

Don't expect another one from me for a long time. Now I am off to the gym for three months to burn off the chocolate.

I do wish all of you the best with your trading. If there is just one thought to leave you with this time it would be:

"It's a marathon, not a sprint."

And even more importantly:

"It's a Marathon, not a Snickers."

Index

Notes

Notes

Notes

Notes

Notes

Notes

Notes

Notes

Notes

Notes

The
Naked
Trader's
Guide to Spread Betting

Available
in paperback and eBook

Brand new
strategies, tips
and tales

Spread Bets
Laid Bare

Get the eBook version of *The Naked Trader* for free!

As a buyer of the printed version of *The Naked Trader*, you can download the electronic version free of charge.

To get hold of your copy of the eBook, simply point your smart phone camera at the following (or go to **ebooks.harriman-house.com/nt3**):

 Harriman House

The free *Naked Trader* eBook is an ePub file, the industry standard developed by the International Digital Publishing Forum. It is compatible with the widest range of eReaders, including Apple iPad, Sony eReader, and Adobe Digital Editions on PC and Mac.